PRINCIPLES OF INTERNATIONAL RELATIONS

Joshua S. Goldstein

American University, Washington, D.C.
University of Massachusetts, Amherst

Jon C. Pevehouse

University of Chicago

PEARSON
Longman

New York   San Francisco   Boston
London   Toronto   Sydney   Tokyo   Singapore   Madrid
Mexico City   Munich   Paris   Cape Town   Hong Kong   Montreal

IN MEMORY OF PROF. HAYWARD R. ALKER

Acquisitions Editor: Vikram Mukhija
Executive Marketing Manager: Ann Stypuloski
Production Coordinator: Scarlett Lindsay
Project Coordination, Text Design, and Electronic Page Makeup: Elm Street Publishing Services
Cover Designer/Manager: Wendy Ann Fredericks
Cover Photo: © Mark Wilson/Liason/Getty Images, Inc.
Senior Manufacturing Buyer: Roy L. Pickering, Jr.
Printer and Binder: RR Donnelley & Sons Company / Crawfordsville
Cover Printer: RR Donnelley & Sons Company / Crawfordsville

Library of Congress Cataloging-in-Publication Data
Goldstein, Joshua S., 1952–
  Principles of international relations / Joshua S. Goldstein and Jon C.
Pevehouse.—1st ed.
    p. cm.
  Includes bibliographical references and index.
  ISBN 978-0-205-65266-2
  1. International relations. I. Pevehouse, Jon C. II. Title.
JZ1242.G68 2009
327—dc22

                                                        2008013773

Visit us at www.ablongman.com/goldstein

ISBN-13: 978-0-205-65266-2
ISBN-10: 0-205-65266-2

1 2 3 4 5 6 7 8 9 10—DOC—11 10 09 08

BRIEF CONTENTS

Detailed Contents

PREFACE

International Relations (IR) is a complicated subject—interdisciplinary, multicultural, both abstract and practical, historical and contemporary, diverse in methodologies, and contested in terms of theoretical approaches. No wonder, then, that professors teach IR in many different ways, drawing on their own particular strengths and interests and the particular needs of their students. And no wonder that professors in this field use a great diversity of course materials, since any one book's approach, coverage, or pedagogy does not fit all professors' ideas about how best to cover the topics in the course.

As the authors of a top-selling introductory college IR textbook, we have often asked ourselves how we could meet the needs of professors who, unlike many others, simply do not want the full textbook treatment. *Principles of International Relations* is our answer to that question. It provides the essential concepts and theories that most IR courses will include, without the other resources found in a textbook. Short enough to fit easily into a diverse range of syllabi, this book does not limit other assigned readings such as topical articles, case studies, or participatory exercises.

FEATURES

Like our textbooks, this book begins with three "core principles"—dominance, reciprocity, and identity—that offer potential solutions to the central recurring problem in IR, the collective goods problem in which autonomous actors have no government to regulate their interactions. These theoretical principles can help unify and make sense of the multitude of situations that make up day-to-day IR.

The overall structure of this book follows the major theoretical approaches to IR, beginning with the core principles and major types of actors (Chapter 1), followed by realist approaches based on rational-actor models (Chapters 2 and 3) and then models of decision making that do not assume rationality (Chapter 3). Liberal alternatives to realism include cooperation based on international organizations (Chapter 4) and the "democratic peace," along with other domestic political influences on IR (Chapter 5). Constructivist theories, international law, and human rights occupy Chapter 6, while more "critical" approaches follow—Marxism, postmodernism, and peace studies (Chapter 7) and gender-based theories of IR (Chapter 8). The last four chapters (9–12) take up more specific explanations of puzzles in the subfields of conflict, trade, globalization, and international development, respectively.

Globalization brings IR into our daily lives in new ways. Although just one chapter focuses entirely on theories of globalization, many chapters touch on the nongovernmental actors and transnational processes that have become central to understanding IR. These actors and processes especially matter in explaining such issues as Islamist politics, terrorism, and human rights.

This book includes the many data graphics and explanatory figures that have helped users of our textbook to understand complex IR concepts visually. We use hard data, presented in a streamlined way, to give students evidence of trends and relationships in IR today that illustrate the theories and concepts discussed in each chapter. For example, graphs in the book compare the great powers' economic and military strength (p. 29), the digital divide in access to telecommunications (p. 168), and China's and India's development paths (p. 185). The use of quantitative data, presented simply and appropriately at a global level, encourages critical thinking by allowing students to form their own judgments and to reason through the implications of different theories.

We also use a few sketch-style graphics (pp. 50–51, 60, 91) to tell a story that illustrates a theoretical point. Maps (pp. 35, 101, 105, 131, 138, and 179) can help students visualize globalization. The real-world orientation of the graphics provides a counterpoint to the more abstract theories that make up the majority of the text.

IR is a large subject that offers many directions for further exploration. The footnotes in this book are not traditional source notes so much as suggested further readings on various topics. (Also, to save space in the notes, publisher locations are omitted and major university or state names refer to their university presses; students should note that this is not a correct research paper style.)

SUPPLEMENTS

Longman is pleased to offer several resources to qualified adopters of this book and their students that will make teaching and learning from *Principles of International Relations* even more effective and enjoyable.

Instructor Resources

MyPoliSciKit Video Case Studies for International Relations and Comparative Politics   Featuring video from major news sources and providing reporting and insight on recent world affairs, this DVD series helps instructors integrate current events into their courses by letting them use the clips as lecture launchers or discussion starters.

Student Resources

Longman Atlas of World Issues (0-321-22456-5)   Introduced and selected by Robert J. Art of Brandeis University and excerpted from the acclaimed Penguin Atlas Series, the *Longman Atlas of World Issues* is designed to help students understand the geography and major issues facing the world today, such as terrorism, debt, and HIV/AIDS. Available at no additional charge when packaged with this book.

New Signet World Atlas (0-451-19732101)   From Penguin Putnam, this pocket-sized yet detailed reference features 96 pages of full-color maps plus statistics, key data, and much more. Available at a discount when packaged with this book.

The Penguin Dictionary of International Relations (0-140-51397-3)   This indispensable reference by Graham Evans and Jeffrey Newnham includes hundreds of cross-referenced entries on the enduring and emerging theories, concepts, and events that are shaping the academic discipline of international relations and today's world politics. Available at a discount when packaged with this book.

Research and Writing in International Relations (0-321-27766-X)   Written by Laura Roselle and Sharon Spray of Elon University, this brief and affordable guide provides the basic step-by-step process and essential resources that are needed to write political science papers that go beyond simple description and into more systematic and sophisticated inquiry. Available at a discount when packaged with this book.

Study Card for International Relations (0-321-29231-6)   Packed with useful information, Allyn & Bacon/Longman's Study Cards make studying easier, more efficient, and more enjoyable. Course information is distilled down to the basics, helping students quickly master the fundamentals, review a subject for understanding, or prepare for an exam. Available at no additional charge when packaged with this book.

Careers in Political Science (0-321-113337-3)   Offering insider advice and practical tips on how to make the most of a political science degree, this booklet by Joel Clark of George Mason University shows students the tremendous potential such a degree offers. Available at a discount when packaged with this book.

ACKNOWLEDGMENTS

Many scholars, colleagues, and friends have contributed ideas that ultimately influenced the eight editions of our textbook and hence this book. We owe a special debt to four beloved and now deceased IR scholars whose ideas particularly influenced our thinking—Robert C. North, Deborah J. "Misty" Gerner, Randall Forsberg, and Hayward R. Alker to whom this book is dedicated and for whom theoretical and methodological diversity in IR were a mission and a way of life. Any errors, of course, remain our own responsibility.

JOSHUA S. GOLDSTEIN
JON C. PEVEHOUSE

A NOTE ON NOMENCLATURE

In international relations, names are politically sensitive; different actors may call a territory or an event by different names. This book cannot resolve such conflicts, but uses the following naming conventions for consistency. The United Kingdom of Great Britain (England, Scotland, Wales) and Northern Ireland is called Britain. Burma, renamed Myanmar by its military government, is referred to as Burma. Bosnia and Herzegovina is shortened to Bosnia. Generally, country names follow common usage, dropping formal designations such as "Republic of." The war between Iran and Iraq in the 1980s is called the Iran-Iraq War. The 1991 U.S.-led multinational campaign that retook Kuwait after Iraq's 1990 invasion is called the Gulf War. The U.S. occupation of Iraq since 2003 is called the Iraq War.

World States and Territories

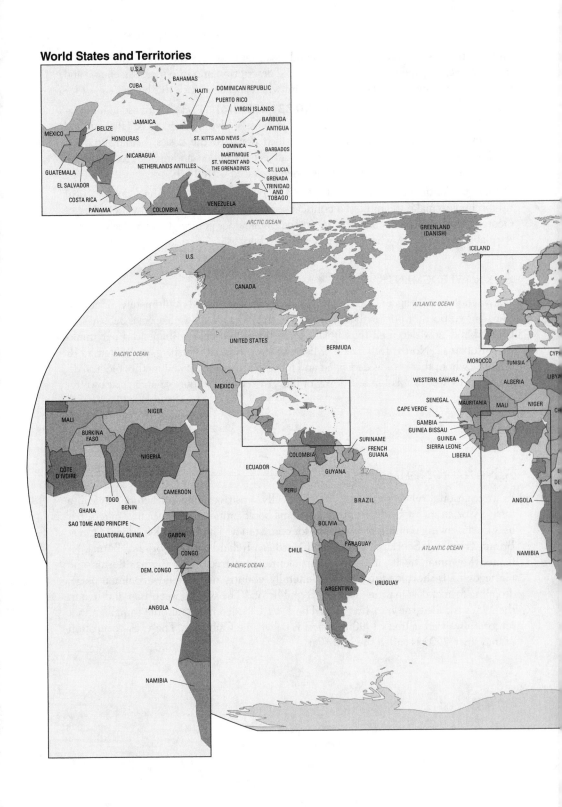

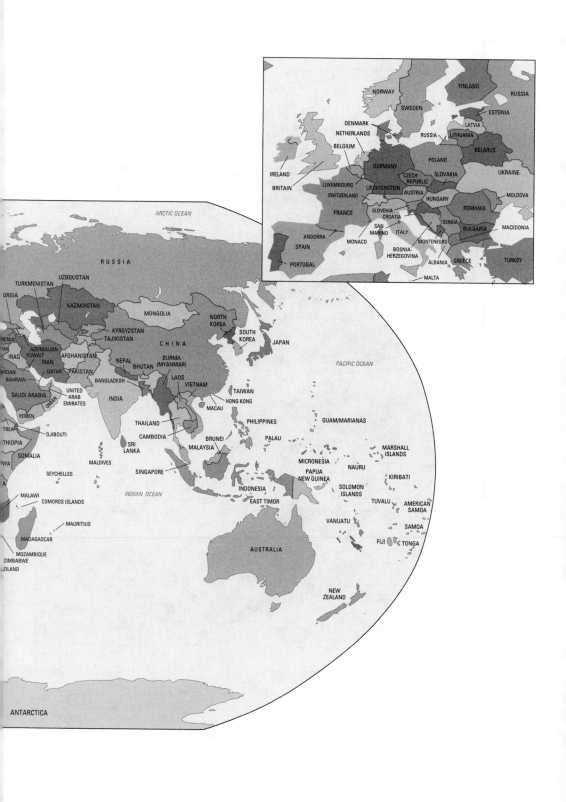

North America

Central America and the Caribbean

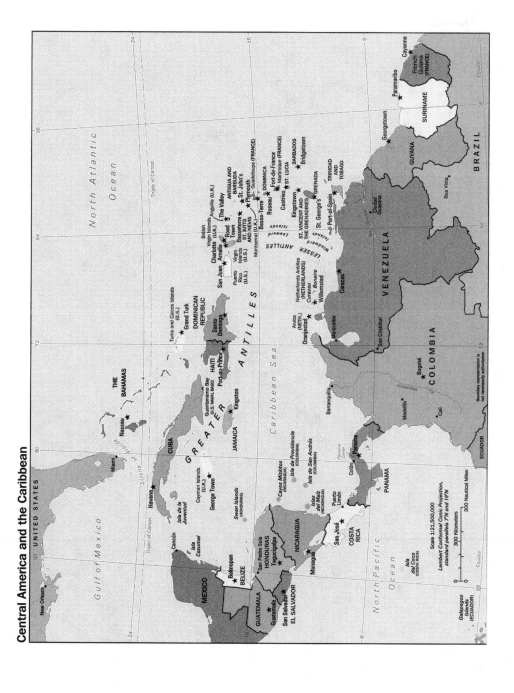

South America

Africa

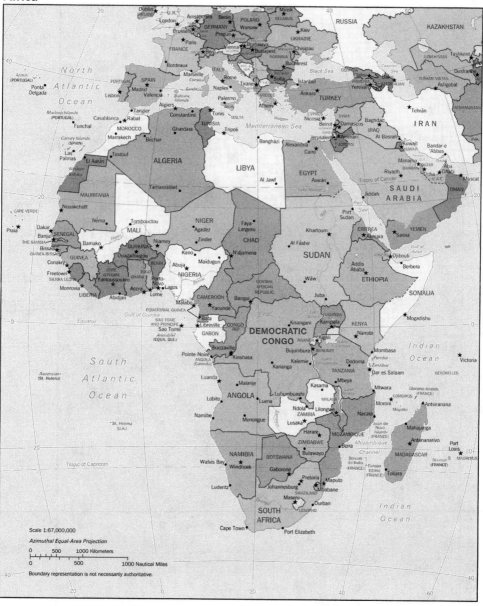

Northern Africa and the Middle East

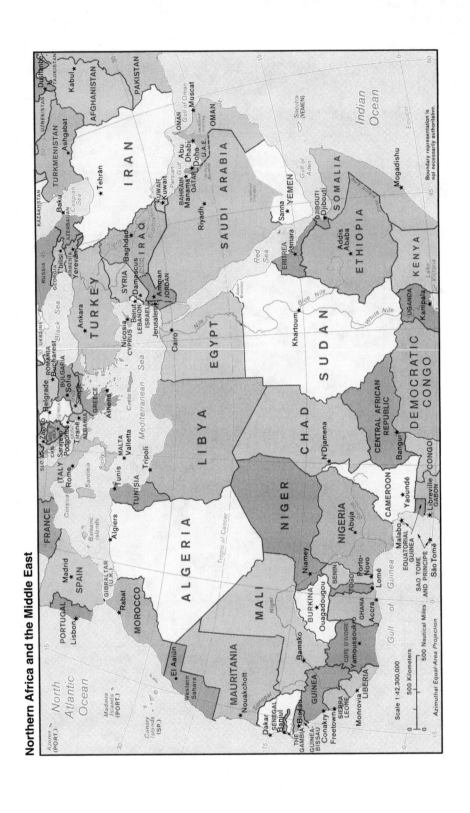

Europe

Serbia and Montenegro have asserted the formation of a joint independent state, but this entity has not been formally recognized as a state by the United States.

Greenland (DENMARK)

Jan Mayen (NORWAY)

Greenland Sea

Norwegian Sea

Barents Sea

Hammerfest

Murmansk

Narvik · Kiruna

Reykjavik ★ **ICELAND**

Arctic Circle

NORWAY

Umea

White Sea

Arkhangel'sk

Oulu

FINLAND

Trondheim

SWEDEN

Tampere

Tórshavn · **Faroe Islands** (DENMARK)

Bergen

Oslo

Gävle

Helsinki

St. Petersburg

Shetland Islands

Stockholm

Åland Islands

Tallinn

ESTONIA

RUSSIA

Rockall (U.K.)

Hebrides

Orkney Islands

Göteborg

Gotland

Riga

LATVIA

Smolensk

Aberdeen

North Sea

Baltic Sea

LITHUANIA

Edinburgh

DENMARK

Öland

Vilnius

Minsk

Belfast **UNITED**

Newcastle

Copenhagen

Bornholm

Kaliningrad (RUSSIA)

BELARUS

Dublin *Irish Sea* Isle of Man

Liverpool

Rostock

Gdansk

KINGDOM

Hamburg

IRELAND

Cardiff

Amsterdam

Berlin

Poznań

Warsaw

Brest

Kiev

London

NETHERLANDS

Hannover

GERMANY

Leipzig

POLAND

Wrocław

English Channel

Brussels

Bonn

Kraków

L'viv

UKRAINE

Guernsey (U.K.) Jersey (U.K.)

Le Havre

BELGIUM

Frankfurt

Prague

Paris

LUX. Luxembourg

CZECH REPUBLIC

Nantes

Strasbourg

Stuttgart

SLOVAKIA

MOLDOVA

Chişinău

Odesa

Munich

Vienna

Bratislava

Budapest

Cluj-Napoca

Bay of Biscay

FRANCE

SWITZ. LIECH.

AUSTRIA

Graz

HUNGARY

ROMANIA

Geneva · Bern

Lyon

Milan

Ljubljana

Pécs

Bucharest

Constanţa

Bordeaux

Turin

Venice

SLOVENIA

Zagreb

Belgrade

Varna

Black Sea

Genoa

SAN MARINO

CROATIA

BOSNIA AND HERZEGOVINA

BULGARIA

Istanbul

Bilbao

MONACO

Florence

Sarajevo

Serbia

Sofia

Porto

Marseille

Podgorica

Skopje

PORTUGAL

SPAIN

ANDORRA

Barcelona

Adriatic Sea

Montenegro

MACEDONIA

Thessaloniki

TURKEY

Madrid

ITALY

Rome

Tirane

ALB.

Lisbon

Corsica

VATICAN CITY

Naples

Ioannina

Valencia

Naples

GREECE

Athens

Sevilla

Sardinia

Tyrrhenian Sea

Ionian Sea

Peloponnisos

Rhodes

Málaga

Balearic Islands

Palermo

Crete

Strait of Gibraltar Gibraltar (U.K.) Ceuta (SPAIN)

Melilla (SPAIN)

Algiers

Mediterranean Sea

Sicily

Rabat ★ **MOROCCO**

ALGERIA

Tunis

TUNISIA

Valletta

MALTA

Scale 1:19,500,000

Lambert Conformal Conic Projection, standard parallels 40°N and 56°N

0   300 Kilometers

0   300 Nautical Miles

Asia

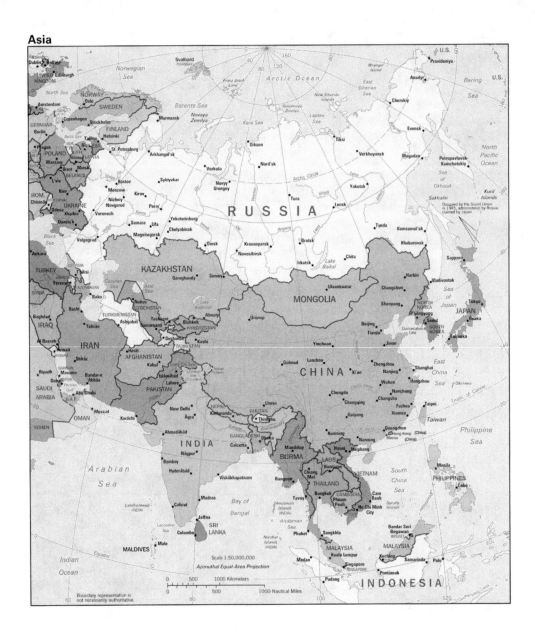

PRINCIPLES OF INTERNATIONAL RELATIONS

FUNDAMENTALS OF IR THEORY

CORE PRINCIPLES

International Relations (IR) directly affects the lives of billions of people, yet scholars and researchers cannot reliably explain and predict the life-and-death outcomes they study. The goal of this book is to lay out the main explanatory principles and theories of IR without exaggerating the successes of the discipline.[1] The field of IR reflects the world's complexity, and IR scholars use many theories, concepts, and buzzwords in trying to describe and explain it. Underneath this complexity, however, lie a few basic principles that shape the field.

IR revolves around one key problem: How can a group—such as two or more nations—serve its *collective* interests when doing so requires its members to forgo their *individual* interests? For example, every country has an interest in stopping global warming, a goal that can be achieved only by many countries acting together. Yet each country also has an individual interest in burning fossil fuels to keep its economy going. Similarly, all members of a military alliance benefit from the strength of the alliance, but each member separately has an interest in minimizing its own contributions in troops and money. Individual nations can advance their own short-term interests by seizing territory militarily, cheating on trade agreements, and refusing to contribute to international efforts such as peacekeeping or vaccination campaigns. But if all nations acted this way, they would find themselves worse off, in a chaotic and vicious environment where mutual gains from security and trade would disappear.

This problem of shared interests versus conflicting interests among members of a group goes by various names in various contexts—the problem of "collective action," "free riding," "burden sharing," the "tragedy of the commons," a "mixed interest game," or the "prisoner's dilemma." We will refer to the general case as the **collective goods problem,*** that is, the problem of how to provide something that benefits all members of a group regardless of what each member contributes to it.[2]

---

[1] Art, Robert J., and Robert Jervis, eds. *International Politics: Enduring Concepts and Contemporary Issues.* 8th ed. Longman, 2006. Dougherty, James E., Jr., and Robert L. Pfaltzgraff. *Contending Theories of International Relations: A Comprehensive Survey.* 5th ed. Longman, 2001. Doyle, Michael W. *Ways of War and Peace: Realism, Liberalism, and Socialism.* Norton, 1997. Viotti, Paul R., and Mark V. Kauppi, eds. *International Relations Theory: Realism, Pluralism, Globalism, and Beyond.* 3rd ed. Allyn & Bacon, 1999. Sterling-Folker, Jennifer, ed. *Making Sense of International Relations Theory.* Rienner, 2005.

[2] Sandler, Todd. *Global Collective Action.* Cambridge, 2004. Olson, Mancur. *The Logic of Collective Action.* Harvard, 1971 [1965].

* Key terms are boldface.

In general, collective goods are easier to provide in small groups than in large ones. In a small group, the cheating (or "free riding") of one member is harder to conceal, has a greater impact on the overall collective good, and is easier to punish. The advantage of small groups helps explain the importance of the great-power system in international security affairs and of the G7 (Group of Seven) industrialized countries in economic matters.

The collective goods problem occurs in all groups and societies, but is particularly acute in international affairs because each nation is sovereign, with no central authority such as a world government to enforce on individual nations the necessary measures to provide for the common good. By contrast, in domestic politics *within* countries, a government can force individuals to contribute in ways that do not serve their individual self-interest, such as by paying taxes or paying to install antipollution equipment on vehicles and in factories. If individuals do not comply, the government can punish them. Although this solution is far from perfect—cheaters and criminals sometimes are not caught, and governments sometimes abuse their power—it mostly works well enough to keep societies going.

Three basic principles—which we call dominance, reciprocity, and identity—offer possible solutions to the core problem of getting individuals to cooperate for the common good without a central authority to make them do so (see Table 1.1). These three principles are fundamental across the social sciences and recur in such disciplines as the study of animal societies, child development, social psychology, anthropology, and economics, as well as political science. To explain each principle, we will apply the three principles to a small-scale human example and an IR example.

The principle of **dominance** solves the collective goods problem by establishing a power hierarchy in which those at the top control those below—a bit like a government but without an actual government. Instead of fighting constantly over who gets scarce resources, the members of a group can just fight occasionally over position in the "status hierarchy." Then social conflicts such as over who gets resources are resolved automatically in favor of the higher-ranking actor. Fights over dominance position have scripted rules that minimize, to some extent, the harm inflicted on the group members. Symbolic acts of submission and dominance reinforce an ever-present status hierarchy. Staying on top of a status hierarchy does not depend on strength alone,

Table 1.1 Core Principles for Solving Collective Goods Problems

Principle	Advantages	Drawbacks
(↓↑) Dominance	Order, Stability, Predictability	Oppression, Resentment
(⇄) Reciprocity	Incentives for Mutual Cooperation	Downward Spirals; Complex Accounting
(→←) Identity	Sacrifice for Group, Redefine Interests	Demonizing an Out-Group

though it helps. Rather, the top actor may be the one most adept at forming and maintaining alliances among the group's more capable members. Dominance is complex, and not just a matter of brute force.

In international relations, the principle of dominance underlies the great-power system, in which a handful of countries dictate the rules for all the others. Sometimes a so-called *hegemon* or superpower stands atop the great powers as the dominant nation. The UN Security Council, in which the world's five strongest military powers hold a veto, reflects the dominance principle.

The advantage of the dominance solution to the collective goods problem is that, like a government, it forces members of a group to contribute to the common good. It minimizes open conflict within the group. However, the disadvantage is that this stability comes at a cost of constant oppression of, and resentment by, the lower-ranking members in the status hierarchy. Also, conflicts over position in the hierarchy can occasionally harm the group's stability and well-being, such as when challenges to the top position lead to serious fights. In the case of international relations, the great-power system and the hegemony of a superpower can provide relative peace and stability for decades on end but then can break down into costly wars among the great powers.

The principle of **reciprocity** solves the collective goods problem by rewarding behavior that contributes to the group and punishing behavior that pursues self-interest at the expense of the group. Reciprocity is very easy to understand and can be "enforced" without any central authority, making it a robust way to get individuals to cooperate for the common good.

But reciprocity operates in both the positive realm ("You scratch my back and I'll scratch yours") and the negative ("An eye for an eye, a tooth for a tooth"). A disadvantage of reciprocity as a solution to the collective goods problem is that it can lead to a downward spiral as each side punishes what it believes to be negative acts by the other. Psychologically, most people overestimate their own good intentions and underestimate the value of the actions of their opponents or rivals. To avoid tit-for-tat escalations of conflict, one or both parties must act generously to get the relationship moving in a good direction.

In international relations, reciprocity forms the basis of most of the norms (habits; expectations) and institutions in the international system. Many central arrangements in IR, such as World Trade Organization agreements, explicitly recognize reciprocity as the linchpin of cooperation. For instance, if one country opens its markets to another's goods, the other opens its markets in return. On the negative side, reciprocity fuels arms races as each side responds to the other's buildup of weapons. But it also allows arms control agreements and other step-by-step conflict-resolution measures, as two sides match each other's actions in backing away from the brink.

A third potential solution to the collective goods problem lies in the identities of participants as members of a community. Although the dominance and reciprocity principles act on the idea of achieving individual self-interest (by taking what you can, or by mutually beneficial arrangements), the **identity** principle does not rely on self-interest. On the contrary, members of an identity community care about the interests of others in the community enough to sacrifice their own interests to benefit others.

The roots of this principle lie in the family, the extended family, and the kinship group. But this potential is not limited to the close family; it can be generalized to any identity community that one feels a part of. As members of a family care about each other, so do members of an ethnic group, a gender group, a nation, or the world's scientists. In each case, individual members will accept solutions to collective goods problems that do not give them the best deal as individuals, because the benefits are "all in the family," so to speak. A biologist retiring at a rich American university may give away lab equipment to a biologist in a poor country because they share an identity as scientists. A European Jew may give money to Israel because of a shared Jewish identity, or a computer scientist from India may return home to work for lower pay after receiving training in Canada, in order to help the community he or she cares about. Millions of Americans contributed to relief for Asian tsunami victims in 2004 because of a shared identity as members of the community of human beings.

In IR, identity communities play important roles in overcoming difficult collective goods problems, including the issue of who contributes to development assistance, world health, and UN peacekeeping missions. The relatively large foreign aid contributions of Scandinavian countries, or Canada's tradition of peacekeeping, cannot be explained well by self-interest, but arise from these countries' self-defined identities as members of the international community. Even in military force and diplomacy (where dominance and reciprocity, respectively, rule the day), the shared identities of military professionals and of diplomats—each with shared traditions and expectations—can take the edge off conflicts. And military alliances also mix identity politics with raw self-interest, as shown by the unusual strength of the U.S.-British alliance, which shared interests alone cannot explain as well as shared identity does.

Nonstate actors, such as nongovernmental organizations or terrorist networks, also rely on identity politics to a great extent. The increasing roles of these actors—feminist organizations, churches, jihadists, and multinational corporations, for example—have brought the identity principle to greater prominence in IR theory in recent years.

To sum up the three core principles, imagine that you have two good friends, a man and a woman, who are in a romantic relationship. They love each other and enjoy the other's company, but they come to you for help with a problem: When they go out together, the man likes to go to the opera, whereas the woman enjoys going to boxing matches.[3] Because of your training in international relations, you quickly recognize this as a collective goods problem, in which the shared interest is spending time together and the conflicting individual interests are watching opera and watching boxing. (Of course, you know that the behavior of states is more complicated than that of individuals, but put that aside for a moment.) You might approach this problem in any of three ways.

First, you could say, "Traditionally, relationships work best when the man wears the pants. For thousands of years the man has made the decision and the woman has followed it. I suggest you do the same, and buy season tickets to the opera." This would be

---

[3] This scenario is adopted from the game theory example "Battle of the Sexes."

a dominance solution. It could be a very stable solution, if the woman cares more about spending time with her true love than she cares about opera or boxing. It would be a simple solution that would settle all future conflicts. It would give one party everything he wants, and the other party some of what she wants (love, company, a stable relationship). This might be better for both of them than spending all their evenings arguing about where to go out. On the other hand, this solution might leave the woman permanently resentful at the unequal nature of the outcome. She might feel her love for her partner diminish, over time, by a longing for respect and a nostalgia for boxing. She might even meet another man who likes her *and* likes boxing.

Second, you could say, "Look, instead of fighting all the time, why don't you establish a pattern and trade off going to boxing one time and opera the next." This would be a reciprocity solution. You could set up agreements, accounting systems, and shared expectations to govern the implementation of this seemingly simple solution. For example, they could go to boxing on Friday nights and opera on Saturday nights. But what if opera season is shorter than boxing season? Then perhaps they would go to opera more often during its season and boxing more often when opera is out of season. What if one of them is out of town on Friday night? Does that night count anyway or does it earn a credit for later? Or does the one who is in town go alone? What if the man *hates* boxing but the woman only mildly dislikes opera? Do you set up a schedule of two operas for each boxing match to keep each side equally happy or unhappy? Clearly, reciprocity solutions can become very complicated (just look at the world trade rules in Chapter 10, for example), and they require constant monitoring to see if obligations are being met and cheating avoided. Your friends might find it an irritant in their relationship to keep close track of who owes whom a night at the opera or the boxing match.

Third, you could say, "Who cares about opera or boxing? The point is that you love each other and want to be together. Get past the superficial issues and strengthen the core feelings that brought you together. Then it won't matter where you go or what you're watching." This would be an identity solution. This approach could powerfully resolve your friends' conflict and leave them both much happier. Over time, one partner might actually begin to prefer the other's favorite activity after more exposure—leading to a change in identity. On the other hand, after a while self-interest could creep back in, because that loving feeling might seem even happier with a boxing match (or opera) to watch. Indeed, one partner can subtly exploit the other's commitment to get past the superficial conflicts. "What's it matter as long as we're together," she says, "and oh, look, there's a good boxing match tonight!" Sometimes the identity principle operates more powerfully in the short term than the long term: the soldier who volunteers to defend the homeland might begin to feel taken advantage of after months or years on the front line, and the American college student who gives money once to tsunami victims may not keep giving year after year to malaria victims.

Now consider an IR example: the problem of nuclear proliferation. All countries share an interest in the collective good of peace and stability, which is hard to achieve in a world where more and more countries make more and more nuclear weapons. Within a society, if individuals acquire dangerous weapons, the government can take them away to keep everyone safe. But in the society of nations, no such central authority exists. In 2006, North Korea tested its first nuclear bomb, and Iran has continued uranium enrichment that could lead to a nuclear bomb—defying UN resolutions in both cases.

One approach to nuclear proliferation legitimizes their ownership by just the few most powerful countries. The "big five" with the largest nuclear arsenals hold veto power on the UN Security Council. Through agreements like the Non-Proliferation Treaty (NPT) and the Proliferation Security Initiative, the existing nuclear powers actively try to keep their exclusive hold on these weapons and prevent smaller nations from getting them. This is a dominance approach. In 2003, when the United States thought Iraq's Saddam Hussein might have an active nuclear weapons program, as he'd had a decade earlier, it invaded Iraq and overthrew its government. Similarly, in 1982 when Iraq had begun working toward a nuclear bomb, Israel sent jets to bomb Iraq's nuclear facility, setting back the program by years. One drawback to these dominance solutions is the resentment they create among the smaller countries. Those countries point to an unenforced provision of the NPT stating that existing nuclear powers should get rid of their own bombs as other countries refrain from making new ones. And they ask what gives Israel the right to bomb another country, or the United States the right to invade one. They speak of a "double standard" for the powerful and the weak.

Reciprocity offers a different avenue for preventing proliferation. It is the basis of the provision in the NPT about the existing nuclear powers' obligation to disarm in exchange for smaller countries' agreement to stay nonnuclear. Reciprocity also underlies arms control agreements, used extensively in the Cold War to manage the buildup of nuclear bombs by the superpowers, and used currently to manage the mutual reduction of their arsenals. Deterrence also relies on reciprocity. The United States warned North Korea in 2006 against selling its bombs (an action that would be in North Korea's short-term self-interest), threatening to retaliate against North Korea if any other actor used such a bomb against the United States. And when Libya gave up its nuclear weapons program in 2003, the international community gave it various rewards, including the ending of economic sanctions, in exchange.

The identity principle has proven equally effective against nuclear proliferation, if less newsworthy. Many nations that have the technical ability to make nuclear weapons have *chosen* not to do so. They have constructed their national identities in ways that shape their self-interests so as to make nuclear bombs undesirable. Some, like Sweden, do not intend to fight wars. Others, like Germany, belong to alliances in which they come under another nation's nuclear "umbrella" and do not need their own bomb. South Africa actually developed nuclear weapons in secret but then dismantled the program before apartheid ended, keeping the bomb out of the hands of the new majority-rule government. Nobody forced South Africa to do this (as in dominance), nor did it respond to rewards and punishments (reciprocity). Rather, South Africa's identity shifted. Similarly, Japan's experience of the catastrophic results of militarism, culminating in the destruction of two of its cities by nuclear bombs in 1945, continues generations later to shape Japan's identity as a country that does not want nuclear weapons, even though it has the know-how and even the stockpile of plutonium to make them.

Collective goods problems fascinate social scientists, and especially scholars of IR, precisely because they have no easy solutions. In later chapters, we will see how these three core principles shape the various approaches to understanding collective goods problems across a broad range of IR issues.

IR AS A FIELD OF STUDY

As a part of political science, IR is about *international politics*—the decisions of governments about foreign actors, especially other governments.[4] To some extent, however, the field is interdisciplinary, relating international politics to economics, history, sociology, and other disciplines. Some universities offer separate degrees or departments for IR. Most, however, teach IR in political science classes. The focus is on the *politics* of economic relationships, or the *politics* of environmental management. (The domestic politics of foreign countries, although overlapping with IR, generally make up the separate field of *comparative politics*.)

Political relations among nations cover a range of activities—diplomacy, war, trade relations, alliances, cultural exchanges, participation in international organizations, and so forth. Particular activities within one of these spheres make up distinct **issue areas** on which scholars and foreign policy makers focus attention. Examples of issue areas include global trade, the environment, and specific conflicts such as the Arab-Israeli conflict. Within each issue area, and across the range of issues of concern in any international relationship, policy makers of one nation can behave in a cooperative manner or a conflictual manner—extending either friendly or hostile behavior toward the other nation. IR scholars often look at international relations in terms of the mix of **conflict and cooperation** in relationships among nations.

The scope of the field of IR may also be defined by the *subfields* it encompasses. Traditionally, the study of IR has focused on questions of war and peace—the subfield of **international security** studies. The movements of armies and of diplomats, the crafting of treaties and alliances, the development and deployment of military capabilities—these are the subjects that dominated the study of IR in the past, especially in the 1950s and 1960s, and they continue to hold a central position in the field. Since the Cold War, regional conflicts and ethnic violence have received more attention, while interdisciplinary peace studies programs and feminist scholarship have sought to broaden concepts of "security" further.[5]

The subfield of **international political economy (IPE),** a second main subfield of IR, concerns trade and financial relations among nations and focuses on how nations have cooperated politically to create and maintain institutions that regulate the flow

---

[4] Carlsnaes, Walter, Thomas Risse, and Beth Simmons, eds. *Handbook of International Relations.* Sage, 2002. Williams, Phil, Donald M. Goldstein, and Jay M. Shafritz. *Classic Readings and Contemporary Debates in International Relations.* Wadsworth, 2005. Clark, Ian, and Iver B. Neumann, eds. *Classical Theories in International Relations.* St. Martin's, 1996.

[5] Neack, Laura. *Elusive Security: States First, People Last.* Rowman & Littlefield, 2007. Booth, Ken, ed. *Critical Security Studies and World Politics.* Rienner, 2005.

of international economic and financial transactions. These topics mainly relate to relations among the world's richer nations. But, since the 1990s, growing attention has been paid to global North-South relations between rich and poor nations, including such topics as economic dependency, debt, foreign aid, and technology transfer. Also increasingly important are problems of international environmental management and of global telecommunications. The subfield of IPE is expanding accordingly.

STATE ACTORS

The principal actors in IR are the world's governments. Scholars of IR traditionally study the decisions and acts of those governments, in relation to other governments. The international stage is crowded with actors large and small, interwoven with the decisions of governments. These actors are individual leaders and citizens. They are bureaucratic agencies in foreign ministries. They are multinational corporations and terrorist groups. But the most important actors in IR are states.

A **state** is a territorial entity controlled by a government and inhabited by a population. The locations of the world's states and territories are shown in the reference map at the front of this book, after the preface. A state government answers to no higher authority; it exercises *sovereignty* over its territory—to make and enforce laws, to collect taxes, and so forth. This sovereignty is recognized (acknowledged) by other states through diplomatic relations and usually by membership in the United Nations (UN). The population inhabiting a state forms a *civil society* to the extent that it has developed institutions to participate in political or social life. All or part of the population that shares a group identity may consider itself a *nation* (see pp. 126–127). The state's government is a *democracy* to the extent that the government is controlled by the members of the population rather than imposed on them. (Note that the word *state* in IR does not mean a state in the United States.) In political life, and to some extent in IR scholarship, the terms *state*, *nation*, and *country* are used imprecisely, usually to refer to state governments.

With few exceptions, each state has a capital city—the seat of government from which it administers its territory—and often a single individual who acts in the name of the state. We will refer to this person simply as the "state leader." Often he or she is the *head of government* (such as a prime minister) or the *head of state* (such as a president, or a king or queen). In some countries, such as the United States, the same person is head of state and government. In other countries, the positions of the president or royalty, or even the prime minister, are symbolic. In any case, the most powerful political figure is the one we mean by "state leader," and these figures are the key individual actors in IR, regardless of whether these leaders are democratically elected or dictators. The state actor includes the individual leader as well as bureaucratic organizations (such as foreign ministries) that act in the name of the state.

The **international system** is the set of relationships among the world's states, structured according to certain rules and patterns of interaction. Some such rules are explicit, some implicit. They include who is considered a member of the system, what rights and responsibilities the members have, and what kinds of actions and responses normally occur between states.

The modern international system has existed for less than 500 years. Before then, people were organized into more mixed and overlapping political units such as city-states, empires, and feudal fiefs. In the past 200 years the idea has spread that nations—groups of people who share a sense of national identity, usually including a language and culture—should have their own states. Most large states today are such **nation-states.** But since World War II, the decolonization process in much of Asia and Africa has added many new states, some not at all nation-states.

A major source of conflict and war at present is the frequent mismatch between perceived nations and actual state borders. When people identify with a nationality that their state government does not represent, they may fight to form their own state and thus to gain sovereignty over their territory and affairs. This substate nationalism is only one of several growing trends that undermine the present system of states. Other such trends include the globalization of economic processes, the power of telecommunications, and the proliferation of ballistic missiles. The independence of former colonies and, more recently, the breakup into smaller states of large multinational states (the Soviet Union, Yugoslavia, and Czechoslovakia) have increased the number of states in the world. The exact total depends on the status of a number of quasi-state political entities, and it changes as political units split apart or merge. The UN had 192 members in 2008.

The population of the world's states varies dramatically, from China and India with more than 1 billion people each to microstates such as San Marino with fewer than 100,000. With the creation of many small states in recent decades, the majority of states now have fewer than 10 million people each, and more than half of the rest have 10 to 50 million each. But the 15 states with populations of more than 70 million people together contain about two-thirds of the world's population. States also differ tremendously in the size of their total annual economic activity—**Gross Domestic Product (GDP)**[6]—from the $13 trillion U.S. economy to the economies of tiny states such as the Pacific island of Vanuatu ($600 million). The world economy is dominated by a few states, just as world population is. Figure 1.1 lists the largest countries by population and economy. Each is an important actor in world affairs. Despite the large number of states in the international system, a much smaller number have the most influence.

A few of these large states possess especially great military and economic strength and influence, and are called *great powers*. They are defined and discussed in Chapter 2.

---

[6] GDP is the total of goods and services produced by a nation; it is very close to the Gross National Product (GNP). Such data are difficult to compare across nations with different currencies, economic systems, and levels of development. In particular, comparisons of GDP in capitalist and socialist economies, or in rich and poor countries, should be treated cautiously. GDP data used in this book are mostly from the World Bank. GDP data are adjusted through time and across countries for "purchasing-power parity" (how much a given amount of money can buy). See Summers, Robert, and Alan Heston. The Penn World Table (Mark 5): An Expanded Set of International Comparisons, 1950–1988. *Quarterly Journal of Economics* 106 (2), 1991: 327–68. GDP and population data are for 2006 unless otherwise noted.

FIGURE 1.1   Largest Countries

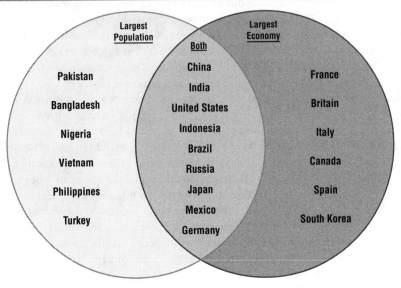

Note: Left and center columns listed in population order, right column in GDP order. GDP calculated by purchasing parity.

The most powerful of great powers, those with truly global influence, have been called *superpowers*. This term generally meant the United States and the Soviet Union during the Cold War, and now refers to the United States alone.

Some other political entities are often referred to as countries although they are not formally recognized as states. Taiwan is the most important of these. It operates independently in practice but is formally a part of China and is not a UN member. Formal colonies and possessions still exist as well. Including various such territorial entities with states brings the world total to about 200 state or quasi-state actors. Other would-be states such as Kurdistan (Iraq), Abkhazia (Georgia), and Somaliland (Somalia) may control the territory they claim but are not internationally recognized.

NONSTATE ACTORS

National governments may be the most important actors in IR, but they are strongly influenced by a variety of **nonstate actors** (see Table 1.2). These actors are also called *transnational actors* when they operate across international borders.

First, states often take actions through, within, or in the context of **intergovernmental organizations (IGOs)**—organizations whose members are national governments. IGOs fulfill a variety of functions and vary in size from just a few states to virtually the whole UN membership. Some IGOs are global in scope; others are regional or just bilateral (having only two states as members). Some are general in their purposes; others have spe-

TABLE 1.2 **Types of Nonstate Actors**

Type		Who Are They?	Examples
IGOs[a]	Intergovernmental Organizations	Members are national governments	United Nations, NATO, Arab League
NGOs[a]	Nongovernmental Organizations	Members are individuals and groups	Amnesty International, Lions Clubs, Red Cross
MNCs	Multinational Corporations	Companies that span borders	ExxonMobil, Toyota, Wal-Mart
Others		Individuals, Cities, Constituencies, etc.	Bono, Iraqi Kurdistan, al Qaeda

[a]Note: IGOs and NGOs together make up International Organizations (IOs).

cific functional purposes. Overall, the success of these IGOs has been mixed; the regional ones have had more success than the global ones, and those with specific functional or technical purposes have worked better than those with broad purposes (see pp. 63–64). IGOs hold together because they promote the national interests (or enhance the leverage) of their member states—not because of vague ideals.

Among *regional* IGOs, the European Union encompasses some of the most important organizations (see Chapter 4), but it is not the only example. Other important regional IGOs are the Association of South East Asian Nations (ASEAN), the Southern Cone Common Market (MERCOSUR), and the African Union. The functional roles of IOs are important to their overall effect on international relations.

Global IGOs (aside from the UN) usually have functional purposes involving coordinating actions of some set of states around the world. For example, members of the Organization of the Petroleum Exporting Countries (OPEC) are major oil producers who set production quotas for members in an effort to keep world oil prices high and stable.

Another type of transnational actor, **nongovernmental organizations (NGOs),** are private organizations, some of considerable size and resources. Increasingly NGOs are being recognized, in the UN and other forums, as legitimate actors along with states, though not equal to them. Sometimes NGOs combine efforts through transnational advocacy networks.[7] There is no single pattern to NGOs.

NGOs tend to be more specialized in function than IGOs. Many NGOs have economic or business-related functions. For instance, the International Air Transport Association coordinates the work of airline companies. Other NGOs have global political purposes—for example, Amnesty International for human rights and Planned Parenthood for reproductive rights and family planning. Still others have cultural purposes—for example, the International Olympic Committee.

---

[7] Keck, Margaret E., and Kathryn Sikkink. *Activists Beyond Borders: Advocacy Networks in International Politics.* Cornell, 1998. Florini, Ann M., ed. *The Third Force: The Rise of Transnational Civil Society.* Carnegie Endowment for International Peace, 2000.

Religious groups are among the largest NGOs—their memberships often span many countries. Both in today's world and historically, sects of Christianity, Islam, Buddhism, Judaism, Hinduism, and other world religions have organized themselves across state borders, often in the face of hostility from one or more national governments. Missionaries have deliberately built and nurtured these transnational links. The Catholic Church historically held a special position in the European international system, especially before the 17th century. NGOs with broad purposes and geographical scope often maintain observer status in the UN so that they can participate in UN meetings about issues of concern. For example, Greenpeace attends UN meetings about the global environment.

Together, IGOs and NGOs are referred to as **international organizations (IOs).**[8] Especially in times of change, when shared norms and habits may not suffice to solve international dilemmas and achieve mutual cooperation, institutions play a key role. They are concrete, tangible structures with specific functions and missions. By one count there are more than 25,000 NGOs and 5,000 IGOs. The number of IOs has grown more than fivefold since 1945 (see Figure 1.2).[9] This weaving together of people

FIGURE 1.2   **States and IGOs in the World, 1815–2000**

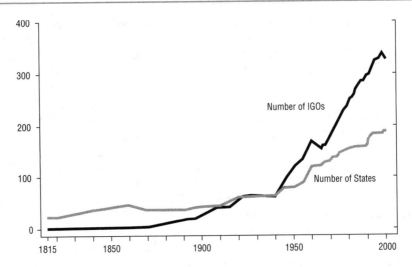

[8] Armstrong, David, Lorna Lloyd, and John Redmond. *International Organization in World Politics.* Palgrave, 2003.

[9] Pevehouse, Jon C., Timothy Nordstrom, and Kevin Warnke. The Correlates of War 2 International Governmental Organizations Data Version 2.0. *Conflict Management and Peace Science* 21 (2), 2004: 101–20.

across national boundaries through specialized groups reflects interdependence (see pp. 159–160).[10]

A web of international organizations of various sizes and types now connects people in all countries. The rapid growth of this network, and the increasingly intense communications and interactions that occur within it, indicate rising international interdependence. These organizations in turn provide the institutional mesh to hold together some kind of world order even when leaders and contexts come and go, and even when norms are undermined by sudden changes in power relations.

Multinational corporations (MNCs) are companies that span multiple countries. The interests of a large company doing business globally do not correspond with any one state's interests. MNCs often control greater resources, and operate internationally with greater efficiency, than many small states. They may prop up (or even create) friendly foreign governments, as the United Fruit Company did in the "banana republics" of Central America a century ago. But MNCs also provide poor states with much-needed foreign investment and tax revenues. MNCs in turn depend on states to provide protection, well-regulated markets, and a stable political environment (see Chapter 11).

Some nonstate actors are *substate actors:* they exist within one country but either influence that country's foreign policy or operate internationally, or both. For instance, the state of Ohio is entirely a U.S. entity but operates an International Trade Division to promote exports and foreign investment, with offices in Belgium, Japan, China, Canada, Israel, and Mexico. The actions of substate economic actors—companies, consumers, workers, investors—help create the context of economic activity against which international political events play out, and within which governments must operate.

Both state and nonstate actors are strongly affected by the revolution in information technologies now under way. The new information-intensive world promises to reshape international relations profoundly. Technological change dramatically affects actors' relative capabilities and even preferences. Telecommunications and computerization allow economics, politics, and culture alike to operate on a global scale as never before (see pp. 166–169).

In this world of globalization, of substate actors and transnational actors, states are still important. But to some extent they are being gradually pushed aside as companies, groups, and individuals deal ever more directly with each other across borders, and as the world economy becomes globally integrated. Now more than ever, IR extends beyond the interactions of national governments.

LEVELS OF ANALYSIS

The many actors involved at once in IR contribute to the complexity of competing explanations and theories. One way that scholars of IR have sorted out this multiplicity

---

[10] Pease, Kelly-Kate S. *International Organizations: Perspectives on Governance in the Twenty-First Century.* 2nd ed. Prentice Hall, 2002. Barnett, Michael N., and Martha Finnemore. *Rules for the World: International Organizations and Global Politics.* Cornell, 2004. Boli, John, and George M. Thomas, eds. *Constructing World Culture: International Nongovernmental Organizations Since 1875.* Stanford, 1999.

of influences, actors, and processes is to categorize them into different *levels of analysis* (see Table 1.3). A level of analysis is a perspective on IR based on a set of similar actors or processes that suggests possible explanations to "why" questions. IR scholars have proposed various level-of-analysis schemes, most often with three main levels (and sometimes a few sublevels between).[11]

The *individual* level of analysis concerns the perceptions, choices, and actions of individual human beings. Great leaders influence the course of history, as do individual citizens, thinkers, soldiers, and voters. Without Lenin, it is said, there might well have been no Soviet Union. The study of foreign policy decision making, discussed in

TABLE 1.3 Levels of Analysis

Many influences affect the course of international relations. Levels of analysis provide a framework for categorizing these influences and thus for suggesting various explanations of international events. Examples include:

Global Level

North-South gap	Religious fundamentalism	Information revolution
World regions	Terrorism	Global telecommunications
European imperialism	World environment	Worldwide scientific and
UN	Technological change	business communities

Interstate Level

Power	Wars	Diplomacy
Balance of power	Treaties	Summit meetings
Alliance formation	Trade agreements	Bargaining
and dissolution	IGOs	Reciprocity

Domestic Level

Nationalism	Dictatorship	Gender
Ethnic conflict	Domestic coalitions	Economic sectors and industries
Type of government	Political parties and elections	Military-industrial complex
Democracy	Public opinion	Foreign policy bureaucracies

Individual Level

Great leaders	Psychology of perception and decision	Citizens' participation (voting,
Crazy leaders	Learning	rebelling, going to war, etc.)
Decision making in	Assassinations, accidents of history	
crises		

---

[11] Singer, J. David. The Level-of-Analysis Problem in International Relations. *World Politics* 14 (1), 1961: 77–92. Waltz, Kenneth. *Man, the State, and War: A Theoretical Analysis.* Rev. ed. Columbia, 2001.

Chapter 3, pays special attention to individual-level explanations of IR outcomes because of the importance of psychological factors in the decision-making process.

The *domestic* (or *state* or *societal*) level of analysis concerns the aggregations of individuals within states that influence state actions in the international arena. Such aggregations include interest groups, political organizations, and government agencies. These groups operate differently (with different international effects) in different kinds of societies and states. For instance, democracies and dictatorships may act differently from one another, and democracies may act differently in an election year from the way they act at other times. The politics of ethnic conflict and nationalism, bubbling up from within states, plays an increasingly important role in the relations among states. Within governments, foreign policy agencies often fight bureaucratic battles over policy decisions.

The *interstate* (or *international* or *systemic*) level of analysis concerns the influence of the international system upon outcomes. This level of analysis therefore focuses on the interactions of states themselves, without regard to their internal makeup or the particular individuals who lead them. This level pays attention to states' relative power positions in the international system and the interactions (trade, for example) among them. It has been traditionally the most important of the levels of analysis.

To these three levels can be added a fourth, the *global* level of analysis, which seeks to explain international outcomes in terms of global trends and forces that transcend the interactions of states themselves.[12] The evolution of human technology, of certain worldwide beliefs, and of humans' relationship to the natural environment are all processes at the global level that reach down to influence international relations. The global level is also increasingly the focus of IR scholars studying transnational integration through worldwide scientific, technical, and business communities. Another pervasive global influence is the lingering effect of historical European imperialism—Europe's conquest of Latin America, Asia, and Africa (discussed in Chapter 7).

Although IR scholars often focus their study mainly on one level of analysis, other levels bear on a problem simultaneously. There is no single correct level for a given "why" question. Rather, levels of analysis help suggest multiple explanations and approaches to consider in explaining an event. They remind scholars and students to look beyond the immediate and superficial aspects of an event to explore the possible influences of more distant causes. Note that the processes at higher levels tend to operate more slowly than those on the lower levels. Individuals go in and out of office often; the structure of the international system changes rarely.

GLOBAL GEOGRAPHY

To highlight the insights afforded by a global level of analysis, this book divides the world into nine regions. These *world regions* differ from each other in the number of states they contain and in each region's particular mix of cultures, geographical

---

[12] North, Robert C. *War, Peace, Survival: Global Politics and Conceptual Synthesis*. Westview, 1990.

16

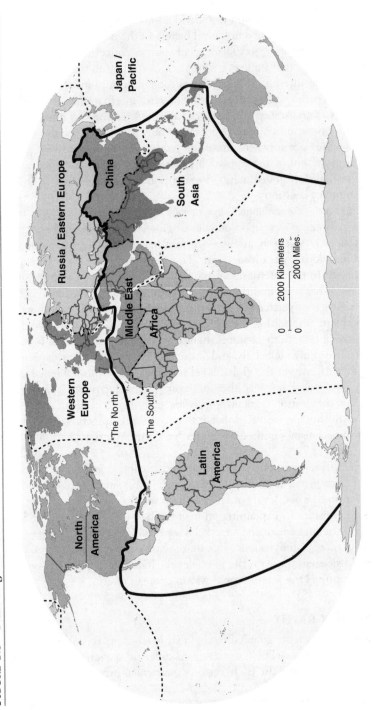

Figure 1.3   Nine Regions of the World

realities, and languages. But each represents a geographical corner of the world, and together they reflect the overall larger divisions of the world.

The global **North-South gap** between the relatively rich industrialized countries of the North and the relatively poor countries of the South is the most important geographical element at the global level of analysis. The regions used in this book have been drawn so as to separate (with a few exceptions) the rich countries from the poor ones. The North includes both the West (the rich countries of North America, Western Europe, and Japan) and the old East (the former Soviet Union and its bloc of allies). The South includes Latin America, Africa, the Middle East, and much of Asia. The South is sometimes called the *third world* (third after the West and East)—a term that is still used despite the second world's collapse. Countries in the South are also referred to as "developing" countries or "less-developed" countries (LDCs), in contrast to the "developed" countries of the North. The overall world regions are shown in Figure 1.3. Of course, no scheme works perfectly, and some states, such as Turkey, are pulled toward two regions.

Table 1.4 shows the approximate population and economic size (GDP) of each region in relation to the world as a whole. As the table indicates, income levels per capita are, overall, more than five times as high in the North as in the South. *The North contains only 20 percent of the world's people but 60 percent of its goods and services.* The other 80 percent of the world's people, in the South, have only 40 percent of the

TABLE 1.4 Comparison of World Regions, 2006

Region	Population (Millions)	GDP (Trillion $)	GDP per Capita (Dollars)
The North			
North America	300	$15	$48,000
Western Europe	400	14	34,000
Japan/Pacific	200	6	27,000
Russia & E. Europe	400	4	7,500
The South			
China	1,400	8	6,000
Middle East	450	4	7,250
Latin America	550	5	9,000
South Asia	2,100	8	4,100
Africa	700	2	3,000
Total North	**1,300 (20%)**	**39 (59%)**	**29,000**
Total South	**5,200 (80%)**	**27 (41%)**	**5,900**
World Total	**6,500**	**$66**	**$10,200**

Note: Data adjusted for purchasing-power parity. 2006 GDP estimates (in 2007 dollars) are based on World Bank data; those for Russia and Eastern Europe, and for China, should be treated especially cautiously.

goods and services. IR scholars have no single explanation of the huge North-South income gap (see Chapter 12).

Unlike the natural sciences, which study very large numbers of identical entities—particles, molecules, genes—IR deals with a mix of entities and processes. The global North and South, the unique cultures of various countries, state and nonstate actors, individuals and organizations, all have their parts in shaping outcomes. This diversity makes IR a fascinating subject but is a major challenge for general theories as useful explanations. Figure 1.4 organizes the various theoretical approaches in IR, discussed in the coming chapters, according to levels of analysis.

FIGURE 1.4 Theories of IR

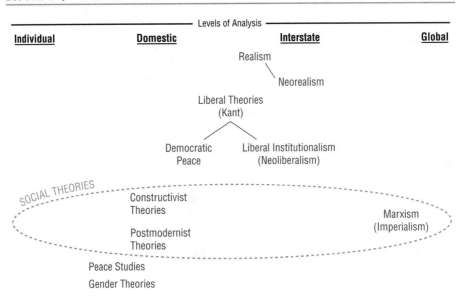

CHAPTER 2

REALISM

REALISM

No single theory reliably explains the wide range of international interactions, but one theoretical framework has traditionally held a central position in the study of IR. This approach, called realism, is favored by some IR scholars and vigorously contested by others, but almost all take it into account. Realism's foundation is the principle of dominance; alternatives based on reciprocity and identity will be reviewed in later chapters.

Realism (or *political realism*) is a school of thought that explains international relations in terms of power. The exercise of power by states toward each other is sometimes called *realpolitik*, or just *power politics*.

Realism as we know it developed in reaction to a liberal tradition that realists called **idealism** (of course, idealists themselves do not consider their approach unrealistic). Idealism emphasizes international law, morality, and international organizations, rather than power alone, as key influences on international events.[1] Idealists think that human nature is basically good. They see the international system as one based on a community of states with the potential to work together to overcome mutual problems (see Chapter 4). For idealists, the principles of IR must flow from morality. Idealists were particularly active between World War I and World War II, following the painful experience of World War I. U.S. president Woodrow Wilson and other idealists placed their hopes for peace in the League of Nations as a formal structure for the community of nations.

Those hopes were dashed when that structure proved helpless to stop German, Italian, and Japanese aggression in the 1930s. Since World War II, realists have blamed idealists for looking too much at how the world *ought* to be instead of how it *really* is. Sobered by the experiences of World War II, realists set out to understand the principles of power politics without succumbing to wishful thinking. Realism provided a theoretical foundation for the Cold War policies of containment and the determination of U.S. policy makers not to appease the Soviet Union and China as the West had appeased Hitler at Munich in 1938. Table 2.1 summarizes some major differences between the assumptions of realism and idealism.

Realists ground themselves in a long tradition. The Chinese strategist *Sun Tzu*, who lived 2,000 years ago, advised the rulers of states how to survive in an era when war had become a systematic instrument of power for the first time (the "warring states" period). Sun Tzu argued that moral reasoning was not very useful to the state

---

[1] Nardin, Terry, and David R. Mapel, eds. *Traditions of International Ethics*. Cambridge, 1992. Long, David, and Peter Wilson, eds. *Thinkers of the Twenty Years' Crisis: Inter-War Idealism Reassessed*. Oxford, 1995.

TABLE 2.1 Assumptions of Realism and Idealism

Issue	Realism	Idealism
Human Nature	Selfish	Altruistic
Most Important Actors	States	States and others including individuals
Causes of State Behavior	Rational pursuit of self-interest	Psychological motives of decision makers
Nature of International System	Anarchy	Community

rulers of the day, faced with armed and dangerous neighbors. He showed rulers how to use power to advance their interests and protect their survival.[2]

At roughly the same time, in Greece, *Thucydides* wrote an account of the Peloponnesian War (431–404 B.C.) focusing on relative power among the Greek city-states. He stated that "the strong do what they have the power to do and the weak accept what they have to accept."[3] Much later, in Renaissance Italy (around 1500), *Niccolò Machiavelli* urged princes to concentrate on expedient actions to stay in power, including the manipulation of the public and military alliances.[4]

The English philosopher *Thomas Hobbes* in the 17th century discussed the free-for-all that exists when government is absent and people seek their own self-interest. He called it the "state of nature" or "state of war"—what we would now call the "law of the jungle" in contrast to the rule of law. Hobbes favored a strong monarchy (which he labeled a *Leviathan*) to tame this condition—essentially advocating a dominance approach to solve the collective goods problem in domestic societies. Realists see in these historical figures evidence that the importance of power politics is timeless and cross-cultural.

After World War II, scholar *Hans Morgenthau* argued that international politics is governed by objective, universal laws based on national interests defined in terms of power (not psychological motives of decision makers). He reasoned that no nation had "God on its side" (a universal morality) and that all nations had to base their actions on prudence and practicality. He opposed the Vietnam War, arguing in 1965 that a communist Vietnam would not harm U.S. national interests.

Similarly, in 2002, before the U.S. invasion of Iraq, leading realists figured prominently among 33 IR scholars signing a *New York Times* advertisement warning that "war with Iraq is *not* in America's national interest."[5] Thus realists do not always favor

---

[2] Sun Tzu. *The Art of War*. Translated by Samuel B. Griffith. Oxford, 1963.

[3] Thucydides. *History of the Peloponnesian War*. Translated by R. Warner. Penguin, 1972, p. 402.

[4] Machiavelli, Niccolò. *The Prince, and the Discourses*. Translated by Luigi Ricci. Revised by E. R. P. Vincent. NY: Modern Library, 1950. Meinecke, Friedrich. *Machiavellism: The Doctrine of Raison d'État and Its Place in Modern History*. Translated by D. Scott. Yale, 1957.

[5] Morgenthau, Hans. We Are Deluding Ourselves in Vietnam. *The New York Times Magazine*, Apr. 18, 1965. Advertisement, *The New York Times*, Sept. 26, 2002.

using military power, although they recognize the necessity of doing so at times. The target of the IR scholars' ad was the group of foreign policy makers in the Bush administration known as *neoconservatives*, who advocated more energetic use of American power, especially military force, to accomplish ambitious goals such as democratizing the Middle East. Neoconservative influence on U.S. foreign policy has diminished, and realist influence has increased, as a result of the problems faced in the war in Iraq. As one journalist put it in 2006, "Iraq has turned conservatives and liberals alike into cold-eyed believers in a foreign policy that narrowly calculates national interest without much concern for what goes on inside other countries."[6]

Realists tend to treat political power as separate from, and predominant over, morality, ideology, and other social and economic aspects of life. For realists, ideologies do not matter much, nor do religions or other cultural factors with which states may explain their actions. Realists see states with very different religions, ideologies, or economic systems as quite similar in their actions with regard to national power.[7]

Thus, realists assume that IR can be best (though not exclusively) explained by the choices of states operating as autonomous actors rationally pursuing their own interests in an international system of sovereign states without central authority.

POWER

Power is a central concept in international relations—*the* central one for realists—but surprisingly difficult to define or measure.[8] Power is often defined as the ability to get another actor to do what it would not otherwise have done (or not to do what it would have done). A variation on this idea is that actors are powerful to the extent that they affect others more than others affect them. These definitions treat power as influence. If actors get their way a lot, they must be powerful.

One problem with this definition is that we seldom know what a second actor would have done in the absence of the first actor's power. There is a danger of circular logic: power explains influence, and influence measures power. Power is not influence itself, however, but the ability or potential to influence others. Many IR scholars believe that such potential is based on specific (tangible and intangible) characteristics or possessions of states—such as their sizes, levels of income, and armed forces. This is power as *capability*. Capabilities are easier to measure than influence and less circular in logic.

Measuring capabilities to explain how one state influences another is not simple, however. It requires summing up various kinds of potentials. States possess varying

---

[6] Packer, George. Unrealistic. *The New Yorker*, Nov. 27, 2006. Safire, William. Realism: The Comeback Word in Foreign Policy. *The New York Times Magazine*, Dec. 24, 2006: 20.

[7] Morgenthau, Hans J., and Kenneth W. Thompson. *Politics among Nations: The Struggle for Power and Peace*. 6th ed. Knopf, 1985. Carr, Edward Hallett. *The Twenty Years' Crisis, 1919–1939: An Introduction to the Study of International Relations*. Macmillan, 1974 [1939]. Aron, Raymond. *Peace and War: A Theory of International Relations*. Translated by R. Howard and A. B. Fox. Doubleday, 1966.

[8] Baldwin, David. Power in International Relations. In Carlsnaes, Walter, Thomas Risse, and Beth Simmons, eds. *Handbook of International Relations*. Sage, 2002, pp. 177–91.

amounts of population, territory, military forces, and so forth. *The best single indicator of a state's power may be its total GDP*, which combines overall size, technological level, and wealth. But even GDP is at best a rough indicator, and economists do not even agree how to measure it. The method followed in this book adjusts for price differences among countries, but an alternative method gives GDP estimates that are on average about 50 percent higher for countries in the global North and about 50 percent lower for the global South including China (see footnote 6 on p. 9). So GDP is a useful estimator of material capabilities but not a precise one.

Power also depends on nonmaterial elements. Capabilities give a state the potential to influence others only to the extent that political leaders can mobilize and deploy them effectively and strategically. This depends on national will, diplomatic skill, popular support for the government (its legitimacy), and so forth. Some scholars emphasize the *power of ideas*—the ability to maximize the influence of capabilities through a psychological process. This process includes the domestic mobilization of capabilities—often through religion, ideology, or (especially) nationalism. International influence is also gained by forming the rules of behavior, to change how others see their own national interests. If a state's own values become widely shared among other states, it will easily influence others. For example, the United States has influenced many other states to accept the value of free markets and free trade. This has been called *soft power*.[9]

As the concept of soft power illustrates, dominance is not the only way to exert power (influence others). The core principles of reciprocity and (in the case of soft power) identity can also work. For example, a mother who wants her toddler to stop screaming in a supermarket might threaten a spanking (dominance); she might promise a candy bar at the checkout as a reward for good behavior (reciprocity); or she could invoke such themes as "Be a big boy/girl" or "You want to help Mommy, don't you?" (identity). Although realists emphasize dominance approaches, they acknowledge that states often achieve their interests in other ways. Furthermore, even realists recognize that power provides only a general understanding of outcomes. Real-world outcomes depend on many other elements, including accidents or luck.

Because power is a relational concept, a state can have power only relative to other states. *Relative power* is the ratio of the power that two states can bring to bear against each other. It matters little to realists whether a state's capabilities are rising or declining in absolute terms, only whether they are falling behind or overtaking the capabilities of rival states.

Elements that an actor can draw on over the *long term* include total GDP, population, territory, geography, and natural resources. These attributes change only slowly. Less tangible long-term power resources include political culture, patriotism, education of the population, and strength of the scientific and technological base. The credibility of its commitments (reputation for keeping its word) is also a long-term power base for a state. So is the ability of one state's culture and values to consistently shape the thinking of other states (the power of ideas).

---

[9] Nye, Joseph S., Jr. *Bound to Lead: The Changing Nature of American Power*. Basic Books, 1990.

Other capabilities allow actors to exercise influence in the *short term*. Military forces are such a capability—perhaps the most important kind. The size, composition, and preparedness of two states' military forces matter more in a short-term military confrontation than do their respective economies or natural resources. Another capability is the military-industrial capacity to quickly produce weapons. The quality of a state's bureaucracy is another type of capability, allowing the state to gather information, regulate international trade, or participate in international conferences. Less tangibly, the *support* and *legitimacy* that an actor commands in the short term from constituents and allies are capabilities that the actor can use to gain influence. So is the *loyalty* of a nation's army and politicians to its leader.

Given the limited resources that any actor commands, trade-offs among possible capabilities always exist. Building up military forces diverts resources that might be put into foreign aid, for instance. Or buying a population's loyalty with consumer goods reduces resources available for building up military capabilities. To the extent that one element of power can be converted into another, it is *fungible*. Generally, money is the most fungible capability because it can buy other capabilities. Realists tend to see *military force* as the most important element of national power in the short term, and they see other elements such as economic strength or diplomatic skill or moral legitimacy as being important to the extent that they are fungible into military power.

Morality can contribute to power by increasing the will to use power and by attracting allies. States have long clothed their actions, however aggressive, in rhetoric about their peaceful and defensive intentions. For instance, the 1989 U.S. invasion of Panama was named "Operation Just Cause." Of course, if a state overuses moralistic rhetoric to cloak self-interest too often, it loses credibility even with its own population.

The use of geography as an element of power is called **geopolitics.** It is often tied to the logistical requirements of military forces. In geopolitics, as in real estate, the three most important considerations are location, location, location. States increase their power to the extent they can use geography to enhance their military capabilities, such as by securing allies and bases close to a rival power or along strategic trade routes, or by controlling key natural resources. Today, control of oil pipeline routes, especially in Central Asia, is a major geopolitical issue.

A recurrent geopolitical theme for centrally located, largely landlocked states such as Germany and Russia is the threat of being surrounded. Militarily, centrally located states often face a *two-front problem*. States less centrally located, such as Britain and the United States, are *insular* because bodies of water protect them against land attacks; their geopolitical problem in the event of war is to move soldiers and supplies over long distances to reach the scene of battle.[10] This capability was demonstrated in the U.S. participation in World War I, World War II, the Cold War, and the Gulf War. But in general, power declines as a function of distance from a home state.

---

[10] Dehio, Ludwig. *The Precarious Balance: Four Centuries of the European Power Struggle*. Translated by Charles Fullman. Vintage Books, 1962 [from the German version of 1948].

ANARCHY AND SOVEREIGNTY

Realists believe that the international system exists in a state of **anarchy**—a term that implies not complete chaos or absence of structure and rules, but rather the lack of a central government that can enforce rules.[11] In domestic society within states, governments can enforce contracts, deter citizens from breaking rules, and use their monopoly on legally sanctioned violence to enforce a system of law. Both democracies and dictatorships provide central government enforcement of a system of rules. Realists contend that no such central authority exists to enforce rules and ensure compliance with norms of conduct. This makes collective goods problems especially acute in IR. The power of one state is countered only by the power of other states. States must rely on *self-help*, which they supplement with allies and the (sometimes) constraining power of international norms.

Some people think that only a world government can solve this problem. Others think that adequate order can be provided by international organizations and agreements, short of world government (see Chapter 4). But most realists think that IR cannot escape from a state of anarchy and will continue to be dangerous as a result.[12] In this anarchic world, realists emphasize prudence as a great virtue in foreign policy. States should pay attention not to the *intentions* of other states but rather to their *capabilities*.

Despite its anarchy, the international system is far from chaotic. The great majority of state interactions closely adhere to **norms** of behavior—shared expectations about what behavior is considered proper (see Chapter 6).[13] Norms change over time, slowly, but the most basic norms of the international system have changed little in recent centuries.

Sovereignty—traditionally the most important norm—means that a government has the right, in principle, to do whatever it wants in its own territory. States are separate and autonomous and answer to no higher authority. In principle, all states are equal in status, if not in power. Sovereignty also means that states are not supposed to interfere in the internal affairs of other states. Although states do try to influence each other (exert power) on matters of trade, alliances, war, and so on, they are not supposed to meddle in the internal politics and decision processes of other states.

In practice, most states have a harder and harder time warding off interference in their affairs. Such "internal" matters as human rights or self-determination are, increasingly, concerns for the international community. For example, election monitors increasingly watch internal elections for fraud, while international organizations monitor ethnic conflicts for genocide. Also, the integration of global economic markets

---

[11] Bull, Hedley. *The Anarchical Society: A Study of Order in World Politics.* Columbia, 2002 [1977]. Taylor, Michael. *Anarchy and Cooperation.* Wiley, 1976. Buzan, Barry, and Richard Little. *International Systems in World History: Remaking the Study of International Relations.* Oxford, 2000. Luard, Evan. *Conflict and Peace in the Modern International System: A Study of the Principles of International Order.* Macmillan, 1988. Wight, Martin. *Systems of States.* Leicester, 1977.

[12] Mearsheimer, John J. *The Tragedy of Great Power Politics.* Norton, 2001.

[13] Franck, Thomas M. *The Power of Legitimacy among Nations.* Oxford, 1990.

and telecommunications (such as the Internet) makes it easier than ever for ideas to penetrate state borders.[14]

States are based on territory. Respect for the territorial integrity of all states, within recognized borders, is an important principle of IR. Many of today's borders are the result of past wars (in which winners took territory from losers) or were imposed arbitrarily by colonizers. The territorial nature of the interstate system developed long ago when agrarian societies relied on agriculture to generate wealth. In today's world, in which trade and technology rather than land create wealth, the territorial state may be less important. Information-based economies are linked across borders instantly, and the idea that the state has a hard shell seems archaic. The accelerating revolution in information technologies may dramatically affect the territorial state system in the coming years.

Realists acknowledge that the rules of IR often create a **security dilemma**—a situation in which states' actions taken to ensure their own security (such as deploying more military forces) threaten the security of other states.[15] The responses of those other states, such as deploying more of their own military forces, in turn threaten the first state. The dilemma is a prime cause of arms races in which states waste large sums of money on mutually threatening weapons that do not ultimately provide security.

The security dilemma is a negative consequence of anarchy in the international system. If a world government could reliably punish aggressors who arm themselves, states would not need to guard against this possibility. Yet the self-help system requires that they prepare for the worst. Realists tend to see the dilemma as unsolvable, whereas liberals think it can be solved through the development of norms and institutions.

As we shall see in later chapters, changes in technology and in norms are undermining the traditional principles of territorial integrity and state autonomy in IR. Some IR scholars find states practically obsolete as the main actors in world politics, as some integrate into larger entities and others fragment into smaller units.[16] Other scholars find the international system quite enduring in its structure and state units.[17] One of its most enduring features is the balance of power.

BALANCE OF POWER

In the anarchy of the international system, the most reliable brake on the power of one state is the power of other states. The term **balance of power** refers to the general concept of one or more states' power being used to balance that of another state or group

---

[14] Finnemore, Martha. *The Purpose of Intervention: Changing Beliefs about the Use of Force.* Cornell, 2004. Krasner, Stephen D. *Sovereignty: Organized Hypocrisy.* Princeton, 1999.

[15] Herz, John. Idealist Internationalism and the Security Dilemma. *World Politics* 2 (2), 1950: 157–80. Jervis, Robert. Cooperation under the Security Dilemma. *World Politics* 30 (2), 1978: 167–214.

[16] Aydinli, Ersel, and James N. Rosenau, eds. *Globalization, Security, and the Nation State: Paradigms in Transition.* SUNY, 2005.

[17] Weiss, Linda. *The Myth of the Powerless State.* Cornell, 1998.

FIGURE 2.1   The Great-Power System, 1500–2000

	1500	1600	1700	1800	1900	2000
Wars		Spain conquers Portugal / Spanish Armada — **30 Years' War**	War of the Spanish Succession — 7 Years' War	**Napoleonic Wars**	Franco-Prussian War — **World War I**	**World War II** / Cold War
Major Alliances	Turkey (Muslim) vs. Europe (Christian)	Hapsburgs (Austria–Spain) vs. France, Britain, Netherlands, Sweden	France vs. Britain, Spain	France vs. Britain, Netherlands	Germany (& Japan) vs. Britain, France, Russia, United States, China	Russia vs. U.S., W. Eur., Japan
Rules & Norms	Nation-states (France, Austria)	Dutch independence / Grotius on int'l law / **Treaty of Westphalia 1648** / Russia	**Treaty of Utrecht 1713**	Congress of Vienna 1815 / Kant on peace / Concert of Europe	League of Nations / Geneva conventions / Communism	UN Security Council 1945– / Human rights
Rising Powers	Britain France	Netherlands		Prussia	United States Germany Japan Italy ↑	China
Declining Powers	Venice	Spain	Netherlands / Sweden / Ottoman Empire		Britain France Austria Italy	Russia

Hegemony bands: **Netherlands hegemony** (c. 1650–1700) · **British hegemony** (c. 1800–1900) · **U.S. hegemony** (1945–)

of states. Balance of power can refer to any ratio of power capabilities between states or alliances, or it can mean only a relatively equal ratio. Alternatively, balance of power can refer to the *process* by which counterbalancing coalitions have repeatedly formed in history to prevent one state from conquering an entire region.[18]

The theory of balance of power argues that such counterbalancing occurs regularly and maintains the stability of the international system. The system is stable in that its rules and principles stay the same: state sovereignty does not collapse into a universal empire. This stability does not, however, imply peace; it is rather a stability maintained by means of recurring wars that adjust power relations.

The modern international system is often dated from the *Treaty of Westphalia* in 1648, which established the principles of independent, sovereign states that continue to shape the international system today (see Figure 2.1). These rules of state relations did not, however, originate at Westphalia; they took form in Europe in the 16th century. Key to this system was the ability of one state, or a coalition, to balance the power of another state so that it could not gobble up smaller units and create a universal empire.

This power-balancing system placed special importance on the handful of great powers with strong military capabilities, global interests and outlooks, and intense interactions with each other. A system of great-power relations has existed since around A.D. 1500, and the structure and rules of that system have remained fairly stable through time, although the particular members change. The structure is a balance of power among the six or so most powerful states, which form and break alliances, fight wars, and make peace, letting no single state conquer the others.[19]

Alliances (to be discussed shortly) play a key role in the balance of power. Building up one's own capabilities against a rival is a form of power balancing, but forming an alliance against a threatening state is often quicker, cheaper, and more effective. In the Cold War, the United States encircled the Soviet Union with military and political alliances to prevent Soviet territorial expansion. Sometimes a particular state deliberately becomes a balancer (in its region or the world), shifting its support to oppose whatever state or alliance is strongest at the moment. Britain played this role on the European continent for centuries, and China played it in the Cold War.

But states do not always balance against the strongest actor. Sometimes smaller states "jump on the bandwagon" of the most powerful state; this has been called bandwagoning as opposed to balancing. For instance, after World War II a broad coalition did not form to contain U.S. power; rather, most major states joined the U.S. bloc. States may seek to balance threats rather than raw power; U.S. power was greater than Soviet power but was less threatening to Europe and Japan (and later to China as well).[20] Furthermore, small states create variations on power-balancing themes when

---

[18] Gulick, Edward V. *Europe's Classical Balance of Power*. Cornell, 1955. Vasquez, John, and Colin Elman, eds. *Realism and the Balance of Power: A New Debate*. Prentice Hall, 2002.

[19] Rabb, Theodore K., ed. *The Thirty Years' War*. University Press of America, 1981. Kissinger, Henry A. *A World Restored*. Houghton Mifflin, 1973 [1957]. Langer, William L. *European Alliances and Alignments, 1871–1890*. Knopf, 1931.

[20] Walt, Stephen M. *The Origins of Alliances*. Cornell, 1987.

they play off rival great powers against each other. For instance, Cuba during the Cold War received massive Soviet subsidies by putting itself in the middle of the U.S.-Soviet rivalry. Other small states may, for domestic reasons, fail to mobilize to balance against threats.[21]

In the post–Cold War era of U.S. dominance, balance-of-power theory would predict closer relations among Russia, China, and even Europe to balance U.S. power. These predictions appear to be on the mark. Russian-Chinese relations have improved dramatically in such areas as arms trade and demilitarization of the border. French leaders have criticized U.S. "hyperpower." Europe and Japan opposed U.S. positions on a range of proposed treaties in 2001 on such subjects as missile defense, biological weapons, small-arms trade, and global warming. The appearance of a common enemy—international terrorists—brought the great powers together temporarily after September 2001. But the 2003 Iraq War brought back a power-balancing coalition of great powers (except Britain)—along with most other countries and world public opinion—against U.S. predominance, as predicted by balance-of-power theory.[22]

GREAT POWERS AND MIDDLE POWERS

The most powerful states in the system exert most of the influence on international events and therefore get the most attention from IR scholars. By almost any measure of power, a handful of states possess the majority of the world's power resources. At most a few dozen states have any real influence beyond their immediate locality. These are called the great powers and middle powers in the international system.

Although there is no firm dividing line, **great powers** are generally considered the half-dozen or so most powerful states. Until the past century the great-power club was exclusively European. Sometimes great powers' status is formally recognized in an international structure such as the 19th-century Concert of Europe or today's UN Security Council. In general, great powers are often defined as states that can be defeated militarily only by another great power. Great powers also tend to share a global outlook based on national interests far from their home territories.

The great powers generally have the world's strongest military forces and the strongest economies to pay for military forces and other power capabilities. These large economies in turn rest on some combination of large populations, plentiful natural resources, advanced technology, and educated labor forces. Because power is based on these underlying resources, membership in the great-power system changes slowly.[23] Only rarely does a great power—even one defeated in a massive war—lose its status as a great power, because its size and long-term economic potential change slowly. Thus Germany and Japan, decimated in World War II, are powerful today, and Russia, after gaining and then losing the rest of the Soviet Union, is still considered a great power.

What states are great powers today? Although definitions vary, seven states appear to meet the criteria: the United States, China, Russia, Japan, Germany, France, and

---

[21] Schweller, Randall L. *Unanswered Threats: Political Constraints on the Balance of Power*. Princeton, 2006.

[22] Walt, Stephen M. *Taming American Power: The Global Response to U.S. Primacy*. Norton, 2005.

O'Connor, Brendon, and Martin Griffiths, eds. *The Rise of Anti-Americanism*. Routledge, 2006.

[23] Levy, Jack S. *War in the Modern Great Power System, 1495–1975*. Kentucky, 1983.

FIGURE 2.2   Great-Power Shares of World GDP and Military Expenditures, 2006

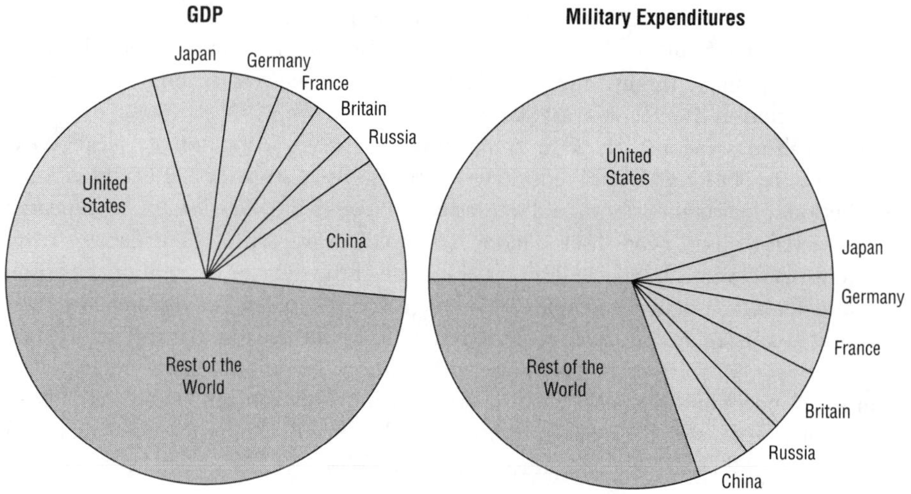

Note: GDP calculated by purchasing-power method. China's GDP using alternate method would be about half as large.
Data sources: World Bank, World Development Indicators 2007; SIPRI, SIPRI Yearbook 2007.

Britain. Together they account for more than half of the world's total GDP and two-thirds of its military spending (see Figure 2.2). They include the five permanent members of the UN Security Council, which are also the members of the "club" openly possessing large nuclear weapons arsenals.

Notable on this list are the United States and China. The United States is considered the world's only superpower because of its historical role of world leadership (especially in and after World War II) and its predominant military might. China has the world's largest population, rapid economic growth (8–10 percent annually over 15 years), and a large though not very modern military including a credible nuclear arsenal. China is likely to play a central role in world politics in the 21st century. Japan and Germany are economically great powers, but both countries have played constrained roles in international security affairs since World War II. Nonetheless, both have large and capable military forces, which they have begun to deploy abroad. Russia, France, and Britain were winners in World War II and have been active military powers since then. Although much reduced in stature from their colonial heydays, they still qualify as great powers.

The slow change in great-power status is evident. Britain and France have been great powers for 500 years, Russia and Germany for more than 250 years, the United States and Japan for about 100 years, and China for 50 years. Only six other states were ever (but no longer are) considered great powers: Italy, Austria (Austria-Hungary), Spain, Turkey (the Ottoman Empire), Sweden, and the Netherlands.

Middle powers rank somewhat below the great powers in terms of their influence on world affairs. Some are large but not highly industrialized; others have specialized capabilities but are small. Some aspire to regional dominance, and many have considerable influence in their regions.

A list of middle powers (not everyone would agree on it) might include midsized countries of the global North such as Canada, Italy, Spain, the Netherlands, Poland, Ukraine, South Korea, and Australia. It could also include large or influential countries in the global South such as India, Indonesia, Brazil, Argentina, Mexico, Nigeria, South Africa, Israel, Turkey, Iran, and Pakistan. Middle powers have not received as much attention in IR as have great powers.

Neorealism, sometimes called *structural realism,* is a 1990s adaptation of realism. It explains patterns of international events in terms of the system structure—the international distribution of power—rather than the internal makeup of individual states.[24] Compared to traditional realism, neorealism is more "scientific" in the sense of proposing general laws to explain events, but neorealism has lost some of the richness of traditional realism, which took account of many complex elements (geography, willpower, diplomacy, etc.).[25] Recently, *neoclassical realists* have sought to restore some of these lost aspects.[26]

The *polarity* of an international power distribution (world or regional) refers to the number of independent power centers in the system. This concept encompasses both the underlying power of various participants and their alliance groupings. Figure 2.3 illustrates several potential configurations of great powers.

FIGURE 2.3   Power Distribution in the International System

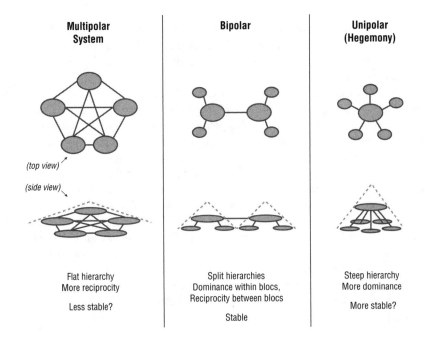

Multipolar System	Bipolar	Unipolar (Hegemony)
Flat hierarchy More reciprocity Less stable?	Split hierarchies Dominance within blocs, Reciprocity between blocs Stable	Steep hierarchy More dominance More stable?

(top view)

(side view)

[24] Waltz, Kenneth. *Theory of International Politics.* Addison-Wesley, 1979.

[25] Keohane, Robert O., ed. *Neorealism and Its Critics.* Columbia, 1986.

[26] Vasquez, John A. *The Power of Power Politics: From Classical Realism to Neotraditionalism.* Cambridge, 1999.

A **multipolar system** typically has five or six centers of power, which are not grouped into alliances. Each state participates independently and on relatively equal terms with the others. In the classical multipolar balance of power, the great-power system itself was stable but wars occurred frequently to adjust power relations. *Tripolar* systems, with three great centers of power, are fairly rare, owing to the tendency for a two-against-one alliance to form. Aspects of tripolarity colored the "strategic triangle" of the United States, the Soviet Union, and China during the 1960s and 1970s. Some scholars imagine a future tripolar world with rival power centers in North America, Europe, and East Asia. A *bipolar* system has two predominant states or two great rival alliance blocs. IR scholars do not agree about whether bipolar systems are relatively peaceful or warlike. The U.S.-Soviet standoff seemed to provide stability and peace to great-power relations, but rival blocs in Europe before World War I did not. At the far extreme, a *unipolar* system has a single center of power around which all others revolve. This is called hegemony, and will be discussed shortly.

Some might argue that peace is best preserved by a relatively equal power distribution (multipolarity) because then no country has an opportunity to win easily. The empirical evidence for this theory, however, is not strong. The opposite proposition has more support: peace is best preserved by hegemony (unipolarity), and next best by bipolarity.

Power transition theory holds that the largest wars result from challenges to the top position in the status hierarchy, when a rising power is surpassing (or threatening to surpass) the most powerful state.[27] At such times, power is relatively equally distributed, and these are the most dangerous times for major wars. Status quo powers that are doing well under the old rules will try to maintain them, whereas challengers that feel locked out by the old rules may try to change them. If a challenger does not start a war to displace the top power, the latter may provoke a "preventive" war to stop the rise of the challenger before it becomes too great a threat.

When a rising power's status (formal position in the hierarchy) diverges from its actual power, the rising power may suffer from relative deprivation: its people may feel they are not doing as well as others or as they deserve, even though their position may be improving in absolute terms. Germany's rise in the 19th century gave it great-power capabilities even though it was left out of colonial territories and other signs of status; this tension may have contributed to the two world wars. China may face a similar problem in the future. It remains to be seen whether, in the coming years, the international system can provide China with appropriate status and respect to reflect its rising power and historical importance, and whether China in turn can come to conform more fully with international rules and norms.

HEGEMONY

Hegemony is the holding by one state of a preponderance of power in the international system, so that it can single-handedly dominate the rules and arrangements by

---

[27] Organski, A. F. K. *World Politics*. Knopf, 1958.

which international political and economic relations are conducted.[28] Such a state is called a *hegemon*. (Usually hegemony means domination of the world, but sometimes it refers to regional domination.) The Italian Marxist theorist Antonio Gramsci used the term hegemony to refer to the complex of *ideas* that rulers use to gain consent for their legitimacy and keep subjects in line, reducing the need to use force to accomplish the same goal.[29] By extension, such a meaning in IR refers to the hegemony of ideas such as democracy and capitalism, and to the global predominance of U.S. culture.

Most studies of hegemony point to two examples: Britain in the 19th century and the United States after World War II. Britain's predominance followed the defeat of its archrival France in the Napoleonic Wars. Both world trade and naval capabilities were firmly in British hands, as "Britannia ruled the waves." U.S. predominance followed the defeat of Germany and Japan (and the exhaustion of the Soviet Union, France, Britain, and China in the effort). In the late 1940s, the U.S. GDP was more than half the world's total; U.S. vessels carried the majority of the world's shipping; the U.S. military could single-handedly defeat any other state or combination of states; and only the United States had nuclear weapons. U.S. industry led the world in technology and productivity, and U.S. citizens enjoyed the world's highest standard of living.

As the extreme power disparities resulting from major wars slowly diminish (states rebuild over years and decades), hegemonic decline may occur, particularly when hegemons have overextended themselves with costly military commitments. IR scholars do not agree about how far or fast U.S. hegemonic decline has proceeded, if at all, and whether international instability will result from such a decline.[30] In the post–Cold War era, international alignments—both military alliances and trade relationships—center on the United States (see Figure 2.4).

Hegemonic stability theory holds that hegemony provides some order similar to a central government in the international system: reducing anarchy, deterring aggression, promoting free trade, and providing a hard currency that can be used as a world standard. Hegemons can help resolve or at least keep in check conflicts among middle powers or small states.[31] When one state's power dominates the world, it can enforce rules and norms unilaterally, avoiding the collective goods problem. In particular, hegemons can maintain global free trade and promote world economic growth, in this view.

---

[28] Kapstein, Ethan B., and Michael Mastanduno. *Unipolar Politics*. Columbia, 1999. Nye, Joseph S. *Paradox of American Power: Why the World's Only Superpower Can't Go It Alone*. Oxford, 2002.

[29] Gramsci, Antonio. *The Modern Prince and Other Writings*. International Publishers, 1959. Cox, Robert W. *Production, Power, and World Order: Social Forces in the Making of History*. Columbia, 1987. Gill, Stephen, ed. *Gramsci, Historical Materialism and International Relations*. Cambridge, 1993.

[30] Kennedy, Paul. *The Rise and Fall of the Great Powers: Economic Change and Military Conflict from 1500–2000*. Random House, 1987. Ikenberry, G. John, ed. *America Unrivaled: The Future of the Balance of Power*. Cornell, 2002.

[31] Keohane, Robert O. The Theory of Hegemonic Stability and Change in International Economic Regimes, 1967–1977. In Holsti, Ole R., R. M. Siverson, and A. L. George, eds. *Change in the International System*. Westview, 1980.

FIGURE 2.4   Current Alignment of Great and Middle Powers

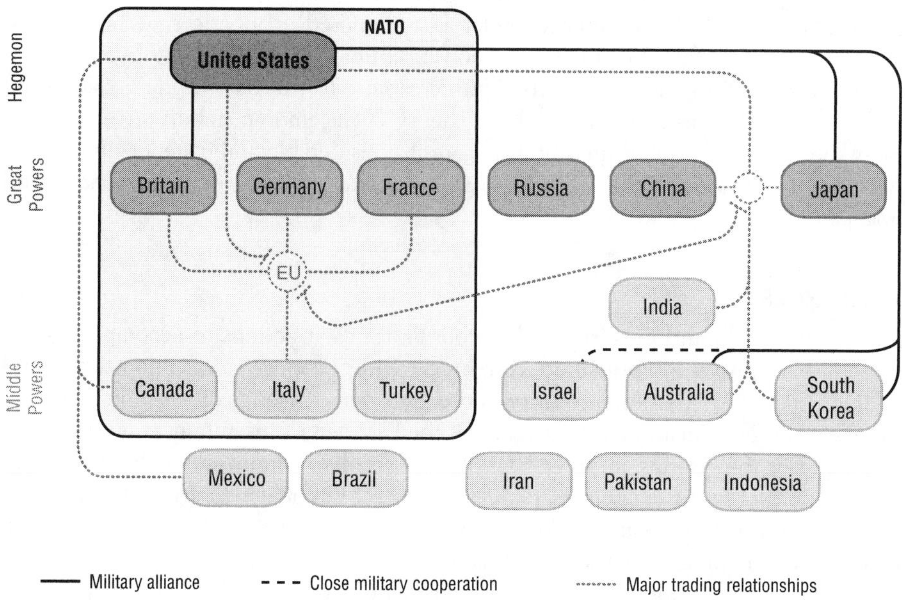

This theory attributes the peace and prosperity of the decades after World War II to U.S. hegemony, which created and maintained a global framework of economic relations supporting relatively stable and free international trade, as well as a security framework that prevented great-power wars. By contrast, the Great Depression of the 1930s and the outbreak of World War II have been attributed to the power vacuum in the international system at that time—Britain was no longer able to act as hegemon, and the United States was unwilling to begin doing so.[32]

Why should a hegemon care about enforcing rules for the international economy that are in the common good? According to hegemonic stability theory, hegemons as the largest international traders have an inherent interest in the promotion of integrated world markets (where the hegemons will tend to dominate). As the most advanced state in productivity and technology, a hegemon does not fear competition from industries in other states; it fears only that its own superior goods will be excluded from competing in other states. Thus hegemons use their power to achieve free trade and the political stability that supports free trade. Hegemony, then, provides both the ability and the motivation to provide a stable political framework for free international trade, according to hegemonic stability theory. This theory is not, however, accepted by all IR scholars.

---

[32] Kindleberger, Charles P. *The World in Depression, 1929–1939.* California, 1973. Lake, David A. *Power, Protection, and Free Trade: International Sources of U.S. Commercial Strategy, 1887–1939.* Cornell, 1988.

From the perspective of less powerful states, of course, hegemony may seem an infringement of state sovereignty, and the order it creates may seem unjust or illegitimate. For instance, China chafed under U.S.-imposed economic sanctions for 20 years after 1949, at the height of U.S. power. China was encircled by U.S. military bases and hostile alliances led by the United States. To this day, Chinese leaders use the term *hegemony* as an insult, and the theory of hegemonic stability does not impress them. Even in the United States there is considerable ambivalence about U.S. hegemony. U.S. foreign policy has historically alternated between *internationalist* and *isolationist* moods.

ALLIANCES

An *alliance* is a coalition of states that coordinate their actions to accomplish some end. Most alliances are formalized in written treaties, concern a common threat and related issues of international security, and endure across a range of issues and a period of time. Shorter-term arrangements, such as the U.S.-led forces in Iraq, may be called a *coalition*. But these terms are somewhat ambiguous. Two countries may have a formal alliance and yet be bitter enemies, such as the Soviet Union and China in the 1960s or NATO members Greece and Turkey today. Or, two countries may create the practical equivalent of an alliance without a formal treaty.

Alliances generally have the purpose of augmenting their members' power by pooling capabilities. For smaller states, alliances can be their most important power element, and for great powers the structure of alliances shapes the configuration of power in the system. Of all the elements of power, none can change as quickly and decisively as alliances. Most alliances form in response to a perceived threat. When a state's power grows and threatens its rivals, the latter often form an alliance to limit that power.

Except in the rare circumstance of hegemony, every state is weaker than some combination of other states. If states overstep norms of international conduct, they may face a powerful alliance of opposing states. This happened to Iraq when it invaded Kuwait in 1990, as it had to Hitler's Germany in the 1940s and to Napoleon's France in the 1800s.

Realists emphasize the fluidity of alliances. They are not marriages of love, but marriages of convenience. Alliances are based on national interests, and can shift as national interests change. This fluidity helps the balance-of-power process operate effectively. Still, it is not simple or costless to break an alliance: one's reputation may suffer and future alliances may be harder to establish. So states often adhere to alliance terms even when it is not in their short-term interest to do so. Nonetheless, because of the nature of international anarchy, the possibility of turning against a friend is always present. Realists would agree with the British statesman Lord Palmerston, who told Parliament in 1848, "We have no eternal allies and we have no perpetual enemies. Our interests are perpetual and eternal and those interests it is our duty to follow."[33]

Examples of fluid alliances are many. Anticommunist Richard Nixon could cooperate with communist Mao Zedong in 1972. Joseph Stalin could sign a nonaggression pact with

---

[33] Remarks in the House of Commons, March 1, 1848.

a fascist, Adolf Hitler, and then cooperate with the capitalist West against Hitler. The United States could back Islamic militants in Afghanistan against the Soviet Union in the 1980s, then attack them in 2001. Every time history brings another such reversal in international alignments, many people are surprised. Realists are not so surprised.

The fluidity of alliances deepens the security dilemma (see p. 25). If there were only two states, each could match capabilities to have adequate defense but an inability to attack successfully. But if a third state is free to ally with either side, then each state has to build adequate defenses against the potential alliance of its enemy with the third state. The threat is greater and the security dilemma is harder to escape.

Alliance cohesion is the ease with which the members hold together an alliance. Cohesion tends to be high when national interests converge and when cooperation within the alliance becomes institutionalized and habitual. When states with divergent interests form an alliance against a common enemy, the alliance may come apart if the threat subsides (as with the U.S.-Soviet alliance in World War II, for instance). Even when alliance cohesion is high, as in NATO during the Cold War, conflicts may arise over who bears the costs of the alliance (**burden sharing**).[34]

Great powers often form alliances (or less formal commitments) with smaller states, sometimes called client states. Extended deterrence refers to a strong state's use of threats to deter attacks on weaker clients—such as the U.S. threat to attack the Soviet Union if it invaded Western Europe. Great powers face a real danger of being dragged into wars with each other over relatively unimportant regional issues if their respective clients go to war. If the great powers do not come to their clients' protection, they may lose credibility with other clients, but if they do, they may end up fighting a costly war.[35]

At present, two important formal alliances dominate the international security scene. By far the more powerful is the **North Atlantic Treaty Organization (NATO),** which encompasses Western Europe and North America. (The second is the U.S.-Japanese alliance.) Using GDP as a measure of power, the 26 NATO members possess nearly half the world total (roughly twice the power of the United States alone). NATO was founded in 1949 to oppose and deter Soviet power in Europe. Its counterpart in Eastern Europe during the Cold War, the Soviet-led **Warsaw Pact,** was founded in 1955 and disbanded in 1991. The biggest issue for NATO is its recent eastward expansion, beyond the East-West Cold War dividing line (see Figure 2.5). NATO expansion was justified by liberals as a way to solidify new democracies while keeping Europe peaceful, and by conservatives as protection against possible future Russian aggression. Russian leaders oppose NATO's expansion into Eastern Europe as aggressive and anti-Russian. NATO forces have participated in the war in Afghanistan, but the 2003 Iraq War bypassed and divided NATO members.

Alliances clearly rank among the most important elements of power. Yet their fluidity makes them a wild card for scholars to understand and for policy makers to anticipate.

---

[34] Martin, Pierre, and Mark R. Brawley, eds. *Alliance Politics, Kosovo, and NATO's War: Allied Force or Forced Allies?* Palgrave, 2000.
[35] Snyder, Glenn H. *Alliance Politics.* Cornell, 1997.

FIGURE 2.5   NATO Expansion

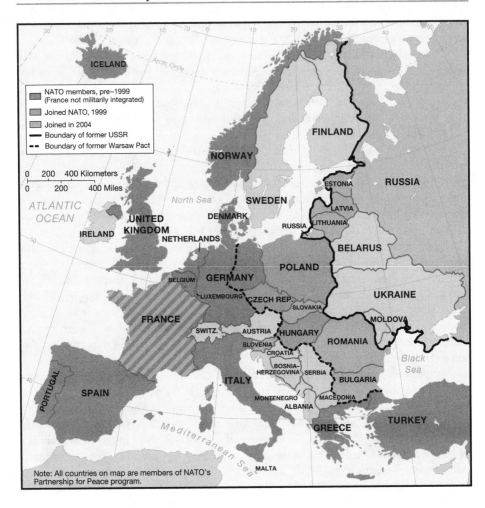

Note: All countries on map are members of NATO's Partnership for Peace program.

CHAPTER 3

FOREIGN POLICY

RATIONALITY

Most realists (and some others) assume that those who wield power while engaging in statecraft behave as **rational actors** in their efforts to influence others.[1] This view has two aspects.

First, the assumption of rationality implies that states and other international actors can identify their interests and put priorities on various interests: A state's actions seek to advance its interests. Many realists assume that the actor (usually a state) exercising power is a single entity that can "think" about its actions coherently and make choices. This is called the *unitary actor* assumption, or sometimes the *strong leader* assumption. The assumption is a simplification, because the interests of particular politicians, parties, economic sectors, or regions of a country often conflict. Yet realists assume that the exercise of power attempts to advance the **national interest**—the interests of the state itself. Some realists simply define the national interest as maximizing power—a debatable assumption. Others compare power in IR with money in economics—a universal measure. In this view, just as firms compete for money in economic markets, states compete for power in the international system.

Second, rationality implies that actors are able to perform a **cost-benefit analysis**—calculating the costs incurred by a possible action and the benefits it is likely to bring. As in the problem of estimating power, one has to add up different dimensions in such a calculation. For instance, states presumably do not initiate wars that they expect to lose, except when they stand to gain political benefits, domestic or international, that outweigh the costs of losing the war. But it is not easy to tally intangible political benefits against the tangible costs of a war. Even victory in a war may not be worth the costs paid. Rational actors can miscalculate costs and benefits, especially when using faulty information (although this does not mean they are irrational). Finally, human behavior and luck can be unpredictable.

These assumptions about rationality and the actors in IR are simplifications that not all IR scholars accept. But realists consider these simplifications useful because they allow scholars to explain in a general way the actions of diverse actors.

The ancient realist Sun Tzu advised that the best general was not the most courageous or aggressive one, but the one who could coolly calculate the costs and benefits

---

[1] Brown, Michael E., Owen R. Cote, Sean M. Lynn-Jones, and Steven E. Miller, eds. *Rational Choice and Security Studies*. MIT, 2000. Lake, David A., and Robert Powell, eds. *Strategic Choice and International Relations*. Princeton, 1999.

of alternative courses. The best war was a short one, in Sun Tzu's view, because wars are costly. Better yet was to take another state intact without fighting—by intimidation, deception, and the disruption of enemy alliances. Capturing an enemy army was better than fighting it. If fighting was necessary, it should occur on another state's territory so the army could live off the land. Attacking cities was too destructive and thus reduced the benefits of war.

Classical realists emphasize *statecraft*—the art of managing state affairs and effectively maneuvering in a world of power politics among sovereign states. Actors use strategy to pursue good outcomes in bargaining with one or more other actors. States deploy power capabilities as leverage to influence each other's actions.[2] Bargaining is interactive, and requires an actor to take account of other actors' interests even while pursuing its own.[3] Sometimes bargaining communication takes place through actions rather than words.

A key aspect of strategy is choosing the kinds of capabilities to develop, given limited resources, in order to maximize international influence. This requires foresight because the capabilities required to manage a situation may need to be developed years before that situation presents itself. Yet the capabilities chosen often will not be fungible in the short term. Central to this dilemma is what kind of standing military forces to maintain in peacetime—enough to prevent a quick defeat if war breaks out, but not so much as to overburden one's economy. Military capabilities are only part of the picture, however, as states also develop a range of nonmilitary forms of leverage (see Figure 3.1).

Strategies also shape policies for when a state is willing to use its power capabilities. The *will* of a nation or leader is hard to estimate. Even if leaders make explicit their intention to fight over an issue, they might be bluffing.

The strategy of **deterrence** uses a threat to punish another actor if it takes a certain negative action (especially attacking one's own state or one's allies). If deterrence works, its effects are almost invisible; its success is measured in attacks that did not occur.[4]

Generally, advocates of deterrence believe that conflicts are more likely to escalate into war when one party to the conflict is weak. In this view, building up military capabilities usually convinces the stronger party that a resort to military leverage would not succeed, so conflicts are less likely to escalate into violence. A strategy of **compellence,** sometimes used after deterrence fails, refers to the use of force to make another actor take some action (rather than refrain from taking an action).[5] Generally it is harder to get another state to change course (the purpose of compellence) than to get it to refrain from changing course (the purpose of deterrence).

---

[2] North, Robert C. *War, Peace, Survival: Global Politics and Conceptual Synthesis.* Westview, 1990.

[3] Snyder, Glenn H., and Paul Diesing. *Conflict among Nations: Bargaining, Decision Making, and System Structure in International Crises.* Princeton, 1977. Starkey, Brigid, Mark A. Boyer, and Jonathan Wilkenfeld. *Negotiating a Complex World: An Introduction to International Negotiation.* 2nd ed. Rowman & Littlefield, 2005.

[4] Morgan, Patrick. *Deterrence Now.* Cambridge, 2003. Zagare, Frank C. *Perfect Deterrence.* Cambridge, 2000. Huth, Paul K. *Extended Deterrence and the Prevention of War.* Yale, 1988. George, Alexander L., and Richard Smoke. *Deterrence in American Foreign Policy: Theory and Practice.* Columbia, 1974.

[5] Schelling, Thomas C. *The Strategy of Conflict.* Harvard, 1960.

FIGURE 3.1   **Military and Nonmilitary Means of Leverage**

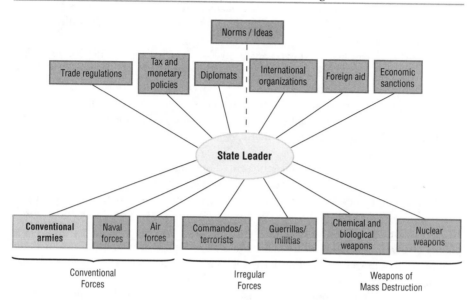

One strategy used to try to compel compliance by another state is *escalation*—a series of negative sanctions of increasing severity applied in order to induce another actor to take some action. In theory, the less severe actions establish credibility—showing the first actor's willingness to exert its power on the issue—and the pattern of escalation establishes the high costs of future sanctions if the second actor does not cooperate. These should induce the second actor to comply, assuming that it finds the potential costs of the escalating punishments greater than the costs of compliance. But escalation can be quite dangerous. During the Cold War, many IR scholars worried that a conventional war could lead to nuclear war if the superpowers tried to apply escalation strategies.

An **arms race** is a reciprocal process in which two (or more) states build up military capabilities in response to each other. Because each wants to act prudently against a threat, the attempt to reciprocate leads to a runaway production of weapons by both sides. The mutual escalation of threats erodes confidence, reduces cooperation, and makes it more likely that a crisis (or accident) could cause one side to strike first and start a war rather than wait for the other side to strike. The arms race process was illustrated vividly in the U.S.-Soviet nuclear arms race, which created arsenals of tens of thousands of nuclear weapons on each side.

FORMAL MODELS

Game theory is a branch of mathematics concerned with predicting bargaining outcomes. A game is a setting in which two or more players choose among alternative moves, either once or repeatedly. Each combination of moves (by all players) results in a set of payoffs (utility) to each player. The payoffs can be tangible items such as money or any intangible items of value. Game theory aims to deduce likely outcomes (what moves players will make), given the players' preferences and the possible moves open to them. Games and related mathematical models are sometimes called **formal models.**

Game theory was first used extensively in IR in the 1950s and 1960s by scholars trying to understand U.S.-Soviet nuclear war contingencies. Moves were decisions to use nuclear weapons in certain ways, and payoffs were outcomes of the war. The use of game theory to study international interactions has become more extensive among IR scholars in recent years, especially among realists, who accept the assumptions about rationality. To analyze a game mathematically, one assumes that each player chooses a move rationally, to maximize its payoff.

Different kinds of situations are represented by different classes of games, as defined by the number of players and the structure of the payoffs. One basic distinction is between **zero-sum games,** in which one player's gain is by definition equal to the other's loss, and *non-zero-sum games,* in which it is possible for both players to gain (or lose). In a zero-sum game there is no point in communication or cooperation between the players because their interests are diametrically opposed. But in a non-zero-sum game, coordination of moves can maximize the total payoff to the players, although each may still maneuver to gain a greater share of that total payoff.[6]

The game called **Prisoner's Dilemma (PD)** captures the kind of collective goods problem common to IR. In this situation, rational players choose moves that produce an outcome in which all players are worse off than under a different set of moves. They all could do better, but as individual rational actors they are unable to achieve this outcome. How can this be?

The original story tells of two prisoners questioned separately by a prosecutor. The prosecutor knows they committed a bank robbery but has only enough evidence to convict them of illegal possession of a gun unless one of them confesses. The prosecutor tells each prisoner that if he confesses and his partner doesn't confess, he will go free. If his partner confesses and he doesn't, he will get a long prison term for bank robbery (while the partner goes free). If both confess, they will get a somewhat reduced term. If neither confesses, they will be convicted on the gun charge and serve a short sentence. The story assumes that neither prisoner will have a chance to retaliate later, that only the immediate outcomes matter, and that each prisoner cares only about himself.

This game has a single solution: both prisoners, if rational, will confess. Each will reason as follows: "If my partner is going to confess, then I should confess too, because I will get a slightly shorter sentence that way. If my partner is not going to confess, then I should still confess because I will go free that way instead of serving a short sentence." The other prisoner follows the same reasoning. The dilemma is that by following their individually rational choices, both prisoners end up serving a fairly long sentence when they could have both served a short one by cooperating (keeping their mouths shut).

6 O'Neill, Barry. A Survey of Game Theory Models on Peace and War. In R. Aumann and S. Hart, eds. *Handbook of Game Theory.* Vol. 2. North-Holland, 1994. Powell, Robert. *In the Shadow of Power: States and Strategies in International Politics.* Princeton, 1999.

The PD game has been used to gain insight into arms races. Consider the decisions of India and Pakistan about whether to build sizable nuclear weapons arsenals. Both have the ability to do so. Neither side can know whether the other is secretly building up an arsenal unless they reach an arms control agreement with strict verification provisions. To analyze the game, we assign values to each possible outcome—often called a *preference ordering*—for each player. This is not simple: if we misjudge the value a player puts on a particular outcome, we may draw wrong conclusions from the game.

The following preferences regarding possible outcomes are plausible: the best outcome would be that oneself but not the other player had a nuclear arsenal (the expense of building nuclear weapons would be worth it because one could then use them as leverage); second best would be for neither to go nuclear (no leverage, but no expense); third best would be for both to develop nuclear arsenals (a major expense without gaining leverage); worst would be to forgo nuclear weapons oneself while the other player developed them (and thus be subject to blackmail).

The game can be summarized in a *payoff matrix* (see Table 3.1). The first number in each cell is India's payoff, and the second number is Pakistan's. To keep things simple, 4 indicates the highest payoff, and 1 the lowest. As is conventional, a decision to refrain from building nuclear weapons is called "cooperation," and a decision to proceed with nuclear weapons is called "defection." The dilemma here parallels that of the prisoners discussed in the text. Each state's leader reasons: "If they go nuclear, we must; if they don't, we'd be crazy not to." The model seems to predict an inevitable Indian-Pakistani nuclear arms race, although both states would do better to avoid one. And indeed, in 1998, India detonated underground nuclear explosions to test weapons designs, and Pakistan promptly followed suit. In 2002, the two states nearly went to war, with projected war deaths of up to 12 million. A costly and dangerous arms race continues, and each side now has dozens of nuclear missiles. This example—a failure to cooperate for mutual benefit—illustrates why realists tend to be pessimistic about cooperative solutions to collective goods problems such as the one that the PD game embodies.

IR scholars have analyzed many other games beyond PD. For example, *Chicken* represents two male teenagers speeding toward a head-on collision. The first to swerve is "chicken." Each reasons: "If he doesn't swerve, I must; but if he swerves, I won't." The player who first commits irrevocably not to swerve (for example, by throwing away the steering wheel or putting on a blindfold while behind the wheel) will win. Similarly, some scholars have argued that in the 1962 Cuban Missile Crisis, President John F.

TABLE 3.1 Payoff Matrix in India-Pakistan PD Game

		Pakistan	
		Cooperate	Defect
India	Cooperate	(3,3)	(1,4)
	Defect	(4,1)	(2,2)

Note: First number in each group is India's payoff, second is Pakistan's. The number 4 is highest payoff, 1 lowest.

Kennedy "won" by seeming ready to risk nuclear war if Soviet Premier Nikita Khrushchev did not back down and remove Soviet missiles from Cuba. (There are, however, alternative explanations of the outcome of the crisis.)

NUCLEAR STRATEGY AND ARMS CONTROL

Theories of rationality underlie *nuclear strategy*, which refers to decisions about how many nuclear weapons to deploy, what delivery systems to put them on, and what policies to adopt regarding the circumstances in which they would be used.[7]

The reason for possessing nuclear weapons is almost always to deter another state from a nuclear or conventional attack by threatening ruinous retaliation. This should work if state leaders are rational actors wanting to avoid the huge costs of a nuclear attack. But it will work only if other states believe that a state's threat to use nuclear weapons is credible. The search for a credible deterrent by two or more hostile states tends to lead to an ever-growing arsenal of nuclear weapons. This is because each side wants to thwart the other's ability to launch a *first strike*—an attack intended to destroy, largely or entirely, a state's nuclear weapons before they can be used. To prevent this, each side builds a *second-strike* capability—enough weapons to take a first strike and still strike back. Possession of second-strike capabilities by both sides is called **mutually assured destruction (MAD)** because neither side can prevent the other from destroying it. The term implies that the strategy, though reflecting "rationality," is actually insane (mad) because deviations from rationality could destroy both countries.

Credibility is key to deterrence. During the Cold War, U.S. war planners wanted to deter a Soviet conventional attack on Western Europe. They could have threatened to use nuclear weapons in response, but rational Soviet leaders would have known that rational U.S. leaders would never act on such a threat and risk escalation to global nuclear war. After all, it would be better for the United States to lose West Germany than to lose both West Germany and New York. To convince the Soviets that such an attack would be too risky, U.S. commanders integrated thousands of tactical nuclear weapons into conventional forces so that the escalation to nuclear war might happen more or less automatically in the event of conventional war. This was the equivalent of "throwing away the steering wheel" in a game of Chicken. China currently uses a similar form of "rational irrationality" in its relations with Taiwan, trying to make credible the threat of war (which would be disastrous for China as well as Taiwan) if Taiwan declares independence.

Defense has played little role in nuclear strategy because no effective defense against missile attack has been devised. However, the United States is spending billions of dollars a year to try to develop defenses that could shoot down incoming ballistic missiles. The program is called the **Strategic Defense Initiative (SDI),** "Star Wars," or Ballistic Missile Defense (BMD).[8] Overall, no reliable defense against ballistic missiles exists, and experts disagree on whether such a defense is just a few or many years away. In addition to the technical challenges of stopping incoming ballistic

---

[7] Rhodes, Edward. *Power and Madness: The Logic of Nuclear Coercion*. Columbia, 1989.

[8] Wirtz, James J., and Jeffrey A. Larsen. *Rocket's Red Glare: Missile Defenses and the Future of World Politics*. Westview, 2001.

missile warheads, a true strategic defense would also have to stop cruise missiles (possibly launched from submarines), airplanes, and more innovative delivery systems. If a rogue state or terrorist group struck the United States with a nuclear weapon, it would probably not use an ICBM to do so. For now, the only real defense against nuclear weapons is keeping those weapons out of new hands, and threatening massive retaliation against states that already have them.

During the Cold War, the superpowers' nuclear forces grew and technologies developed. Those evolving force structures were codified (more than constrained) by a series of arms control agreements. *Arms control* is an effort by two or more states to regulate by formal agreement their acquisition of weapons,[9] using the reciprocity principle to solve the collective goods problem of expensive arms races that ultimately benefit neither side. Arms control is broader than just nuclear weapons—for instance, after World War I the great powers negotiated limits on sizes of navies—but in the Cold War nuclear weapons were the main focus of arms control. Arms control agreements typically require long formal negotiations with many technical discussions, culminating in a treaty. Some arms control treaties are multilateral, but during the Cold War most were bilateral (U.S.-Soviet). Some stay in effect indefinitely; others have a limited term. Under the management of arms control treaties, the U.S. arsenal peaked in the 1960s at more than 30,000 warheads and the Soviet arsenal peaked in the 1980s at more than 40,000. Now each side is reducing deployed warheads to 2,200 by 2012, in addition to the elimination of most tactical nuclear weapons. The reciprocity principle that helped fuel the arms race also enables its step-by-step reversal.

The spread of ballistic missiles has been difficult to control.[10] Through the **Missile Technology Control Regime,** industrialized states try to limit the flow of missile-relevant technology to states in the global South. One success was the interruption of an Egyptian-Argentinean-Iraqi partnership in the 1980s to develop a medium-range missile. But in general, the regime has had limited success. Short- and medium-range missiles (with ranges of up to about 2,000 miles) apparently are being developed by Iran, Israel, Saudi Arabia, Pakistan, India, North Korea, and possibly Argentina and Brazil. Soviet-made short-range ballistic missiles are owned by a number of states. Currently India and Pakistan are following the path of the Cold War superpowers, matching each other's expanding nuclear arsenals and upgrading their missile capabilities (see Figure 3.2). The proliferation of missiles and nuclear capabilities complicates arms control compared with the Cold War era.

MODELS OF DECISION MAKING

In an ideal world, perhaps, rational decisions by state actors would make reciprocity effective and deterrence secure, preventing unnecessary conflicts. But ours is not an ideal world. In reality, the actions of states result from individual human choices—by citizens,

---

[9] Larsen, Jeffrey A. *Arms Control: Cooperative Security in a Changing Environment.* Rienner, 2002. Adler, Emanuel, ed. *The International Practice of Arms Control.* Johns Hopkins, 1992.
[10] Mistry, Dinshaw. *Containing Missile Proliferation: Strategic Technology, Security Regimes, and International Cooperation in Arms Control.* University of Washington, 2003.

FIGURE 3.2   **Expanding Ranges of Indian and Pakistani Missiles, 1998–2003**

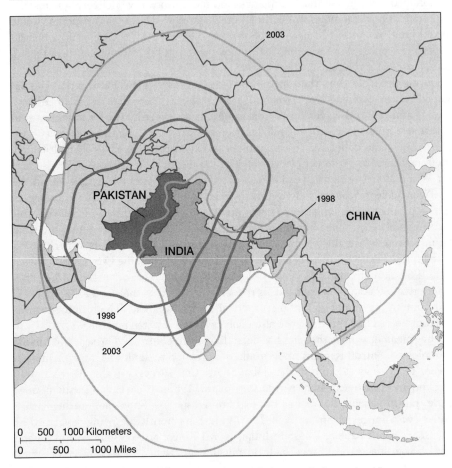

Source: *The Washington Post,* May 29, 1999: A32; Carnegie Endowment for International Peace.

political leaders, diplomats, and bureaucrats—aggregated through the states' internal structures. The study of foreign policy looks at the state from the inside out, trying to understand the processes and structures *within* states that make them behave as they do.

Foreign policies are the strategies governments use to guide their actions in the international arena. Foreign policies spell out the objectives state leaders have decided to pursue in a given relationship or situation. But in general, IR scholars are less interested in specific policies than in the **foreign policy process**—how policies are arrived at and implemented. States establish various organizational structures and functional relationships to create and carry out foreign policies. Officials and agencies collect information about a situation through various channels; they write memoranda outlining possible options for action; they hold meetings to discuss the matter; some of them meet privately outside these meetings to decide how to steer the meetings. IR scholars are especially interested in exploring whether certain kinds of policy processes lead to certain kinds of decisions—whether certain processes produce better outcomes (for the state's self-defined interests) than do others.

Comparative foreign policy is the study of foreign policy in various states in order to discover whether similar types of societies or governments consistently have similar types of foreign policies (comparing across states or across different time periods for a single state). Such studies have focused on three characteristics: size, wealth, and extent of democratic participation in government.[11] Unfortunately, no simple rule has been found to predict a state's warlike tendencies based on these attributes. States vary greatly among each other and even within a single state over time. For example, both capitalist and communist states have proven capable of naked aggression or peaceful behavior, depending on circumstances. Some political scientists have tried to interpret particular states' foreign policies in terms of each one's *political culture and history*.

Foreign policy outcomes result from multiple forces at various levels of analysis. The outcomes depend on individual decision makers, on the type of society and government they are working within, and on the international and global context of their actions. The study of foreign policy processes runs counter to realism's assumption of a unitary state actor. Because the study of foreign policy concentrates on forces within the state, its main emphasis is on the individual and domestic levels of analysis.

The foreign policy process is a process of *decision making*. States take actions because people in governments—*decision makers*—choose those actions.[12] Decision making is a *steering* process in which adjustments are made as a result of feedback from the outside world. Decisions are carried out by actions taken to change the world, and then information from the world is monitored to evaluate the effects of actions. These evaluations—along with information about other, independent changes in the environment—go into the next round of decisions (see Figure 3.3).

FIGURE 3.3   Decision Making as Steering

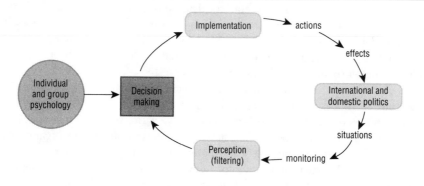

---

[11] Beasley, Ryan K., et al., eds. *Foreign Policy in Comparative Perspective: Domestic and International Influences on State Behavior*. CQ Press, 2002.

[12] Stein, Janice Gross. Psychological Explanations of International Conflict. In Carlsnaes, Walter, Thomas Risse, and Beth A. Simmons, eds. *Handbook of International Relations*. Sage, 2002, pp. 292–308.

FIGURE 3.4   Rational Model of Decision Making

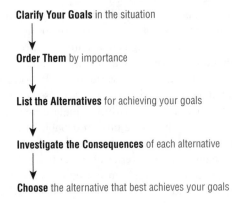

A common starting point for studying the decision-making process is the **rational model.**[13] In this model, decision makers set goals, evaluate their relative importance, calculate the costs and benefits of each possible course of action, then choose the one with the highest benefits and lowest costs (see Figure 3.4).

The choice may be complicated by *uncertainty* about the costs and benefits of various actions. In such cases, decision makers must attach probabilities to each possible outcome of an action. For example, will pressuring a rival state to give ground in peace talks work or backfire? Some decision makers are relatively *accepting of risk*, whereas others are *averse to risk*. These factors affect the importance that decision makers place on various alternative outcomes that could result from an action.

The goals of different individuals involved in making a decision may diverge, as may the goals of different state agencies. For example, the U.S. secretary of state may have a different goal than the secretary of defense, just as the Central Intelligence Agency may view a situation differently than the National Security Council does. The rational model of decision making thus is somewhat complicated by uncertainty and the multiple goals of decision makers. The rational model may imply that decision making is simpler than is actually the case.

An alternative to the rational model of decision making is the **organizational process model.** In this model, foreign policy decision makers generally skip the labor-intensive process of identifying goals and alternative actions, relying instead for most decisions on standardized responses or *standard operating procedures*. The organizational process model implies that much of foreign policy results from "management by muddling through."[14] Another alternative to the rational model is the **government bargaining** (or *bureaucratic politics*) **model,** in which foreign policy decisions result from

---

[13] The rational model, along with the organizational process and bureaucratic politics models discussed later, derives from Graham Allison; see Allison, Graham T., and Philip Zelikow. *Essence of Decision: Explaining the Cuban Missile Crisis.* 2nd ed. Longman, 1999.

[14] Avant, Deborah D. *Political Institutions and Military Change: Lessons from Peripheral Wars.* Cornell, 1995.

the bargaining process among various government agencies with somewhat divergent interests in the outcome.

INDIVIDUAL DECISION MAKERS

Every international event is the result, intended or unintended, of decisions made by individuals. The study of individual decision making revolves around the question of rationality. To what extent are national leaders (or citizens) able to make rational decisions in the national interest—if indeed such an interest can be defined—and thus to conform to a realist view of IR? Individual rationality is not equivalent to state rationality: states might filter individuals' irrational decisions so as to arrive at rational choices, or states might distort individually rational decisions and end up with irrational state choices. But realists tend to assume that both states and individuals are rational and that the goals or interests of states correlate with those of leaders.

The most simplified rational-actor models assume that interests are the same from one actor to another. If this were so, individuals could be substituted for each other in various roles without changing history very much. And states would all behave similarly to each other (or rather, the differences between them would reflect different resources and geography, not differences in the nature of national interests). This assumption is at best a great oversimplification; individual decisions reflect the *values* and *beliefs* of the decision maker.

Individual decision makers not only have differing values and beliefs, but also have unique personalities—their personal experiences, intellectual capabilities, and personal styles of making decisions. Some IR scholars study individual psychology to understand how personality affects decision making. Psychoanalytic approaches hold that personalities reflect the subconscious influences of childhood experiences. For instance, Bill Clinton drew much criticism in his early years as president for a foreign policy that seemed to zigzag. A notable Clinton personality trait was his readiness to compromise. Clinton himself once noted that his experience of growing up with a violent, alcoholic stepfather shaped him into a "peacemaker, always trying to minimize the disruption."[15]

Beyond individual *idiosyncrasies* in goals or decision-making processes, individual decision making diverges from the rational model in at least three *systematic* ways. First, decision makers suffer from **misperceptions** and **selective perceptions** (taking in only some kinds of information) when they compile information on the likely consequences of their choices.[16] Decision-making processes must reduce and filter the incoming information on which a decision is based; the problem is that such filtration often is biased. **Information screens** are subconscious filters through which people put the information coming in about the world around them. Often they simply ignore any information that does not fit their expectations. Information is also screened out as it passes from one person to another in the decision-making process. For example, prior

---

[15] Collins, Nancy. A Legacy of Strength and Love [interview with President Clinton]. *Good Housekeeping* 221 (5), 1995: 113–15.

[16] Jervis, Robert. *Perception and Misperception in International Politics*. Princeton, 1976.

to the September 2001 terrorist attacks, U.S. intelligence agencies failed to adequately interpret available evidence because too few analysts were fluent in Arabic. Similarly, Soviet leaders in 1941 and Israeli leaders in 1973 ignored evidence of pending invasions of their countries.

Misperceptions can affect the implementation of policy by low-level officials as well as its formulation by high-level officials. For example, in 1988, officers on a U.S. warship in the Persian Gulf shot down a civilian Iranian jet that they believed to be a military jet attacking them. The officers were trying to carry out policies established by national leaders, but because of misperceptions their actions instead damaged their state's interests.

Second, the rationality of individual cost-benefit calculations is undermined by emotions that decision makers feel while thinking about the consequences of their actions—an effect referred to as *affective bias*. (*Positive* and *negative affect* refer to feelings of liking or disliking someone.) As hard as a decision maker tries to be rational in making a decision, the decision-making process is bound to be influenced by strong feelings held about the person or state toward which a decision is directed. (Affective biases also contribute to information screening, as positive information about disliked people or negative information about liked people is screened out.)

Third, *cognitive biases* are systematic distortions of rational calculations based not on emotional feelings but simply on the limitations of the human brain in making choices. The most important seems to be the attempt to produce *cognitive balance*—or to reduce *cognitive dissonance*. These terms refer to the tendency people have to try to maintain mental models of the world that are logically consistent (this seldom succeeds entirely).[17]

One implication of cognitive balance is that decision makers place greater value on goals that they have put much effort into achieving—the *justification of effort*. This is especially true in a democracy, in which politicians must face their citizens' judgment at the polls and so do not want to admit failures. The Vietnam War trapped U.S. decision makers in this way in the 1960s. After sending half a million troops halfway around the world, U.S. leaders found it difficult to admit to themselves that the costs of the war were greater than the benefits.

Decision makers also achieve cognitive balance through *wishful thinking*—an overestimate of the probability of a desired outcome. A variation of wishful thinking is to assume that an event with a *low probability* of occurring will *not* occur. This could be a dangerous way to think about catastrophic events such as accidental nuclear war or a terrorist attack.

Cognitive balance often leads decision makers to maintain a hardened image of an *enemy* and to interpret all of the enemy's actions in a negative light (because the idea of bad people doing good things would create cognitive dissonance).[18] A *mirror image* refers to two sides in a conflict maintaining very similar enemy images of each other ("we are defensive, they are aggressive," etc.). A decision maker may also experience

---

[17] Sylvan, Donald A., and James F. Voss. *Problem Representation in Foreign Policy Decision Making.* Cambridge, 1998.

[18] Mercer, Jonathan L. *Reputation and International Politics.* Cornell, 1996.

psychological *projection* of his or her own feelings onto another actor. For instance, if one country wanted to gain superiority over another, but found that goal inconsistent with its self-image, the resulting cognitive dissonance might be resolved by believing that the other country was trying to gain superiority.

Another form of cognitive bias, related to cognitive balance, is the use of *historical analogies* to structure one's thinking about a decision. This can be quite useful or quite misleading, depending on whether the analogy is appropriate.[19] As each historical situation is unique in some way, when a decision maker latches onto an analogy and uses it as a shortcut to a decision, the rational calculation of costs and benefits may be cut short as well. In particular, decision makers often assume that a solution that worked in the past will work again—without fully examining how similar the situations really are.

All of these psychological processes—misperception, affective biases, and cognitive biases—interfere with the rational assessment of costs and benefits in making a decision.[20] Two specific modifications to the rational model of decision making have been proposed to accommodate psychological realities.

First, the model of *bounded rationality* takes into account the costs of seeking and processing information. Nobody thinks about every single possible course of action when making a decision. Instead of **optimizing,** or picking the very best option, people usually work on the problem until they come up with a "good enough" option that meets some minimal criteria; this is called **satisficing,** or finding a satisfactory solution.[21] The time constraints faced by top decision makers in IR—who are constantly besieged with crises requiring their attention—generally preclude their finding the very best response to a situation. These time constraints were described by U.S. defense secretary William Cohen in 1997: "The unrelenting flow of information, the need to digest it on a minute-by-minute basis, is quite different from anything I've experienced before. ... There's little time for contemplation; most of it is action."[22]

Second, **prospect theory** provides an alternative explanation (rather than simple rational optimization) of decisions made under risk or uncertainty.[23] According to this theory, decision makers go through two phases. In the *editing phase,* they frame the options available and the probabilities of various outcomes associated with each option. Then, in the *evaluation phase,* they assess the options and choose one. Prospect theory holds that evaluations take place by comparison with a *reference point,* which is often the status quo but might be some past or expected situation. The decision maker asks whether he or she can do better than that reference point, but the value placed on outcomes depends on how far from the reference point they are.

---

[19] Neustadt, Richard E., and Ernest R. May. *Thinking in Time: The Uses of History for Decision Makers.* Free Press, 1986.

[20] Tuchman, Barbara W. *The March of Folly: From Troy to Vietnam.* Knopf/Random House, 1984. Bennett, Andrew. *Condemned to Repetition? The Rise, Fall, and Reprise of Soviet-Russian Military Interventionism, 1973–1996.* MIT, 1999.

[21] Simon, Herbert A. *Models of Bounded Rationality.* MIT, 1982.

[22] *Washington Post,* March 5, 1997: A22.

[23] Davis, James W. *Threats and Promises: The Pursuit of International Influence.* Johns Hopkins, 2000. McDermott, Rose. *Risk-Taking in International Politics: Prospect Theory in American Foreign Policy.* Michigan, 1998.

Individual decision making thus follows an imperfect and partial kind of rationality at best. Not only do the goals of different individuals vary, but decision makers face a series of obstacles in receiving accurate information, constructing accurate models of the world, and reaching decisions that further their own goals. The rational model is only a simplification at best and must be supplemented by an understanding of individual psychological processes that affect decision making.

GROUP PSYCHOLOGY

What are the implications of group psychology for foreign policy decision making? In one respect, groups promote rationality by balancing out the blind spots and biases of any individual. Advisors or legislative committees may force a state leader to reconsider a rash decision. And the interactions of different individuals in a group may result in the formulation of goals that more closely reflect state interests rather than individual idiosyncrasies. However, group dynamics also introduce new sources of irrationality into the decision-making process.

Groupthink refers to the tendency for groups to reach decisions without accurately assessing their consequences, because individual members tend to go along with ideas they think the others support.[24] The basic phenomenon is illustrated by a simple psychology experiment. A group of six people is asked to compare the lengths of two lines projected onto a screen. When five of the people are secretly instructed to say that line A is longer—even though anyone can see that line B is actually longer—the sixth person is likely to agree with the group rather than believe his or her own eyes.

Unlike individuals, groups tend to be overly optimistic about the chances of success and are thus more willing to take risks. Participants suppress their doubts about dubious

FIGURE 3.5   **Some Psychological Pitfalls of Decision Making**

Note: Conflictland could be Vietnam in 1968, Bosnia in 1994, or Iraq in 2006.

---

[24] Janis, Irving L. *Victims of Groupthink: A Psychological Study of Foreign-Policy Decisions and Fiascoes.* Houghton Mifflin, 1972. Hart, Paul, Eric K. Stern, and Bengt Sundelius, eds. *Beyond Groupthink: Political Group Dynamics and Foreign Policy-Making.* Michigan, 1997.

undertakings because everyone else seems to think an idea will work. Also, because the group diffuses responsibility from individuals, nobody feels accountable for actions.

In a spectacular case of groupthink, President Ronald Reagan's close friend and director of the U.S. Central Intelligence Agency (CIA) bypassed his own agency and ran covert operations spanning three continents using the National Security Council (NSC) staff in the White House basement. The NSC sold weapons to Iran in exchange for the freedom of U.S. hostages held in Lebanon, and then used the Iranian payments to illegally fund Nicaraguan Contra rebels. The **Iran-Contra scandal** resulted when these operations, managed by an obscure NSC aide named Oliver North, became public.

The U.S. war in Iraq may also provide cautionary examples to future generations about the risks of misinformation, misperception, wishful thinking, and groupthink in managing a major foreign policy initiative.[25] Some of the problems of individual and group psychology in the policy process—be they in Vietnam, Bosnia, or Iraq—are illustrated in Figure 3.5.

The difficulties in reaching rational decisions, both for individuals and for groups, are heightened during a crisis.[26] *Crises* are foreign policy situations in which outcomes are very important and time frames are compressed. Crisis decision making is harder to understand and predict than is normal foreign policy making.

In a crisis, decision makers operate under tremendous time constraints. The normal checks on unwise decisions may not operate. Communications become shorter and more stereotyped, and information that does not fit a decision maker's expectations is more likely to be discarded simply because there is no time to consider it. In framing options decision makers tend to restrict the choices, again to save time, and tend to overlook creative options while focusing on the most obvious ones. (In the

FIGURE 3.5 *(continued)*

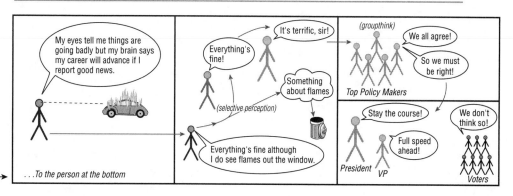

---

[25] Woodward, Bob. *State of Denial: Bush at War III.* Simon & Schuster, 2006.
[26] Brecher, Michael, and Jonathan Wilkenfeld. *A Study of Crisis.* Michigan, 2000. Gelpi, Christopher. *The Power of Legitimacy: Assessing the Role of Norms in International Crisis Bargaining.* Princeton, 2003.

United States, shifting time constraints are measurable in a doubling or tripling in pizza deliveries to government agencies, as decision makers work through mealtimes.)

Groupthink occurs easily during crises. During the 1962 Cuban Missile Crisis, President John F. Kennedy created a small, closed group of advisors who worked together intensively for days on end, cut off from outside contact and discussion. Even the president's communication with Soviet leader Nikita Khrushchev was rerouted through Kennedy's brother Robert and the Soviet ambassador, cutting out the State Department. Recognizing the danger of groupthink, Kennedy left the room from time to time—removing the authority figure from the group—to encourage free discussion. Through this and other means, the group managed to identify an option (a naval blockade) between their first two choices (bombing the missile sites or doing nothing). Sometimes leaders purposefully designate someone in the group (known as a *devil's advocate*) to object to ideas.

Participants in crisis decision making not only are rushed, but experience severe psychological *stress*, amplifying the biases just discussed. Decision makers tend to overestimate the hostility of adversaries and to underestimate their own hostility toward those adversaries. Dislike easily turns to hatred, and anxiety to fear. More and more information is screened out in order to come to terms with decisions being made and to restore cognitive balance. Crisis decision making also leads to physical exhaustion. *Sleep deprivation* sets in within days as decision makers use every hour to stay on top of the crisis. Unless decision makers are careful about getting enough sleep, they may make vital foreign policy decisions under shifting perceptual and mood changes.

To summarize, foreign policy is a complex outcome of a complex process. No single individual, agency, or guiding principle determines the outcome. Yet foreign policy does achieve a certain overall coherence. States form foreign policy on an issue or toward a region; it is not just an incoherent collection of decisions and actions taken from time to time. Out of the turbulent internal processes of foreign policy formation come relatively coherent interests and policies that states pursue.

CHAPTER 4

LIBERAL
INSTITUTIONALISM

LIBERAL THEORIES

If realism offers mostly dominance solutions to the collective goods problems of IR, several alternative theoretical approaches draw mostly on the reciprocity and identity principles. Among other common elements, these approaches generally are more optimistic than realism about the prospects for peace. Although realists see the laws of power politics as relatively timeless and unchanging, liberal theorists generally see the rules of IR as slowly, incrementally evolving through time and becoming more and more peaceful.

The German philosopher Immanuel Kant 200 years ago offered three reasons to believe that lasting peace is possible.[1] The first, based on the reciprocity principle, was that states could develop the organizations and rules to facilitate cooperation, specifically by forming a world federation resembling today's United Nations (UN). This reason forms the foundation of present-day liberal institutionalism, discussed in this chapter. Kant's second reason, operating at a lower level of analysis, was that peace depends on the internal character of governments—specifically that republics, with a legislative branch that can hold the monarch in check, will be more peaceful than autocracies. This argument, along with Kant's related point that citizens of any country deserve hospitality in any other country, relies more on the identity principle and will be taken up in Chapter 5.

Kant's third reason, that trade promotes peace, relies on the presumption that trade increases wealth, cooperation, and global well-being—all while making conflict less likely in the long term because governments will not want to disrupt any process that adds to the wealth of their states.[2] Realists are skeptical, however, arguing that one state's reliance on another creates *more* tensions in the short term because states are nervous that another actor has an important source of leverage over them. Critics of the trade-brings-peace theory note that World War I followed a period of high economic interdependence.

Now consider Kant's first reason, namely the ability of states to develop and follow mutually advantageous rules, with international institutions to monitor and enforce

---

[1] Kant, Immanuel. *Perpetual Peace*. Edited by Lewis White Beck. Bobbs-Merrill, 1957 [1795]. Russett, Bruce, and John Oneal. *Triangulating Peace: Democracy, Interdependence, and International Organizations*. Norton, 2000.

[2] Angell, Norman. *The Foundations of International Polity*. Heinemann, 1914. Schrodt, Philip A. Democratic Peace or Liberal Peace: The Debate. *International Studies Review* 6 (2), 2004: 292.

them. The core principle of reciprocity lies at the heart of this approach, because international institutions operate by reciprocal contributions and concessions of formally equal members. Kant argued that states, although autonomous, could join a worldwide federation like today's UN and respect its principles even at the cost of forgoing certain short-term individual gains. To Kant, international cooperation was a more rational option for states than resorting to war. Thus, in realist conceptions of rationality, war and violence appear rational (because they often advance short-term state interests), but in liberal theories war and violence appear as irrational deviations that result from defective reasoning and that harm the (collective, long-term) interests of warring states.

The **neoliberal** approach differs from earlier liberal approaches in that it concedes to realism several important assumptions—among them, that states are unitary actors rationally pursuing their self-interests in a system of anarchy. Neoliberals say to realists, "Even if we grant your assumptions about the nature of states and their motives, your pessimistic conclusions do not follow." States achieve cooperation fairly often because it is in their interest to do so, and they can learn to use institutions to ease the pursuit of mutual gains and the reduction of possibilities for cheating or taking advantage of another state.[3] Neoliberal scholars try to show that even in a world of unitary rational states, the neorealists' pessimism about international cooperation is not valid. States can create mutual rules, expectations, and institutions to promote behavior that enhances (or at least doesn't destroy) the possibilities for mutual gain.

In particular, reciprocity in IR helps international cooperation emerge despite the absence of central authority. Through reciprocity, not a world government, norms and rules are enforced. In international security, reciprocity underlies the gradual improvement of relations sought by arms control agreements and peacekeeping missions. In international political economy (IPE), in which cooperation can create great benefits through trade, the threat to restrict trade in retaliation for unfair practices is a strong incentive to comply with rules and norms. But side by side with the potential for eliciting cooperation, reciprocity contains a danger of runaway hostility. When two sides both reciprocate but never manage to put relations on a cooperative footing, the result can be a drawn-out exchange of punishments.

Neoliberals use the *Prisoner's Dilemma (PD)* game (see pp. 40–41) to illustrate their argument that cooperation is possible. Each actor can gain by individually defecting, but both lose when both defect. Similarly, in IR, states often have a mix of conflicting and mutual interests. The dilemma can be resolved if the game is played over and over again—an accurate model of IR, in which states deal with each other in repeated interactions. In that case, a strategy of strict reciprocity after an initial cooperative move (nicknamed *tit-for-tat*) can bring about mutual cooperation in a repeated PD game, because the other player must conclude that any defection will merely provoke a like defection in response.[4]

---

[3] Baldwin, David A., ed. *Neorealism and Neoliberalism: The Contemporary Debate*. Columbia, 1993. Oye, Kenneth A., ed. *Cooperation under Anarchy*. Princeton, 1986.

[4] Axelrod, Robert. *The Evolution of Cooperation*. Basic, 1984.

INTERNATIONAL REGIMES

Achieving good outcomes is not simple. Because of the contradictory interpretations that parties to a conflict usually have, it is difficult to resolve conflicts without a third party to arbitrate or an overall framework to set common expectations for all parties. These considerations underlie the creation of International Organizations.

An **international regime** is a set of rules, norms, and procedures around which the expectations of actors converge in a certain issue area (whether arms control, international trade, or Antarctic exploration).[5] The convergence of expectations means that participants in the international system have similar ideas about what rules will govern their mutual participation: each expects to play by the same rules. (This meaning of regime is not the same as that referring to the domestic governments of states, especially governments considered illegitimate, as in *regime change*.)

Regimes can help solve collective goods problems by increasing transparency—because everyone knows what everyone is doing, cheating is more costly. The current revolution in information technologies is strengthening regimes particularly in this aspect. Also, with better international communication, states can identify conflicts and negotiate solutions through regimes more effectively.

IR scholars conceive of regimes in several different ways, and the concept has been criticized as too vague. But the most common conception of regimes combines elements of realism and liberalism. States are seen as autonomous units maximizing their own interests in an anarchic context. Regimes do not play a role in issues in which states can realize their interests directly through unilateral applications of leverage. Rather, regimes come into existence to overcome collective goods dilemmas by coordinating the behaviors of individual states. Although states continue to seek their own interests, they create frameworks to coordinate their actions with those of other states if and when such coordination is necessary to realize self-interest (that is, in collective goods dilemmas). In part, the survival of regimes rests on their embedding in permanent *institutions* such as the UN, NATO, and the International Monetary Fund.

Regimes do not substitute for the basic calculations of costs and benefits by states; they just open up new possibilities with more favorable benefit-cost ratios. Regimes do not constrain states, except in a very narrow and short-term sense. Rather they facilitate and empower national governments faced with issues in which collective goods or coordination problems would otherwise prevent governments from achieving their ends. Regimes can be seen as *intervening variables* between the basic causal forces at work in IR—for realists, the relative power of state actors—and the outcomes such as international cooperation (or lack thereof). For realists in particular, regimes do not negate the effects of power; more often they codify and normalize existing power relations in accordance with the dominance principle. For example, the nuclear nonproliferation regime protects the status quo in which only a few states have nuclear weapons.

The concept of **collective security,** which grows out of liberal institutionalism, refers to the formation of a broad alliance of most major actors in an international

---

[5] Hasenclever, Andreas, Peter Mayer, and Volker Rittberger. *Theories of International Regimes*. Cambridge, 1997. Keohane, Robert O. *After Hegemony: Cooperation and Discord in the World Political Economy*. Princeton, 1984. Krasner, Stephen D., ed. *International Regimes*. Cornell, 1983.

system for the purpose of jointly opposing aggression by any actor. Kant laid out the rationale for this approach. Because past treaties ending great-power wars had never lasted permanently, Kant proposed a federation (league) of the world's states. Through such a federation, Kant proposed, the majority of states could unite to punish any one state that committed aggression, safeguarding the collective interests of all the nations while protecting the self-determination of small nations that all too easily became pawns in great-power games.

After the horrors of World War I, the *League of Nations* was formed. But it was flawed in two ways. Its membership did not include all the great powers (notably the most powerful one, the United States), and its members proved unwilling to bear the costs of collective action to oppose aggression when it did occur in the 1930s, starting with Japan and Italy. After World War II, the UN was created as the League's successor to promote collective security. Several regional IGOs also currently perform collective security functions (deterring aggression) as well as economic and cultural ones—the *Organization of American States (OAS)*, the *Arab League*, and the *African Union*.

THE UNITED NATIONS

The UN and other international organizations have both strengths and weaknesses in the anarchic international system. State sovereignty creates a real need for such organizations on a practical level, because no central world government performs the function of coordinating the actions of states for mutual benefit. However, state sovereignty also severely limits the power of the UN and other IOs, because governments reserve power to themselves and are stingy in delegating it to the UN or anyone else. The UN has had a mixed record with these strengths and weaknesses—in some ways providing remarkable global-level management and in other ways appearing helpless against the sovereignty of even modest-sized states.[6]

The **UN Charter** is based on the principles that states are *equal* under international law; that states have full *sovereignty* over their own affairs; that states should have full *independence* and *territorial integrity;* and that states should carry out their international *obligations*—such as respecting diplomatic privileges, refraining from committing aggression, and observing the terms of treaties they sign. The Charter also lays out the structure of the UN and the methods by which it operates.

The UN is a *symbol* of international order and even of global identity. It is also a *forum* where states promote their views and bring their disputes. And it is a *mechanism* for conflict resolution in international security affairs. The UN also promotes and coordinates development assistance (see Chapter 12) and other programs of economic and social development in the global South. These programs reflect the belief that economic and social problems—above all, poverty—are an important source of inter-

---

[6] Kennedy, Paul. *The Parliament of Man: The Past, Present, and Future of the United Nations.* Random House, 2006. Mingst, Karen A., and Margaret P. Karns. *The United Nations in the Twenty-First Century.* 3rd ed. Westview, 2006. Krasno, Jean E. *The United Nations: Confronting the Challenges of a Global Society.* Rienner, 2004.

national conflict and war. Finally, the UN is a coordinating system for *information* and planning by hundreds of internal and external agencies and programs, and for the publication of international data.

Despite its heavy tasks, the UN is still a small and fragile institution. Every year, the world spends about $1.2 trillion on the military, and less than $2 billion on the UN regular budget. The whole budget of UN operations, peacekeeping, programs, and agencies combined is less than $20 billion, or less than 2 percent of world military spending. Sometimes the UN succeeds and sometimes it fails. The UN deals with some of the most difficult issues in the world, such as ethnic conflicts, human rights, refugees, and world hunger.[7]

The UN's structure, shown in Figure 4.1, centers on the **UN General Assembly,** where representatives of all states sit together in a huge room, listen to speeches, and pass resolutions.[8] The General Assembly, with little power except over budgets and the admission of new members, coordinates a variety of development programs and other autonomous agencies through the *Economic and Social Council (ECOSOC).*

FIGURE **4.1   The United Nations**

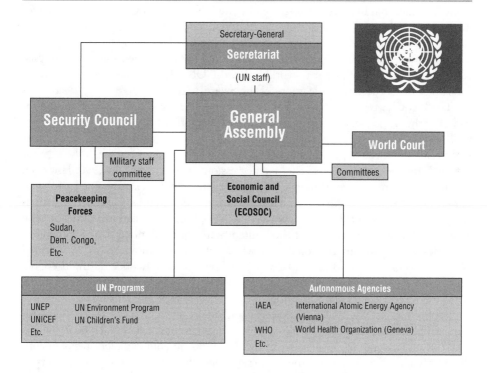

[7] Price, Richard M., and Mark W. Zacher. *The United Nations and Global Security.* Palgrave, 2004.
Newman, Edward, and Oliver P. Richmond. *The United Nations and Human Security.* Palgrave, 2001.
[8] Peterson, M. J. *The United Nations General Assembly.* Routledge, 2005.

Parallel to the General Assembly is the **UN Security Council,** in which five great powers and ten rotating member states make decisions about international peace and security. The Security Council dispatches peacekeeping forces to trouble spots. The *World Court* (International Court of Justice), which is discussed in Chapter 6, is a judicial arm of the UN.

The administration of the UN takes place through the **UN Secretariat** (executive branch), led by the secretary-general of the UN, who is nominated by the Security Council—requiring the consent of all five permanent members—and approved by the General Assembly. The term of office is five years and may be renewed. Past secretaries-general have come from various regions of the world but never from a great power. The UN staff numbers about 15,000 people, and the total number of employees in the UN system (including the World Bank and IMF) is around 60,000. One purpose of the UN Secretariat is to develop an *international civil service* of diplomats and bureaucrats whose loyalties lie at the global level, not with their states of origin.

A major strength of the UN structure is the *universality of its membership*. The UN had 192 members in 2008. In contrast to the old League of Nations, virtually every territory in the world is either a UN member or formally a province or colony of a UN member (the latter category including Taiwan, which functions autonomously in many international matters but is treated by the UN as part of China). Formal agreement on the Charter, even if sometimes breached, commits all states to a set of basic rules governing their relations. One way the UN induced all the great powers to join was to reassure them that their participation would not harm their national interests. Recognizing the role of power in world order, the UN Charter gave five great powers each a veto over substantive decisions of the Security Council.

The UN Charter establishes a mechanism for collective security—the banding together of the world's states to stop an aggressor. Chapter 7 of the Charter explicitly authorizes the Security Council to use military force against aggression if the nonviolent means called for in Chapter 6 have failed. For example, under Chapter 7, the UN authorized the use of force to reverse Iraqi aggression against Kuwait in 1990. However, because of the great-power veto, the UN cannot effectively stop aggression by (or supported by) a great power. As often happens with the dominance principle, this structure creates resentments by smaller powers. In 2006, Iran's president asked the General Assembly, "If the governments of the United States or the United Kingdom commit atrocities or violate international law, which of the organizations in the United Nations can take them to account?" Chapter 7 was used only once during the Cold War—in the Korean War when the Soviet delegation unwisely boycotted the proceedings (and when China's seat was still held by the nationalists on Taiwan).

After the Cold War, the great powers could finally agree on measures regarding international security, and the UN moved to center stage in international security affairs. The UN had several major successes in the late 1980s in ending violent regional conflicts (in Central America and the Iran-Iraq War) while introducing peacekeepers to monitor the cease-fires. Between 1987 and 1993, Security Council resolutions increased from 15 to 78, peacekeeping missions from 5 to 17, peacekeepers from 12,000 to 78,000, and countries sending troops from 26 to 76. The new missions ran into serious problems, however. Inadequate funding and management problems undermined peacekeeping efforts in Angola, Somalia, and Cambodia. In the former Yugoslavia in 1993–1995, the UN undertook a large peacekeeping mission before a cease-fire was in place—"peace-keeping where there is no peace to keep." In response to these problems (and to unpaid U.S. dues), the UN scaled back peacekeeping operations in 1995–1997 (from 78,000 to 19,000 troops) and carried out reductions and reforms in the UN Secretariat and UN programs. Peacekeeping missions expanded again in the new century.

The 2001 terrorist attacks increased U.S. participation in the UN, where a deci-sive coalition of member states initially supported U.S. positions on terrorism in Afghanistan. The 2003 Iraq War, however, triggered serious divisions among the great powers that sidelined the UN. After reaching consensus to insist on Iraqi disarmament and send back UN weapons inspectors, the Security Council split on whether to au-thorize force against Iraq—the United States and Britain in favor; France, Russia, and China against. After France threatened to veto a UN resolution authorizing war, a U.S.-British coalition toppled the Iraqi government without explicit UN backing. UN secretary-general Kofi Annan later called the war "illegal." The UN sent a team to Iraq to help with reconstruction, but suicide truck-bombers destroyed it, killing the chief of the mission and dozens of others. Another bomber destroyed the Red Cross headquar-ters in Baghdad. The UN withdrew its staff from Iraq in 2003 and found itself largely sidelined in the world's most prominent international conflict.

Currently, the UN follows a principle of "three pillars"—security, economic devel-opment, and human rights—which are considered mutually necessary for any of them to succeed. In a postwar conflict situation, in particular, the three reinforce each other.

THE SECURITY COUNCIL AND PEACEKEEPING

The Security Council is responsible for maintaining international peace and security and for restoring peace when it breaks down. Its decisions are *binding* on all UN mem-ber states. The Security Council has tremendous power to *define* the existence and na-ture of a security threat, to *structure* the response to such a threat, and to *enforce* its de-cisions through mandatory directives to UN members (such as to halt trade with an aggressor). However, the Council's decisions depend entirely on the particular inter-ests of its member states, which may diverge (see Figure 4.2).

The five *permanent members* of the Council—the United States, Britain, France, Russia, and China—are the most important. What they can agree on, generally the world must go along with. Substantive Security Council resolutions require 9 votes from among the 15 members. But a "no" vote by any permanent member defeats the resolution—the *veto* power. Many resolutions have been vetoed by the permanent members, but since 1991, with the great powers getting along better, the use of the veto has dropped sharply. By factoring in the importance of the great military pow-ers, the UN Security Council relies strongly on the dominance principle to maintain world order. In six decades, the Council has passed more than 1,700 resolutions, with new ones added every week. These resolutions represent the great powers' blue-prints for resolving the world's various security disputes, especially in regional con-flicts. (Because of the veto system, the Council avoids conflicts among great powers themselves.)

FIGURE 4.2   **Divergent Interests on the UN Security Council**

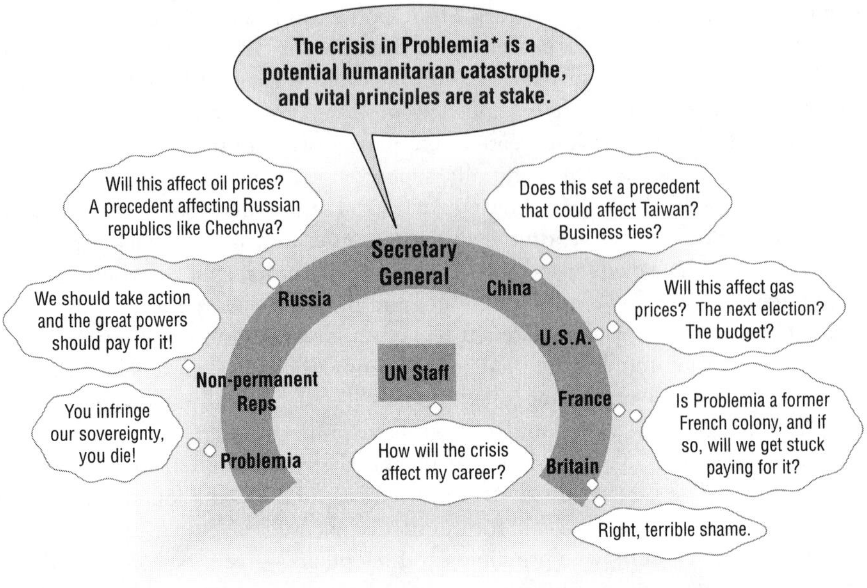

*Problemia could be Kurdish Iraq in 1991 or Darfur, Sudan, in 2007.

The Council's 10 *nonpermanent members* rotate onto the Council for two-year terms. Nonpermanent members are elected (5 each year) by the General Assembly from a list prepared by informal regional caucuses. Usually there is a mix of regions and country sizes, though not by any strict formula. The Council's *chairperson* rotates among the Council members monthly. Table 4.1 shows the recent rotations of members onto the Security Council. The system of nomination by regional caucuses has worked to keep the regional balance on the Council fairly constant as individual states come and go. Major regional actors tend to rotate onto the Council more often than do less important states.

The structure of the Security Council is not without problems. Japan and Germany would like seats, as great powers that contribute substantial UN dues and make large contributions to UN programs and peacekeeping operations. But if Germany joined, three permanent members would be European, giving that region unfair weight. The three European seats could be combined into one (a rotating seat or one representing the European Union), but this would water down the power of Britain and France, which can veto any such change in the Charter. Japan's bid for a seat faces Chinese opposition. Also, if Japan or Germany got a seat, then what about India, what about an Islamic country such as Indonesia, and what about Latin America and Africa? Any overhaul of the Security Council would require a change in the UN Charter, and would reduce the power of the current five permanent members, any of which could veto the change.

Peacekeeping forces are not mentioned in the UN Charter. Secretary-General Dag Hammarskjöld in the 1960s joked that they were allowed under "Chapter Six

TABLE **4.1** Regional Representation on the UN Security Council

Region	Permanent Members[a]	NONPERMANENT MEMBERS[b]			Possible Contenders for New Permanent Seats[c]
		2008	2007	2006	
North America	United States				
W. Europe	Britain France	Italy Belgium	Italy Belgium	Denmark Greece	Germany
Japan/ Pacific				Japan	Japan
Russia & E. Europe	Russia	Croatia	Slovakia	Slovakia	
China	China				
Middle East		Libya	Qatar	Qatar	Egypt?
Latin America		Costa Rica Panama	Peru Panama	Peru Argentina	Brazil, Mexico?
South Asia		Indonesia Vietnam	Indonesia		India, Indonesia?
Africa		South Africa Burkina Faso	South Africa Ghana Congo Republic	Tanzania Ghana Congo Republic	Nigeria? South Africa?

[a]The five permanent members hold veto power.
[b]Nonpermanent members are elected for two-year terms by the General Assembly, based on nominations by regional caucuses.
[c]Possible new permanent seats might have fewer if any veto powers.

and a Half"—somewhere between the nonviolent dispute resolution called for in Chapter 6 of the Charter and the authorization of force provided for in Chapter 7. The Charter requires member states to place military forces at the disposal of the UN, but such forces were envisioned as being used in response to aggression (under collective security). In practice, when the UN has authorized force to reverse aggression—as in the Gulf War in 1990—the forces involved have been *national* forces not under UN command.

The UN's *own* forces—borrowed from armies of member states but under the flag and command of the UN—have been *peacekeeping* forces to calm regional conflicts, playing a neutral role between warring parties.[9] The secretary-general assembles a peacekeeping force for each mission, usually from a few states totally uninvolved in the

---

[9] Doyle, Michael W., and Nicholas Sambanis. *Making War and Building Peace: United Nations Peace Operations*. Princeton, 2006. Whitworth, Sandra. *Men, Militarism and UN Peacekeeping: A Gendered Analysis*. Rienner, 2004. Findlay, Trevor. *The Use of Force in UN Peace Operations*. Oxford, 2002.

conflict, and puts it under a single commander. The soldiers are commonly called *blue helmets*. They perform two different functions. *Observers* are unarmed military officers sent to a conflict area in small numbers simply to watch what happens and report back to the UN. *Peacekeepers* per se are lightly armed soldiers (in armored vehicles with automatic rifles but without artillery, tanks, and other heavy weapons) who can interpose themselves between hostile forces. Both types serve at the invitation of a host government and must leave if that government orders them out.

The Security Council grants authority for peacekeeping forces, usually for a period of three to six months that may be renewed (in some cases for decades). Funds must be voted on by the General Assembly. Special assessments against member states pay for peacekeeping operations. With the expansion of peacekeeping since 1988, the expenses of these forces (about $7 billion) are several times larger than the regular UN budget.

TABLE 4.2   UN Peacekeeping Missions as of March 2008

Location	Region	Size	Annual Cost (million $)	Role	Since
Democratic Congo	Africa	19,300	$1,100	Observe cease-fire; protect civilians	1999
Liberia	Africa	15,200	690	Assist transitional govt.	2003
Sudan	Africa	10,900	850	Support agreement; monitor war	2005
Sudan/Darfur*a*	Africa	10,300	1,275	Protect civilians	2007
Ivory Coast	Africa	10,000	470	Help implement peace agreement	2004
Ethiopia/Eritrea	Africa	850	110	Monitor postwar border	2000
Western Sahara	Africa	300	45	Organize referendum in territory	1991
Central Afr. Rep./ Chad	Africa	120	180	Assist in repatriation of refugees	2007
India/Pakistan	South Asia	70	15	Observe India-Pakistan cease-fire	1949
Kosovo	Russia/E. Eur.	2,500	210	Civil administration; relief	1999
Georgia	Russia/E. Eur.	250	35	Observe cease-fire in civil war	1993
Lebanon	Middle East	13,500	715	Monitor cease-fire on Israeli border	1978
Syria (Golan Heights)	Middle East	1,100	40	Monitor Israel-Syria cease-fire	1974
Cyprus	Middle East	1,000	50	Monitor Greek-Turkish cease-fire	1964
Israel	Middle East	250	60	Observe Arab-Israeli truce	1948
Haiti	Latin America	10,500	535	Assist transitional govt.	2004
East Timor	Japan/Pacific	1,860	150	Observe cease-fire; policing	2006
Total		98,000	6,530		

Note: Size indicates total international personnel (mostly troops but some civilian administrators and police).

*a*The Sudan/Darfur force is a joint African Union–United Nations peacekeeping force that has not achieved its authorized strength.

In early 2008, the UN maintained nearly 100,000 troops (including some police) in 17 separate peacekeeping or observing missions, using military personnel from more than a hundred countries, spanning five world regions (see Table 4.2). In some conflicts, peacekeepers have been organized outside the UN framework. For instance, 3,500 French peacekeepers—not under UN command—serve in Ivory Coast alongside 9,000 UN peacekeepers from other countries.

Peacekeeping forces have generally been unable to make peace, only to keep it. To go into a shooting war and suppress hostilities requires military forces far beyond those of past UN peacekeeping missions. Thus, peacekeepers are usually not sent until a cease-fire has been arranged, has taken effect, and has held up for some time. Wars may simmer along for years, taking a terrible toll, before the UN gets its chance. To begin to address this problem, 16 countries participate in a Multinational Standby High Readiness Brigade, controlled by the Security Council, with several thousand troops available to deploy to conflict areas within about a month.

INTEGRATION THEORY

The UN and other international organizations are **supranational** in that they subsume a number of states and their functions within a larger whole. Such arrangements embody a struggle between the contradictory forces of *nationalism* and *supranationalism*—between state sovereignty and the higher authority of supranational structures.

International integration refers to the process by which supranational institutions replace national ones—the gradual shifting upward of sovereignty from state to regional or global structures. The ultimate expression of integration would be the merger of several (or many) states into a single state—or ultimately into a single world government. In practice, the process of integration has never gone beyond a partial and uneasy sharing of power between state and supranational levels. States have been unwilling to give up their exclusive claim to sovereignty and have limited the power and authority of supranational institutions.

The most successful example of the process of integration by far is the European Union.[10] Elsewhere in the world, economies have become more interdependent at both the regional and global levels. But other regional organizations have not experienced the success of the EU, despite their similar aims.[11]

Integration comes at a price. It reduces states' ability to shield themselves from the world's many problems and conflicts. The centralization of political authority, information, and culture as a result of integration can threaten both individual and group freedom. Ethnic groups want to safeguard their own cultures, languages, and institutions against the bland homogeneity that a global or regional melting pot would create. As a

[10] Eichengreen, Barry. *The European Economy since 1945: Coordinated Capitalism and Beyond*. Princeton, 2006. Dinan, Desmond. *Europe Recast: A History of the European Union*. Rienner, 2004. Moravcsik, Andrew. *The Choice for Europe: Social Purpose and State Power from Messina to Maastricht*. Cornell, 1998.
[11] Thomas, Kenneth P., and Mary Ann Tétreault, eds. *Racing to Regionalize: Democracy, Capitalism, and Regional Political Economy*. Rienner, 1999. Gleditsch, Kristian S. *All International Politics Is Local: The Diffusion of Conflict, Integration, and Democracy*. Michigan, 2002.

result, many states and citizens, in Europe and elsewhere, have at times responded to integration with resurgent nationalism. Indeed, these forces have set in motion a wave of *disintegration* of states running counter to (though simultaneous with) the integrating tendencies in today's world. The wave of disintegration in some ways began with the decolonization of former European empires in Africa, Asia, and the Middle East after World War II. After the Cold War, disintegration centered on Russia and Eastern Europe—especially in the former Soviet Union and former Yugoslavia. States in other regions—Somalia, Democratic Congo, and Iraq—appear in danger of breaking into pieces, in practice if not formally.

That Western European states began forming supranational institutions and creating an economic community to promote free trade and coordinate economic policies caught the attention of IR scholars, who used the term *integration* to describe what they observed. Seemingly, integration challenged the realist assumption that states were strictly autonomous and would never yield power or sovereignty. These scholars proposed that European moves toward integration could be explained by *functionalism*—growth of specialized technical organizations that cross national borders.[12] According to functionalists, technological and economic development lead to more and more supranational structures as states seek practical means to fulfill necessary *functions* such as delivering mail from one country to another or coordinating the use of rivers that cross borders. As these connections became denser and the flows faster, functionalism predicted, states would be drawn together into stronger international economic structures.

The European experience, however, went beyond the creation of specialized agencies to include the development of more general, more political supranational bodies, such as the European Parliament. **Neofunctionalism** modifies functional theory by arguing that economic integration (functionalism) generates a *political* dynamic that drives integration further. Closer economic ties require more political coordination in order to operate effectively and eventually lead to political integration as well—a process called *spillover*. Some scholars focused on the less tangible *sense of community* ("we" feeling) that began to develop among Europeans, running contrary to nationalist feelings that still existed as well. The low expectation of violence among the states of Western Europe created a **security community** in which such feelings could grow.[13] This theory reflects the identity principle.

THE EUROPEAN UNION

Like the UN, the **European Union (EU)** was created after World War II and has developed since. But whereas the UN structure has changed little since its Charter was adopted, the EU has gone through several waves of expansion in its scope, member-

---

[12] Mitrany, David. *The Functional Theory of Politics.* London School of Economics/M. Robertson, 1975. Haas, Ernst B. *Beyond the Nation-State: Functionalism and International Organization.* Stanford, 1964.
[13] Adler, Emanuel, and Michael Barnett, eds. *Security Communities.* Cambridge, 1998. Deutsch, Karl W., et al. *Political Community and the North Atlantic Area: International Organization in the Light of Historical Experience.* Princeton, 1957.

ship, and mission over the past 50 years.[14] The EU today has nearly 500 million citizens and surpasses the U.S. economy in GDP.

If ever there were a candidate for the failure of integration, Europe would appear to be it. For 500 years, until 1945, the states of Europe were locked in chronic intermittent warfare; in the 20th century alone two world wars left the continent in ruins. The European states have historical and present-day religious, ethnic, and cultural differences. The 27 members of the EU in 2008 spoke 23 different official languages.

Europe in 1945 was decimated by war. Most of the next decade was spent recovering with help from the United States through the Marshall Plan. But already two French leaders, Jean Monnet and Robert Schuman, were developing a plan to implement the idea of functionalism in Europe—that future wars could be prevented by creating economic linkages that would eventually bind states together politically. In 1950, Schuman as French foreign minister proposed a first modest step—the merger of the French and German steel (iron) and coal industries into a single framework that could most efficiently use the two states' coal resources and steel mills. Coal and steel were key to European recovery and growth. The Schuman plan gave birth in 1952 to the *European Coal and Steel Community (ECSC)*, in which France and Germany were joined by Italy (the third large industrial country of continental Europe) and by three smaller countries. German and French steel experts had more in common than German and French politicians.

Although technical cooperation succeeded in 1952, political and military cooperation proved much more difficult. In line with the vision of a united Europe, the six ECSC states signed a second treaty in 1952 to create a European Defense Community to work toward integrating Europe's military forces under one budget and command. But the French parliament failed to ratify the treaty, and Britain refused to join such a force. The ECSC states also discussed formation of a European Political Community in 1953, but could not agree on its terms. Thus, in economic cooperation the supranational institutions succeeded but in political and military affairs state sovereignty prevailed.

In the **Treaty of Rome** in 1957, the same six states formed the *European Economic Community (EEC)*, later renamed the *European Community (EC)*. The EEC created a **free-trade area,** lifting tariffs and restrictions on the movement of goods across borders. In the 1960s it expanded this arrangement into a **customs union,** in which participating states adopt a unified set of tariffs with regard to goods coming in from outside the free-trade area. The customs union remains the heart of the EU and the one aspect widely copied elsewhere in the world. The EEC also moved Europe toward a **common market** (still incompletely achieved today) in which member states allow labor and capital as well as goods to flow freely across borders.

One key aspect of this common market was the **Common Agricultural Policy (CAP),** which began in the 1960s. In practice, it has led to recurrent conflicts among member states, and tensions between nationalism and regionalism. The CAP was

[14] Caporaso, James A. *The European Union: Dilemmas of Regional Integration.* Westview, 2000. Nelsen, Brent F., and Alexander Stubb. *European Union: Readings on the Theory and Practice of European Integration.* Rienner, 2003.

based on the principle that a subsidy extended to farmers in any member state should be extended to farmers in all EU countries. That way, no member government was forced to alienate politically powerful farmers by removing subsidies, yet the overall policy would be equalized throughout the community in line with the common market principle. As a result, subsidies to farmers today absorb about 40 percent of the total EU budget, with France as the main beneficiary, and are the single greatest source of trade friction between Europe and the United States (see pp. 152–153).

The next step in the plan for European integration after a free-trade area, customs union, and common market was an *economic and monetary union (EMU)* in which a single currency replaced separate national currencies (see p. 68). A future step could be the supranational coordination of economic policies such as budgets and taxes.

To reduce state leaders' fears of losing sovereignty, the Treaty of Rome provided that changes in its provisions must be approved by all member states. The requirement for consensus, only now being eased in a new treaty for the EU's 27 members, slowed down integration over the decades but reduced conflict among member states.

The structure of the EU reflects its roots in technical and economic cooperation. The coal and steel experts have been joined by experts on trade, agriculture, and finance at the heart of the community. The EU headquarters and staff have the reputation of colorless bureaucrats—sometimes called *Eurocrats*—who care more about technical problem solving than about politics. These supranational bureaucrats are balanced in the EU structure by provisions that uphold the power of states and state leaders.

Although the rule of Eurocrats follows the functionalist plan, it has created problems as the EU has progressed. Politicians in member states have qualms about losing power to the Eurocrats. Citizens in those states have become more uncomfortable in recent years with the growing power of faceless Eurocrats over their lives. Citizens can throw their own political leaders out of office in national elections, but the Eurocrats seem less accountable.

The EU's structure is illustrated in Figure 4.3. The Eurocrats consist of a staff of 24,000, organized under the **European Commission** at EU headquarters in Brussels, Belgium. The Commission has 27 individual members—one from each member state—who are chosen for four-year renewable terms. Their role is to identify problems and propose solutions. They select one of their members as the commission president. These individuals are supposed to represent the interests of Europe as a whole (supranational interests), not their own states, but this goal has been only imperfectly met.

The European Commission lacks formal autonomous power except for day-to-day EU operations. Formally, the Commission reports to, and implements policies of, the **Council of the European Union.** The Council is a meeting of the relevant ministers (foreign, economic, agriculture, finance, etc.) of each member state—politicians who control the bureaucrats (or who try to). This formal structure reflects states' resistance to yielding sovereignty. It also means that the individuals making up the Council of the EU vary from one meeting to the next, and that technical issues receive priority over political ones. The arrangement thus gives some advantage back to the Commission staff.[15]

---

[15] Pollack, Mark A. *The Engines of Integration: Delegation, Agency, and Agenda Setting in the European Union.* Oxford, 2003. Nugent, Neill. *The Government and Politics of the European Union.* 5th ed. Duke, 2003.

FIGURE 4.3   Structure of the European Union (EU)

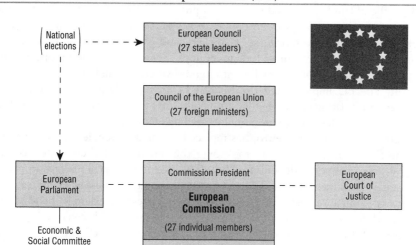

There is a **European Parliament,** which falls somewhat short of a true legislature passing laws for all of Europe.[16] It must approve the Commission's budget but cannot control it item by item. The parliament shares power with the Council under a "co-decision procedure" in such areas as migration, employment, health, and consumer protection.

The **European Court of Justice** in Luxembourg adjudicates disputes on matters covered by the Treaty of Rome—which includes many issues. The European Court can overrule national laws that conflict with EU law—giving it unique powers among international courts. It hears cases brought by individuals, not just governments. In hundreds of cases, the Court has ruled on matters ranging from discrimination in the workplace to the pensions of Commission staff members.

European integration has proceeded in a step-by-step process that produces tangible successes, reduces politicians' fears of losing sovereignty, and creates pressures to continue the process. Often major steps forward are followed by periods of stagnation or even reversals in integration. The first major revision of the Treaty of Rome—the 1985 **Single European Act**—began a new phase of accelerated integration. The EU set a target date of the end of 1992 for the creation of a true common market in Europe. This comprehensive set of changes was nicknamed *Europe 1992* and centered on about 300 directives from the European Commission, aimed at eliminating nontariff barriers to free trade in goods, services, labor, and capital within the EC. However, Europe 1992 continued to put aside for the future the difficult problems of political and military integration.[17]

---

[16] Judge, David, and David Earnshaw. *The European Parliament.* Palgrave, 2003.

[17] Salmon, Trevor C., and Alistair J. K. Shepherd. *Toward a European Army: A Military Power in the Making?* Rienner, 2003.

The **Maastricht Treaty,** signed in the Dutch city of Maastricht in 1992, renamed the EC as the EU and committed it to further progress in three main areas—monetary union, justice (creating a European police agency and responding to the opening of borders to immigrants, criminals, sex traffickers, and contraband), and political and military integration (a common foreign policy). Some citizens of Europe reacted strongly against the loss of national identity and sovereignty implicit in Maastricht.[18] Eventually, the EU implemented the Maastricht Treaty, although more slowly and with fewer participating countries than originally hoped. Economic and technical integration, including monetary union, maintained momentum.

A European currency, the **euro,** has replaced national currencies in 15 EU members. The European Central Bank took over the functions of these states' central banks.[19] Monetary union is difficult for both economic and political reasons. In participating states, fundamental economic and financial conditions must be equalized. One state cannot stimulate its economy with low interest rates (for example, because of a recession) while another cools inflation with high interest rates (because of high economic growth). In an integrated economy that is also politically centralized, the central government can reallocate resources, but the EU does not have centralized powers of taxation or control of national budgets. This split of fiscal and monetary policy is unusual. Furthermore, money is more political than steel tariffs. A monetary union infringes on a core prerogative of states—the right to print currency. Because citizens use money every day, the euro could deepen citizens' sense of identification with Europe—a victory for supranationalism over nationalism. With the euro in 2002, people for the first time could "put Europe in their pocket." Despite all these challenges, the creation of a European currency—arguably the largest financial overhaul ever attempted in history—has been very successful so far. Having survived its birth and gained the confidence of investors, the euro gained value from $1.17 at the outset to $1.55 in June 2008. It has become a major world currency.

The larger and more integrated the EU becomes, the less attractive is the prospect of remaining outside it for any state in the vicinity of Europe. The EU has expanded from 15 members to 27 since 2004, with potentially far-reaching changes in how the EU operates, in particular its ability to reach decisions by consensus. To grapple with the implications of an expanding EU, the members signed an EU constitution in late 2004 and the European Parliament gave it a strong vote of support in 2005. To take effect, it had to be ratified by all 25 states, including several requiring referendums. The constitution was to establish a stronger president of the EU, and a foreign minister. It was to replace the requirement for consensus in EU decision making with majority voting in more cases. And it was to guarantee fundamental rights to all EU citizens. But voters in France and the Netherlands rejected the constitution and the process halted.

---

[18] Cowles, Maria Green, James Caporaso, and Thomas Risse, eds. *Transforming Europe: Europeanization and Domestic Change.* Cornell, 2001.

[19] De Grauwe, Paul. *The Economics of Monetary Union.* 5th ed. Oxford, 2004.

Putting behind the failed constitution, the EU moved forward at the end of 2007 with a new treaty, the Lisbon Treaty, embodying many of the same concepts. It provided for an EU president with a term of two and a half years, a powerful foreign policy representative, and the use of majority votes instead of unanimity in more decisions. The treaty had to be approved by all 27 member states, but faced a popular referendum only in Ireland, with the others facing the lesser challenge of parliamentary approval. However, Irish voters defeated the referendum in June 2008, putting the future of EU reforms in doubt.

Turkey continues to seek membership, but the EU has not reached a consensus on admitting Turkey as a full member. Proponents note that Turkey has made major economic and political changes, including abolishing the death penalty and improving human rights, to try to win EU membership. Granting full membership would reward these changes, keeping an implicit promise to reciprocate Turkey's actions. Turkey's size and growth would contribute to the EU economy, and Turkish workers could help alleviate a labor shortage in Western Europe. Supporters also argue that Turkey as an EU member would serve as a bridge between Europe and the important but unstable Middle East region and as an example of secular democracy to other Middle Eastern countries.

Opponents note that Turkey would be the only Muslim country in the EU, yet would become the second most populous EU member after Germany. With 2 million Turks already living in Germany, opponents argue that EU membership would open the floodgates for immigration from a large, poor country, overwhelming the smaller and richer EU members. In France, opposition to Turkey's admission, and to immigration generally, created a backlash that helped derail a proposed EU constitution in 2005. In economic terms, Turkey would be the poorest member, even including the new Eastern European members (see Figure 4.4). Finally, opponents want Turkey to remove its military forces from Cyprus, where a Greek-Turkish partition has endured for decades.

Beyond the EU itself, Europe is a patchwork of overlapping structures with varying memberships (see Figure 4.5). NATO membership overlaps partly with the EU. Russia and even the United States are European actors in some respects but not others. One truly universal intergovernmental organization exists in Europe—the *Organization for Security and Cooperation in Europe (OSCE)*. Operating by consensus, it has little power except to act as a discussion forum for security issues and an election monitor.

Thus, international integration is not a matter of a single group or organization but more a mosaic of structures tying states together. These various structures of the European political system, centered on the EU, are IGOs composed of states as members. But a less-tangible aspect of integration is the sense of identity that develops over time as economic (and other functional) ties bring people closer together across borders. Supranational identity, culture, and communication are also aspects of international integration.

FIGURE 4.4   Income Levels of Old and New EU Members, 2005

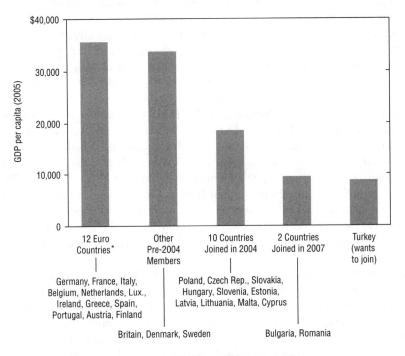

* Slovenia adopted the euro in 2007, Cyprus and Malta did so in 2008.

Source: World Bank data.

FIGURE 4.5 Overlapping Memberships of European States

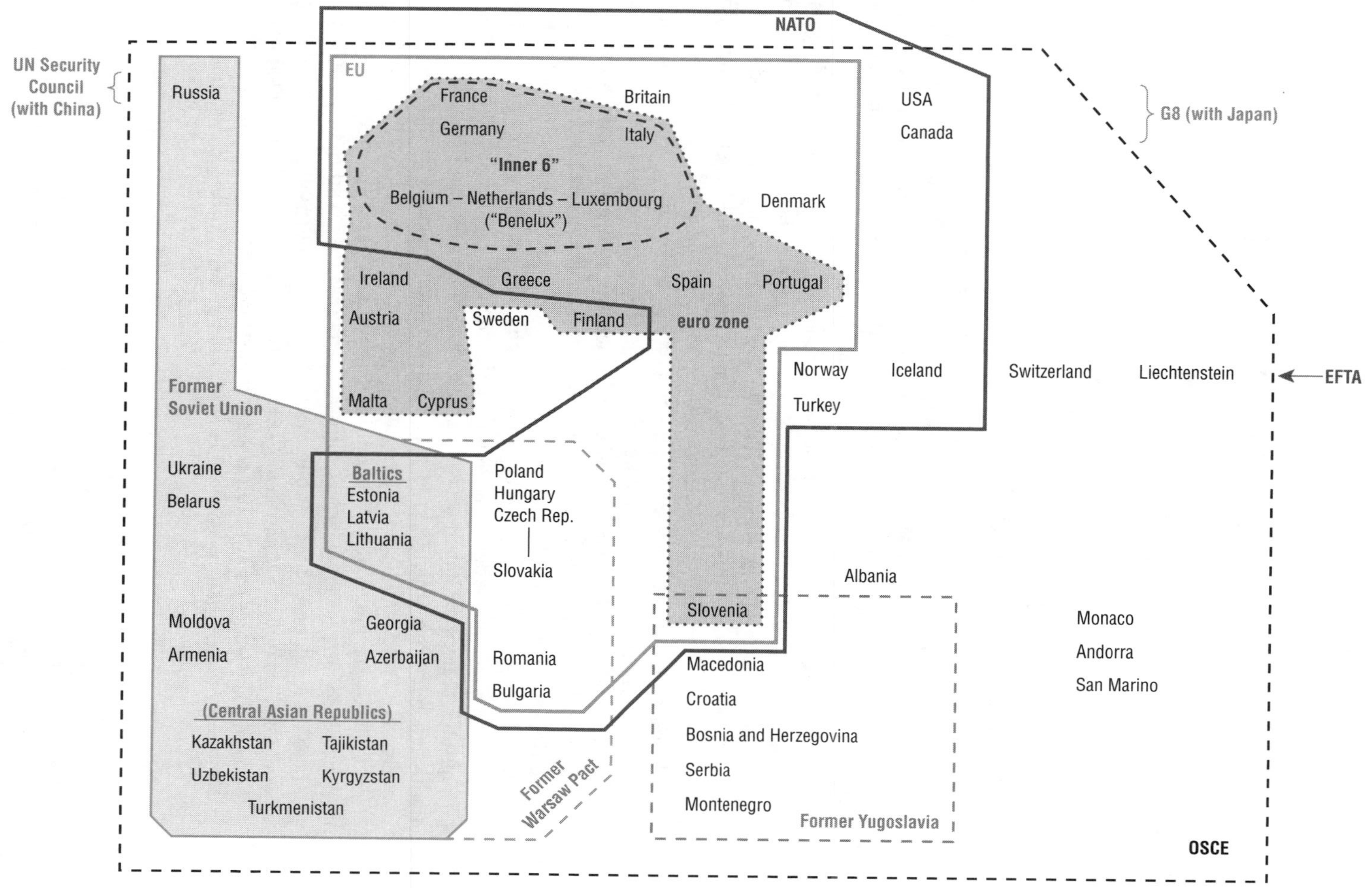

CHAPTER 5

DOMESTIC INFLUENCES

THE DEMOCRATIC PEACE

Several distinct approaches in IR theory may be grouped together as *social theories*, meaning that they rely on social interaction to explain individuals' and states' preferences. These theories contrast with realism's assumption of fixed, timeless preferences (states want more power). Most prominent of these approaches is democratic peace theory.

Kant (see pp. 53–54) argued that lasting peace would depend on states' becoming republics, with legislatures to check the power of monarchs (or presidents) to make war. Somewhat similarly, IR scholars have linked democracy with a kind of foreign policy fundamentally different from that of authoritarianism.[1] One theory they considered was that democracies are generally *more peaceful* than authoritarian governments (fighting fewer, or smaller, wars). This turned out to be false. Democracies fight as many wars as do authoritarian states. Indeed, the three most war-prone states of the past two centuries (according to political scientists who count wars) were France, Russia, and Britain. Britain was a democracy throughout, France for part of the period, and Russia not at all. (Kant himself distrusted democracies as subjecting policy to mob rule rather than rationality, a view influenced by witnessing the French Revolution.)

What *is* true about democracies is that although they fight wars against authoritarian states, *democracies almost never fight each other*. No major historical cases contradict this generalization, which is known as the **democratic peace.** Why this is so is not entirely clear. As there have not been many democracies for very long, the generalization could be just a coincidence, though this seems unlikely. It may be that democracies do not tend to have severe conflicts with each other, as they tend to be capitalist states whose trade relations create strong interdependence (war would be costly because it would disrupt trade). Or, citizens of democratic societies (whose support is necessary for wars to be waged) may simply not see the citizens of other democracies as enemies. By contrast, authoritarian governments of other states can be seen as enemies. Note

---

[1] Huth, Paul, and Todd Allee. *The Democratic Peace and the Territorial Conflict in the Twentieth Century.* Cambridge, 2003. Lipson, Charles. *Reliable Partners: How Democracies Have Made a Separate Peace.* Princeton, 2003. Reiter, Dan, and Allan C. Stam. *Democracies at War.* Princeton, 2002. Gowa, Joanne. *Ballots and Bullets: The Elusive Democratic Peace.* Princeton, 1999. Rummel, R. J. *Power Kills: Democracy as a Method of Nonviolence.* Transaction, 1997.

that the peace among democracies gives empirical support to a long-standing liberal claim that, because it is rooted in the domestic level of analysis, contradicts realism's claim that the most important explanations are at the interstate level.

Over the past two centuries, democracy has become more widespread as a form of government, and this trend is changing the nature of the foreign policy process world-wide.[2] Many states do not yet have democratic governments (the most important of these is China). And existing democracies are imperfect in various ways—from political apathy in the United States and corruption in Japan to autocratic traditions in Russia. Nonetheless, the trend is toward democratization in most of the world's regions.

In the past two decades the trend has accelerated in several ways. New democracies emerged in several (though not all) states of the old Soviet bloc. Military governments were replaced with democratically elected civilian ones throughout most of Latin America as well as in several African and Asian countries. In the late 1990s, long-standing dictatorships and military governments gave up power peacefully to democratic governments in Indonesia and Nigeria, both regional giants. In late 2004 and early 2005, pro-democracy forces won a string of victories in Ukraine, Palestine, Afghanistan, Iraq, and Kyrgyzstan. In 2006 in Nepal, massive popular protests forced the king to reverse his seizure of absolute power and reinstate the parliament, leading Maoist rebels to join the political process as a party and win elections in 2008. However, movement in the other direction still occurs. Military governments took over Pakistan and Ivory Coast in 1999, a military coup took place in Thailand in 2006, and Russia's government has constrained democracy in recent years while China's communist party has maintained its iron grip on politics.

We do not know where these trends toward democracy will lead, but it is now conceivable that someday nearly all of the world's states will be democratically governed. As Kant envisaged, an international community based on peaceful relations may emerge.

However, although mature democracies almost never fight each other, a period of *transition* to democracy may be more prone to war than either a stable democracy or a stable authoritarian government.[3] Therefore the process of democratization does not necessarily bode well for peace in the short term. This theory gained support in early 2006 when Iraqi elections were followed by a rise in sectarian violence, and then Palestinian elections brought to power the militant faction Hamas, which rejects Israel's right to exist.

BUREAUCRACIES

Democracy is not the only aspect of domestic politics to affect foreign policy. The decisions of governments, whether in democratic or authoritarian societies, are influenced by substate actors such as government agencies, political interest groups, and industries. The substate actors closest to the foreign policy process are the state's bureaucratic agencies maintained for developing and carrying out foreign policy.

---

[2] Pevehouse, Jon C. *Democracy from Above? Regional Organizations and Democratization.* Cambridge, 2005.
[3] Mansfield, Edward D., and Jack Snyder. *Electing to Fight: Why Emerging Democracies Go to War.* MIT, 2005.

Different states maintain different foreign policy bureaucracies but share some common elements.

Virtually all states maintain a *diplomatic corps*, or *foreign service*, of diplomats working in *embassies* in foreign capitals (and in *consulates* located in noncapital foreign cities), as well as diplomats who remain at home to help coordinate foreign policy. States appoint *ambassadors* as their official representatives to other states and to international organizations. Diplomatic activities are organized through a *foreign ministry* or the equivalent (for example, the U.S. State Department).

In many democracies, some diplomats are *political appointees* who come and go with changes in government leaders (often as patronage for past political support). Others are *career diplomats* who come up through the ranks of the foreign service and tend to outlast changes in administration. Diplomats provide much of the information that goes into making foreign policies, but their main role is to carry out rather than create policies. Nonetheless, foreign ministry bureaucrats often make foreign relations so routine that top leaders and political appointees can come and go without greatly altering the country's relations. The national interest is served, the bureaucrats believe, by the stability of overall national goals and positions in international affairs.

Tension is common between state leaders and foreign policy bureaucrats. Career diplomats try to orient new leaders and their appointees, and to control the flow of information they receive (creating information screens). Politicians struggle to exercise power over the formal bureaucratic agencies because the latter can be too "bureaucratic" (cumbersome, routinized, conservative) to easily control. Also, these agencies are often staffed (at lower levels) mostly by career officials who may not owe loyalty to political leaders.

Interagency tension also affects the formulation of foreign policy. Certain agencies traditionally clash, and an endless tug-of-war shapes the foreign policies that emerge. In an extreme example of interagency rivalry, the U.S. State Department and the CIA backed opposite sides in a civil war in Laos in 1960.

In general, bureaucracies promote policies under which their own capabilities will be effective and their power will increase. There is a saying that "where you stand" on an issue "depends on where you sit" (in the bureaucratic structure). One can often predict just from the job titles of participants how they will argue on a policy issue. The government bargaining model (see p. 46) pays special attention to the interagency negotiations that result from conflicts of interest between agencies of the same government.

Although representatives of bureaucratic agencies usually promote the interests of their own bureaucracies, sometimes heads of agencies try to appear loyal to the state leader by forgoing the interests of their own agencies. Also, the preferences of leaders of bureaucratic agencies cannot always be predicted given the goal of their institution.

Units within agencies have similar tensions. In many countries, the different military services (army, navy, air force) pull in somewhat different directions, even if they ultimately unite to battle the foreign ministry. Bureaucrats working in particular units or projects become attached to them. Officials responsible for a new weapon system lose bureaucratic turf, and perhaps their jobs, if the weapon's development is canceled.

Of special concern in many poor states is the institutional interest that military officers have in maintaining a strong military. If civilian state leaders allow officers' salaries to fall or the size of the military forces to be cut, they may well face institutional resistance from the military—in the extreme case a military takeover of the government.[4]

In general, bureaucratic rivalry as an influence on foreign policy challenges the notion of states as unitary actors in the international system. Such rivalries suggest that a state does not have any single set of goals—a national interest—but that its actions may result from the bargaining of subunits, each with its own set of goals. Furthermore, such a perspective extends far beyond bureaucratic agencies because other substate actors have their own goals, which they seek to advance by influencing foreign policy.

INTEREST GROUPS

In all states, societal pressures influence foreign policy, although these are aggregated and made effective through different channels in different societies. In pluralistic democracies, interested parties influence foreign policy through interest groups and political parties. In dictatorships, similar influences occur but less visibly. Thus foreign policies adopted by states generally reflect some kind of process of domestic coalition formation.[5] Of course, international factors in turn also have strong effects on domestic politics.[6]

Interest groups are coalitions of people who share a common interest in the outcome of some political issue and who organize themselves to try to influence the outcome. For instance, French farmers have a big stake in international negotiations in the European Community (which subsidizes agriculture) and in world trade talks (which set agricultural tariffs). The farmers exert political pressure on the French government through long-established and politically sophisticated associations and organizations. They lobby for desired legislation and contribute to politicians' campaigns. More dramatically, when their interests have been threatened—as during a U.S.-European trade dispute in 1992—French farmers have turned out in large numbers across the country to block roads, stage violent street demonstrations, and threaten to grind the national economy to a halt unless the government adopts their position. Similarly (but often less dramatically), interest groups form around businesses, labor unions, churches, veterans, senior citizens, members of an occupation, or citizens concerned about an issue such as the environment.

Lobbying is the process of talking with legislators or officials to influence their decisions on some set of issues. Three important elements that go into successful lobbying

---

[4] Feaver, Peter D., and Christopher Gelpi. *Choosing Your Battles: American Civil-Military Relations and the Use of Force.* Princeton, 2004.

[5] Smith, Tony. *Foreign Attachments: The Power of Ethnic Groups in the Making of American Foreign Policy.* Harvard, 2000. Solingen, Etel. *Regional Orders at Century's Dawn: Global and Domestic Influences on Grand Strategy.* Princeton, 1998. Snyder, Jack. *Myths of Empire: Domestic Politics and International Ambition.* Cornell, 1991.

[6] Gourevitch, Peter. The Second Image Reversed: International Sources of Domestic Politics. *International Organization* 32 (4), 1978: 881–911. Rogowski, Ronald. *Commerce and Coalitions: How Trade Affects Domestic Political Alignments.* Princeton, 1989.

are the ability to gain a hearing with busy officials, the ability to present cogent arguments for one's case, and the ability to trade favors in return for positive action on an issue. These favors—legal and illegal—range from campaign contributions through dinners at nice restaurants, trips to golf resorts, securing illicit sexual liaisons, and paying bribes. In many states, corruption is a major problem in governmental decision making (see p. 188), and interest groups may induce government officials by illegal means to take certain actions.

Ethnic groups within one state often become interest groups concerned about their ancestral nation outside that state. Many members of ethnic groups feel strong emotional ties to their relatives in other countries; because the rest of the population generally does not care about such issues one way or the other, even a small ethnic group can have considerable influence on policy toward a particular country. Such ethnic ties are emerging as a powerful foreign policy influence in various ethnic conflicts in poor regions. The effect is especially strong in the United States, which is ethnically mixed and has a pluralistic form of democracy. But whether or not a foreign country has a large constituency of ethnic nationals within another country, it can lobby that country's government.

Clearly, interest groups have goals and interests that may or may not coincide with the national interest as a whole (if indeed such an interest can be identified). As with bureaucratic agencies, the view of the state as a unitary actor can be questioned. Defenders of interest-group politics argue that various interest groups tend to push and pull in different directions, with the ultimate decisions generally reflecting the interests of society as a whole. But according to *Marxist* theories of international relations, the key domestic influences on foreign policy in capitalist countries are rich owners of big businesses (see Chapter 7).

THE MILITARY-INDUSTRIAL COMPLEX

A **military-industrial complex** refers to the huge interlocking network of governmental agencies, industrial corporations, and research institutes working together to supply a nation's military forces. The military-industrial complex was a response to the growing importance of technology (nuclear weapons, electronics, and others) and of logistics in Cold War military planning. Because of the domestic political clout of these actors, the complex was a powerful influence on foreign policy in both the United States and the Soviet Union during the Cold War and, to a lesser extent, since then.[7]

PUBLIC OPINION

Many domestic actors seek to influence **public opinion**—the range of views on foreign policy issues held by the citizens of a state. Public opinion has greater influence on foreign policy in democracies than in authoritarian governments. But even dictators must

---

[7] Der Derian, James. *Virtuous War: Mapping the Military-Industrial-Media-Entertainment Network.* Westview, 2001.

pay attention to what citizens think. No government can rule by force alone: it needs legitimacy to survive. It must persuade people to accept (if not to like) its policies, because in the end, policies are carried out by ordinary people—soldiers, workers, and bureaucrats. Occasionally a foreign policy issue is decided directly by a referendum of the entire citizenry (the United States lacks such a tradition, which is strong in Switzerland and Denmark, for example).

Because of the need for public support, even authoritarian governments spend great effort on *propaganda*—the public promotion of their official line—to win support for foreign policies. States use television, newspapers, and other information media in this effort. In many countries, the state owns or controls major mass media such as television and newspapers, mediating the flow of information to its citizens; however, new information technologies with multiple channels make this harder to do.

Public opinion can constrain government choices in both democracies and authoritarian states. For example, the shrinking public support for the United States worldwide during the Iraq War (see Figure 5.1) limited the options of governments allied with U.S. goals. In Turkey, a NATO member, favorable opinions of the United States shrank from 50 percent of the public to below 15 percent in 2000–2007, and Turkey opposed U.S. policies in Iraq at several key points in the war.

Although the democratic peace theory implies that the citizenry is a force for peace, public opinion can also inflame international hostilities. For instance, in recent

FIGURE 5.1   Views of the United States in Nine Countries, 2000–2007

(Percent favorable view in public opinion polls)

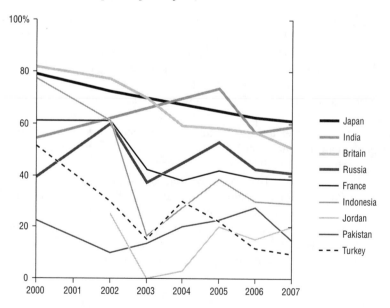

Source: *New York Times* from data of Pew Global Attitudes Project. 2000 data from State Department surveys.

FIGURE 5.2   Public Opinion in Muslim and Non-Muslim Countries, 2005

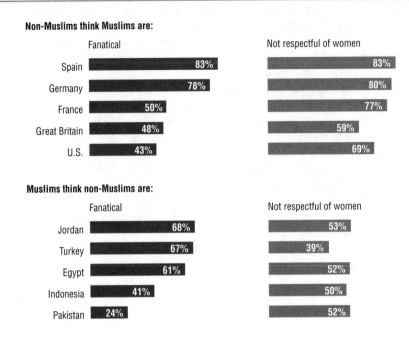

Non-Muslims think Muslims are:

Fanatical
- Spain — 83%
- Germany — 78%
- France — 50%
- Great Britain — 48%
- U.S. — 43%

Not respectful of women
- Spain — 83%
- Germany — 80%
- France — 77%
- Great Britain — 59%
- U.S. — 69%

Muslims think non-Muslims are:

Fanatical
- Jordan — 68%
- Turkey — 67%
- Egypt — 61%
- Indonesia — 41%
- Pakistan — 24%

Not respectful of women
- Jordan — 53%
- Turkey — 39%
- Egypt — 52%
- Indonesia — 50%
- Pakistan — 52%

Source: Pew Global Attitudes Survey.

years public opinion in both Muslim and non-Muslim countries reflects some notable misunderstandings. A 2005 poll, illustrated in Figure 5.2, recalls "mirror image" perceptions (see p. 48). In five Western industrialized countries, about 40 to 80 percent thought Muslims were "fanatical" and 60 to 80 percent thought they did not respect women. But in three of five Muslim countries, more than 60 percent thought non-Muslims were "fanatical" and in four of those five countries a majority thought non-Muslims did not respect women. These negative views held sway in democracies such as Spain and Turkey as well as in authoritarian states such as Jordan and Egypt.

The public may also, however, embody evolving norms that favor peace. Some IR scholars argue that war and military force are becoming *obsolete* because these means of influence are not very effective in today's highly complex, interdependent world. These scholars make historical analogies to the decline of the practices of slavery and dueling—once considered normal by publics but now obsolete.[8]

Journalists serve as the gatekeepers of information passing from foreign policy elites to the public. The media and government often conflict, because of the traditional role of the press as a watchdog and critic of government actions and powers. The media try

---

[8] Mueller, John. *Retreat from Doomsday: The Obsolescence of Major War.* Basic Books, 1989.

to uncover and publicize what the government wants to hide. Foreign policy decision makers also rely on the media for information about foreign affairs.

Yet the media also depend on government for information; the size and resources of the foreign policy bureaucracies dwarf those of the press. These advantages give the government great power to *manipulate* journalists by feeding them information, in order to shape the news and influence public opinion. Government decision makers can create dramatic stories in foreign relations—through summit meetings, crises, actions, and so forth. Bureaucrats can also *leak* secret information to the press in order to support their own point of view and win bureaucratic battles. Finally, the military and the press have a running battle about journalists' access to military operations, but both sides gained from the open access given to journalists "embedded" with U.S. forces in Iraq in 2003.

In democracies, where governments must stand for election, an unpopular war can force a leader or party from office, as happened to U.S. president Lyndon Johnson in 1968 during the Vietnam War. Or a popular war can help secure a government's mandate to continue in power, as happened to Margaret Thatcher in Britain after the 1982 Falkland Islands War. A key influence on public opinion is the content of scenes appearing on television: U.S. soldiers were sent to Somalia to assist in relief efforts in 1992 after TV news showed the heartrending results of civil war and famine there. But after TV news showed an American soldier's body being dragged through the streets by members of a Somali faction after a deadly firefight that killed 18 U.S. soldiers, public opinion shifted quickly against the Somalia operation.

Even in the most open democracies, states do not merely *respond* to public opinion. Decision makers enjoy some autonomy to make their own choices, and they are pulled in various directions by bureaucracies and interest groups, whose views often conflict with the direction favored by public opinion at large. Furthermore, public opinion is seldom unified on any policy, and sophisticated polling can show that particular segments of the population (regions of the country, genders, income groups, races, etc.) often differ in their perceptions of foreign policy issues. So a politician may respond to the opinion of one constituency rather than the whole population. Public opinion varies considerably over time on many foreign policy issues. States use propaganda (in dictatorships) or try to manipulate the media (in democracies) to keep public opinion from diverging too much from state policies.

In democracies, public opinion generally has less effect on foreign policy than on domestic policy. National leaders traditionally have additional latitude to make decisions in the international realm. This derives from the special need of states to act in a unified way to function effectively in the international system, as well as from the traditions of secrecy and diplomacy that remove IR from the realm of ordinary domestic politics.

The *attentive public* in a democracy is the minority of the population that stays informed about international issues. This segment varies somewhat from one issue to another, but there is also a core of people who care in general about foreign affairs and follow them closely. The most active members of the attentive public on foreign affairs constitute a foreign policy *elite*—people with power and influence who affect foreign policy. This elite includes people within governments as well as outsiders such as businesspeople, journalists, lobbyists, and professors of political science. Public opinion polls show that

FIGURE 5.3   The "Rally 'Round the Flag" Syndrome

President Bush's ratings demonstrate that war triggers a short-term boost in public approval.

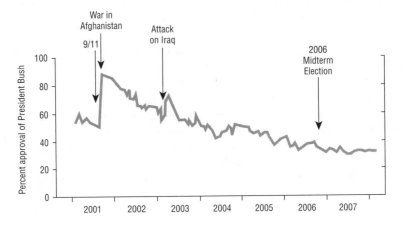

Source: Gallup poll.

elite opinions sometimes (but not always) differ considerably from those of the general population, and sometimes from those of the government as well.[9]

Governments sometimes adopt foreign policies for the specific purpose of generating public approval and hence gaining domestic legitimacy. This is the case when a government undertakes a war or foreign military intervention at a time of domestic difficulty, to distract attention and gain public support—taking advantage of the **"rally 'round the flag" syndrome** (the public's increased support for government leaders during wartime, at least in the short term). Citizens who would readily criticize their government's policies on education or health care often refrain from criticism when the government is at war and the lives of the nation's soldiers are on the line. Policies of this sort are often labeled **diversionary foreign policy.** Unfortunately, it is always difficult to tell whether a state adopts a foreign policy to distract the public, because leaders would never admit to trying to divert public attention.

However, wars that go on too long or are not successful can turn public opinion against the government and even lead to a popular uprising to overthrow the government. For example, in 2006, President Bush's popularity, which had soared early in the Iraq War, deflated as the war dragged on (see Figure 5.3), and voters threw his party out of power in Congress.

LEGISLATURES

One conduit through which interest groups and public opinion may wield influence is legislatures. Some democracies, such as the United States, have presidential systems, in which legislative bodies are elected apart from the president (also referred to as

---

[9] Holsti, Ole R. *Public Opinion and American Foreign Policy (Revised)*. Michigan, 2004.

executives). In these systems, legislatures play a direct role in making foreign policy by passing budgets, regulating bureaucratic rules, creating trade law, even controlling immigration policy. Although executives may attend summits and talks, any agreement they sign must be approved by their domestic legislature.[10]

Although few would argue that legislatures in presidential democracies do not influence foreign policy generally, different rules may apply to the use of military force. Some contend that legislatures, like public opinion, rally around the flag during times of international crises. For example, three days after the September 11, 2001, attacks, the U.S. Congress voted to give President Bush full authority to prosecute a war in Afghanistan. In October 2002, Congress passed a resolution authorizing the use of force in Iraq. Thus, legislatures rarely if ever challenge an executive on important military matters.

Others point to a different dynamic in which legislatures do stand up to executive power regarding military force. For example, because legislatures hold the "purse strings" (the ability to approve or reject new spending), they have the ability to stop a war in its tracks. In the United States, the War Powers Act, enacted during the close of the Vietnam War, requires the president to notify Congress when U.S. troops are deployed for combat. After this notification, the president has 60 days (plus a possible 30-day extension) to recall the troops unless Congress explicitly approves the military action.[11]

In parliamentary systems, such as Great Britain, executives (for example, prime ministers) are chosen by the political parties that hold a dominant position in the legislative bodies. Often parliamentary executives do not need to submit treaties or policies for formal approval by the legislature. Yet legislatures in parliamentary systems still hold power regarding foreign policy. In Great Britain, for example, Parliament is not required to vote on international agreements negotiated by the prime minister, but it must approve any change to British laws that such agreements entail. Because most international agreements do involve these types of changes, Parliament effectively exercises a right of ratification over international agreements.

In many parliamentary systems, if a policy is particularly controversial, parties that do not have a majority in the legislature can attempt to call elections—meaning that the country votes again on which parties will hold seats in the legislature. If a different group of parties wins a majority of seats, a new executive is appointed. Thus, in parliamentary systems, legislatures play a key role in designing and implementing foreign policy.

The differences in the foreign policy process from one state to another are also influenced by a state's type of government, such as military dictatorship, communist party rule, one-party (noncommunist) rule, and various forms of multiparty democracy. Relatively democratic states tend to share values and interests, and hence to get along better with each other than with nondemocracies (see "The Democratic Peace" pp. 72–73). In practice, most states lie along a spectrum with some mix of democratic and authoritarian elements.

---

[10] Milner, Helen. *Interests, Institutions, and Information: Domestic Politics and International Relations.* Princeton, 1997. Evans, Peter B., Harold K. Jacobson, and Robert D. Putnam, eds. *Double-Edged Diplomacy: International Bargaining and Domestic Politics.* California, 1993.

[11] Howell, Will, and Jon C. Pevehouse. *While Dangers Gather: Congressional Checks on Presidential War Powers.* Princeton, 2007.

CHAPTER 6

CONSTRUCTIVISM, LAW, AND HUMAN RIGHTS

CONSTRUCTIVISM

Constructivism is best described as an approach rather than a theory. Strongly based on the identity principle, constructivism considers how actors define their national interests, threats to those interests, and their relationships to one another. Realists (and neoliberals) tend to simply take state interests as given. Thus, constructivism puts IR in the context of broader social relations.[1] Constructivist research has many strands. One prominent line examines how states' interests and identities are intertwined, as well as how those identities are shaped by interactions with other states.[2] For example, why is the United States concerned when North Korea builds nuclear weapons, but not when Great Britain does? Realists would quickly answer that North Korea poses a bigger threat, yet from a pure military power perspective, Great Britain is a *far* superior military force to North Korea. Yet, no one would argue that Great Britain is a threat to the United States no matter how many nuclear weapons it builds and no matter how deep disagreements about foreign policy become. Constructivist scholars would point out the shared history, shared alliances, and shared norms that tell Americans and the British they are not a threat to one another although they are very powerful militarily. The identity of the potential adversary matters, not just its military capabilities and interests.

This is a rejection of the realist assumption that states always want more rather than less power and wealth as well as the assumption that state interests exist independently of a context of interactions among states.[3] Constructivists hold that these state identities are complex and changing, and arise from interactions with other states— often through a process of *socialization*. Some constructivist scholars contend that over time, states can conceptualize one another in such a way that there is no danger of a security dilemma, arms races, or the other effects of anarchy. They point to Europe as an example—a continent that was the center of two military conflicts in the first half

---

[1] Legro, Jeffrey W. *Rethinking the World: Great Power Strategies and International Order.* Cornell, 2005. Hopf, Ted. *Social Construction of International Politics: Identities and Foreign Policies, Moscow, 1955 and 1999.* Cornell, 2002. Crawford, Neta C. *Argument and Change in World Politics: Ethics, Decolonization, and Humanitarian Intervention.* Cambridge, 2002. Katzenstein, Peter, ed. *The Culture of National Security.* Columbia, 1996.

[2] Hall, Rodney Bruce. *National Collective Identity: Social Constructs and International Systems.* Columbia, 1999. Reus-Smit, Christian. *The Moral Purpose of the State: Culture, Social Identity, and Institutional Rationality in International Relations.* Princeton, 1999.

[3] Wendt, Alexander. *Social Theory of International Politics.* Cambridge, 1999. Guzzini, Stefano, and Anna Leander, eds. *Constructivism and International Relations: Alex Wendt and His Critics.* Routledge, 2006.

of the 20th century that killed millions. By the end of that century, war had become unthinkable. European identities are now intertwined with the European Union, not with the violent nationalism that led to two world wars. For constructivists, power politics, anarchy, and military force cannot explain this change. Institutions, regimes, norms, and changes in identity are better explanations.

States may also come to value and covet something like status or reputation, which are social, not material concepts. Switzerland, for example, values its role as a neutral, nonaligned state (it belongs to neither the European Union nor NATO, and joined the UN only in 2002). This status as a neutral gives Switzerland prestige and power— not a material power like money or guns—but a normative power to intervene diplomatically in important international affairs. Similarly, Canada's foreign policy contains its own identity-driven imperatives usually revolving around peacekeeping and humanitarian operations.

Another field of constructivist research also relies heavily on international norms and their power to constrain state action. Although realists (and neoliberals) contend that states make decisions based on a *logic of consequences* ("What will happen to me if I behave a certain way?"), constructivist scholars note that there is a powerful *logic of appropriateness* ("How should I behave in this situation?").[4] For example, some cases of humanitarian intervention—military intervention by a state or states to protect citizens or subjects of another—seem difficult to explain in realist or liberal terms. Why, for example, did the United States in 1992 send troops to Somalia—a country of minimal strategic and economic importance to the United States—as Somalia descended into political chaos and faced the possibility of mass starvation (see p. 79)? A constructivist explanation might point to changing norms about which kinds of people are worthy of protection. In the 19th century, European powers occasionally intervened to protect Christian subjects of the Ottoman Empire from massacres, but generally ignored non-Christian victims. However, as decolonization enshrined the principle of self-determination and as human rights became widely valued, the scope of humanitarian intervention expanded. Although the international community does not always respond effectively to humanitarian crises, it is no longer acceptable to view only Christians as deserving protection.[5] The United States in this example tried to act in an appropriate fashion rather than according to the dictates of cost-benefit calculations.

Examples can be found in the developing world as well. Some constructivists have argued that countries in Latin America, Africa, and the Middle East have adopted or changed policies in response to international norms—not because it provided large benefits, but rather because it was perceived as the appropriate course of action. For example, many developing states have raced to create science bureaucracies and/or begin technological modernization of their militaries. Constructivists point out that the reason developing states choose to spend their limited resources on such projects is their desire to be perceived as "modern" by the international system. "Modern" states have science bureaucracies and advanced militaries. Ironically, many states that build

[4] March, James G., and Johan Olsen. The Institutional Dynamics of International Political Orders. *International Organization* 52 (4), 1998, 943–69.

[5] Finnemore, Martha. *The Purpose of Intervention: Changing Beliefs about the Use of Force*. Cornell, 2004.

science bureaucracies have few scientists while many states that build advanced militaries have few enemies. Thus, constructivists emphasize that identities and norms must be used to explain this seemingly puzzling behavior.

How are these international norms spread around the world? In an age of global communication and relative ease of transportation, many possibilities exist. Constructivists emphasize different sets of actors who spread norms. Some contend that individuals, labeled *norm entrepreneurs*, through travel, writing, and meeting with elites change ideas and encourage certain types of norms. Some point to broad-based social movements and nongovernmental organizations, such as the anti-apartheid movement encouraging the development of a global norm of racial equality. Others show how international organizations (such as the UN and NATO) can diffuse norms of what is appropriate and inappropriate behavior. In each case, however, new ideas and norms, rather than power and self-interest, drive state behavior.[6] Research in the constructivist tradition has expanded rapidly in recent years. Scholars have examined the role of the European Union in socializing elites in new member states. Others have investigated how international organizations gain authority through their expertise (e.g., the IMF on international financial issues) to make decisions that run counter to what their member states desire.[7] Finally, constructivist scholars have begun to investigate how notions of identity and symbolism are important for understanding terrorist movements and counterterrorism policy.

INTERNATIONAL NORMS

Most international conflicts are not settled by military force. Despite the anarchic nature of the international system based on state sovereignty, the security dilemma does not usually lead to a breakdown in basic cooperation among states. States generally refrain from taking maximum short-term advantage of each other (such as by invading and conquering). States work *with* other states for mutual gain and take advantage of each other only "at the margin." Unfortunately, the day-to-day cooperative activities of international actors often are less newsworthy than their conflicts.

States work together by following rules they develop to govern their interactions. States usually *do* follow the rules. Over time, the rules become more firmly established and institutions grow up around them. States then develop the habit of working through those institutions and within the rules. They do so because of self-interest. Great gains can be realized by regulating international interactions through institutions and rules, thereby avoiding the costly outcomes associated with a breakdown of cooperation (see pp. 2–4).

The rules that govern most interactions in IR are rooted in norms. **International norms** are the expectations that actors hold about normal international relations. Some norms, such as sovereignty and respect for treaties, are widely held; they shape expectations about state behavior and set standards that make deviations stand out.

---

[6] Keck, Margaret, and Kathryn Sikkink. *Activists Beyond Borders: Advocacy Networks in International Politics.* Cornell, 1998. Klotz, Audie. *Norms in International Relations: The Struggle against Apartheid.* Cornell, 1995. Finnemore, Martha. *National Interests in International Society.* Cornell, 1996.

[7] Barnett, Michael, and Martha Finnemore. *Rules for the World.* Cornell, 2004.

Constructivist scholars in IR emphasize the importance of these global norms and standards. The attempt to define universal norms follows a centuries-long philosophical tradition. Philosophers such as Kant argued that it was natural for autonomous individuals (or states) to cooperate for mutual benefit because they could see that pursuing their narrow individual interests would end up hurting all. Thus, sovereign states could work together through structures and organizations (such as Kant's proposed world federation) that would respect each member's autonomy and not create a world government over them. In the 19th century, such ideas were embodied in practical organizations in which states participated to manage specific issues such as international postal service and control of traffic on European rivers.

Agreed norms of behavior, institutionalized through such organizations, become *habitual* over time and gain *legitimacy*. State leaders become used to behaving in a normal way and stop calculating, for each action, whether violating norms would pay off. For example, at the turn of the 19th century, U.S. war planners had active war plans for the possibility of a major naval conflict between the United States and Great Britain. Today, such plans would seem ridiculous. Over time, states refrain from behavior not just for cost-benefit reasons (as emphasized by realists and liberals) but also for normative reasons having little to do with material calculations (as emphasized by constructivists). Legitimacy and habit explain why international norms can be effective even when they are not codified and enforced.

The power of international norms and standards of morality, however, may vary when different states or world regions hold different expectations of what is normal. To the United States, it was a moral imperative to remove Saddam Hussein from power. But from the perspective of Arab populations, the U.S. invasion was an unjust violation of territorial sovereignty. In cases of diverging norms, morality can be a factor for misunderstanding and conflict rather than a force of stability. Realists point to examples such as these to suggest that international norms do not hold much sway on important matters of IR. Yet constructivist scholars point out that even if international norms are violated, states (even the United States) go to tremendous lengths to justify behaviors that violate the norms. This suggests that strong norms do exist and are recognized by even the most powerful states.

INTERNATIONAL LAW

International law, unlike national laws, derives not from actions of a legislative branch or other central authority, but from tradition and agreements signed by states. It also differs in the difficulty of enforcement, which depends not on the power and authority of central government but on reciprocity, collective action, and international norms.[8]

Laws within states come from central authorities—legislatures or dictators. Because states are sovereign and recognize no central authority, international law rests on a different basis. The declarations of the UN General Assembly are not laws, and

---

[8] Shaw, Malcolm N. *International Law*. 4th ed. Cambridge, 1998. Scott, Shirley V. *International Law in World Politics: An Introduction*. Rienner, 2004. Ku, Charlotte, and Paul F. Diehl. *International Law: Classic and Contemporary Readings*. 2nd ed. Rienner, 2003.

most do not bind the members. The Security Council can compel certain actions by states, but these are commands rather than laws: they are specific to a situation. Four sources of international law are recognized: treaties, custom, general principles of law (such as equity), and legal scholarship (including past judicial decisions).

Treaties and other written conventions signed by states are the most important source.[9] International treaties now fill more than a thousand thick volumes, with tens of thousands of individual agreements. A principle in international law states that treaties, once signed and ratified, must be observed (*pacta sunt servanda*). States violate the terms of treaties they have signed only if the matter is very important or the penalties for such a violation seem very small. In the United States, treaties duly ratified by the Senate are considered the highest law of the land, equal with acts passed by Congress.

Treaties and other international obligations such as debts are binding on successor governments whether the new government takes power through an election, a coup, or a revolution. After the revolutions in Eastern Europe around 1990, newly democratic governments were held responsible for debts incurred by their communist predecessors. Even when the Soviet Union broke up, Russia as the successor state had to guarantee that Soviet debts would be paid and Soviet treaties honored. Although revolution does not free a state from its obligations, some treaties have built-in escape clauses that let states legally withdraw from them, after giving due notice, without violating international law. The United States in 2001 invoked the six-month opt-out provision of the ABM treaty.

Because of the universal commitment by all states to respect certain basic principles of international law, the UN Charter is one of the world's most important treaties. Its implications are broad and far-reaching, in contrast to more specific treaties such as a fishery management agreement. The specialized agreements are usually easier to interpret and more enforceable than broad treaties such as the Charter.

Custom is the second major source of international law. If states behave toward each other in a certain way for long enough, their behavior may become generally accepted practice with the status of law. Western international law (though not Islamic law) tends to be *positivist* in this regard—it draws on actual customs, the practical realities of self-interest, and the need for consent rather than on an abstract concept of divine or natural law.

General principles of law also serve as a source of international law. Actions such as theft and assault recognized in most national legal systems as crimes tend to have the same meaning in an international context. Iraq's 1990 invasion of Kuwait was illegal under treaties signed by Iraq (including the UN Charter and that of the Arab League) and under the custom Iraq and Kuwait had established of living in peace as sovereign states. Beyond treaty or custom, the invasion violated international law because of the general principle that one state may not overrun its neighbor's territory and annex it by force. (Of course, a state may still think it can get away with such a violation of international law.)

The fourth source of international law, recognized by the World Court as subsidiary to the others, is *legal scholarship*—the written arguments of judges and lawyers

---

[9] Reuter, Paul. *Introduction to the Law of Treaties*. Pinter, 1992. Aust, Anthony. *Modern Treaty Law and Practice*. Cambridge, 2000.

around the world on the issues in question. Only the writings of the most highly qualified and respected legal figures can be taken into account, and then only to resolve points not resolved by the first three sources of international law.

Often international law lags behind changes in norms; law is quite tradition-bound. Certain activities such as espionage are technically illegal but are so widely condoned that they cannot be said to violate international norms. Other activities are still legal but have come to be frowned upon and seen as abnormal. For example, China's shooting of student demonstrators in 1989 violated international norms but not international law.

Although these sources of international law distinguish it from national law, an even greater difference exists as to the *enforcement* of the two types of law. International law is much more difficult to enforce. There is no world police force. Enforcement of international law depends on the power of states themselves, individually or collectively, to punish transgressors.

Enforcement of international law depends heavily on the reciprocity principle (see p. 3). States follow international law most of the time because they want other states to do so. The reason neither side in World War II used chemical weapons was not that anyone could *enforce* the treaty banning use of such weapons. It was that the other side would probably respond by using chemical weapons, too, and the costs would be high to both sides. International law recognizes in certain circumstances the legitimacy of *reprisals*: actions that would have been illegal under international law may sometimes be legal if taken in response to the illegal actions of another state.

A state that breaks international law may face a collective response by a group of states, such as the imposition of *sanctions*—agreements among other states to stop trading with the violator, or to stop some particular commodity trade (most often military goods) as punishment for its violation. Over time, a sanctioned state can become a pariah in the community of nations, cut off from normal relations with others. This is very costly in today's world, in which economic well-being everywhere depends on trade and economic exchange in world markets. Libya suffered for decades from its isolated status in the international community, and decided in 2003 to make a clean break and regain normal status. Libya admitted responsibility for past terrorism, began to compensate victims, and agreed to disclose and dismantle its nuclear, chemical, and biological weapons programs.

Even the world's superpower constrains its behavior, at least some of the time, to adhere to international law. For example, in late 2002 a North Korean freighter was caught en route to Yemen with a hidden load of 15 Scud missiles. The United States, fighting the war on terrorism, had an evident national interest in preventing such proliferation, and had the power to prevent it. But when U.S. government lawyers determined that the shipment did not violate international law, the United States backed off and let the delivery continue.

International law enforcement through reciprocity and collective response has one great weakness—it depends entirely on national power. Reciprocity works only if the aggrieved state has the power to inflict costs on the violator. Collective response works only if the collective cares enough about an issue to respond. Thus, it is relatively easy to cheat on small issues (or to get away with major violations if one has enough power).

Without common expectations regarding the rules of the game and adherence to those rules most of the time by most actors, power alone would create great instability in the anarchic international system. International law, even without perfect enforcement, creates expectations about what constitutes legal behavior by states. Because violations or divergences from those expectations stand out, it is easier to identify and punish states that deviate from accepted rules. When states agree to the rules by signing treaties (such as the UN Charter), violations become more visible and clearly illegitimate. In most cases, although power continues to reside in states, international law establishes workable rules for those states to follow. The resulting stability is so beneficial that usually the costs of breaking the rules outweigh the short-term benefits that could be gained from such violations.

Traditionally, the bedrock of international law is respect for the rights of diplomats. The standards of behavior in this area are spelled out in detail, applied universally, and taken very seriously. The status of embassies and of an ambassador as an official state representative is explicitly defined in the process of **diplomatic recognition.** Diplomats are *accredited* to each other's governments (they present "credentials"), and thereafter the individuals so defined enjoy certain rights and protections as foreign diplomats in the host country. Diplomats have the right to occupy an *embassy* in the host country as though it were their own state's territory.

Diplomats enjoy **diplomatic immunity** even when they leave the embassy grounds. Alone among all foreign nationals, diplomats are beyond the jurisdiction of the host country's national courts. Because of diplomatic immunity, espionage activities are commonly conducted through the diplomatic corps, out of an embassy. A *diplomatic pouch* is a package sent between an embassy and its home country. Diplomatic pouches, too, enjoy the status of home country territoriality: they cannot be opened, searched, or confiscated by a host country.

When two countries lack diplomatic relations, they often do business through a third country willing to represent a country's interests formally through its own embassy. This is called an *interests section* in the third country's embassy. Thus, the practical needs of diplomacy can overcome a formal lack of relations between states.

After the law of diplomacy, international law regarding war is one of the most developed areas of international law. Laws concerning war are divided into two areas—laws *of* war (when war is permissible) and laws *in* war (how wars are fought). To begin with the laws of war, international law distinguishes **just wars,** which are legal, from wars of aggression, which are illegal. (We discuss laws *in* war shortly in the context of human rights.) This area of law grows out of centuries-old religious writings about just wars (which once could be enforced by threats to excommunicate individuals from the church). Today, the legality of war is defined by the UN Charter, which outlaws aggression. Above and beyond its legal standing, just-war doctrine has become a strong international norm, not one that all states follow but an important part of the modern intellectual tradition governing matters of war and peace that evolved in Europe.[10]

---

[10] Walzer, Michael. *Arguing about War.* Yale, 2004. Walzer, Michael. *Just and Unjust Wars: A Moral Argument with Historical Illustrations.* 2nd ed. Basic, 1992.

The idea of aggression, around which the doctrine of just war evolved, is based on a violation of the sovereignty and territorial integrity of states. *Aggression* refers to a state's use of force, or an imminent threat to do so, against another state's territory or sovereignty—unless the use of force is in response to aggression. Tanks swarming across the border constitute aggression, but so do tanks massing at the border if their state has threatened to invade. The lines are somewhat fuzzy. But for a threat to constitute aggression (and justify the use of force in response), it must be a clear threat of using force, not just a hostile policy or general rivalry.

States have the right to respond to aggression in the only manner thought to be reliable—military force. Just-war doctrine is not based on nonviolence. Responses can include both *repelling* the attack itself and *punishing* the aggressor. Responses can be made by the victim of aggression or by other states not directly affected—as a way of maintaining the norm of nonaggression in the international system.

Response to aggression is the only allowable use of military force according to just-war doctrine. The just-war approach thus explicitly rules out war as an instrument to change another state's government or policies, or in ethnic and religious conflicts. In fact, the UN Charter makes no provision for "war" but rather for "international police actions" against aggressors. The analogy is with law and order in a national society, enforced by police when necessary. Because only aggression justifies military force, if all states obeyed the law against aggression, there would be no international war.

Just-war doctrine has been undermined, even more seriously than have laws of war crimes, by the changing nature of warfare.[11] In civil wars and low-intensity conflicts, the belligerents range from poorly organized militias to national armies, and the battleground is often a patchwork of enclaves and positions with no clear front lines (much less borders). It is harder to identify an aggressor in such situations, and harder to balance the relative merits of peace and justice.

THE WORLD COURT AND NATIONAL COURTS

As international law has developed, a general world legal framework in which states can pursue grievances against each other has begun to take shape. The rudiments of such a system now exist in the **World Court** (formally called the **International Court of Justice**), although its jurisdiction is limited and its caseload light.[12] Only states, not individuals or businesses, can sue or be sued in the World Court. When a state has a grievance against another, it can take the case to the World Court for an impartial hearing. The Security Council or General Assembly may also request advisory Court opinions on matters of international law.

The World Court is a panel of 15 judges elected for nine-year terms (5 judges every three years) by a majority of both the Security Council and General Assembly. The Court meets in The Hague, the Netherlands. It is customary for permanent members of the Security Council to have one of their nationals as a judge at all times. Ad hoc judges may be added to the 15 if a party to a case does not already have one of its nationals as a judge.

---

[11] Johnson, James Turner. *Can Modern War Be Just?* Yale, 1984.
[12] Meyer, Howard N. *The World Court in Action: Judging among Nations.* Rowman & Littlefield, 2002.

The great weakness of the World Court is that states have not agreed in a comprehensive way to subject themselves to its jurisdiction or obey its decisions. Almost all states have signed the treaty creating the Court, but only about a third have signed the *optional clause* in the treaty agreeing to give the Court jurisdiction in certain cases—and even many of those signatories have added their own stipulations reserving their rights and limiting the degree to which the Court can infringe on national sovereignty. The United States withdrew from the optional clause when it was sued by Nicaragua in 1986 (over the CIA's mining of Nicaraguan harbors). Similarly, Iran refused to acknowledge the jurisdiction of the Court when sued by the United States in 1979 over its seizure of the U.S. embassy in Iran. In such a case, the Court may hear the case anyway and usually rules in favor of the participating side—but has no means to enforce the ruling. Justice can also move slowly.

A main use of the World Court now is to arbitrate issues of secondary importance between countries with friendly relations overall. The United States has settled commercial disputes with Canada and with Italy through the Court. Because security interests are not at stake, and because the overall friendly relations are more important than the particular issue, states have been willing to submit to the Court's jurisdiction. Figure 6.1 illustrates one of the Court's recent cases, a dispute between Argentina and Uruguay.

Because of the difficulty of winning enforceable agreements on major conflicts through the World Court, states have used the Court infrequently over the years—a dozen or fewer cases per year (about 100 judgments and advisory opinions since 1946).

Notwithstanding the World Court's prominence, most legal cases concerning international matters—whether brought by governments or by private individuals or companies—remain entirely within the legal systems of one or more states. National courts hear cases brought under national laws and can enforce judgments by collecting damages (in civil suits) or imposing punishments (in criminal ones). Their judgments are enforceable. Individuals and companies, not just states, can bring actions. And a litigant can choose a country whose legal system is most favorable to one's case. For instance, U.S. juries have a reputation for awarding bigger settlements in lawsuits. Each state's court system must decide whether it has *jurisdiction* in a case (the right to hear it), and courts tend to extend their own authority with a broad interpretation. Traditionally, a national court may hear cases concerning any activity on its national territory, any actions of its own citizens anywhere in the world, and actions taken toward its citizens elsewhere in the world.

There are important limits to the use of national courts to resolve international disputes, however. Most important is that the authority of national courts stops at the state's borders, where sovereignty ends. To act beyond national borders, states must persuade other states to cooperate. To bring a person outside a state's territory to trial, the state's government must ask a second government to arrest and *extradite* the suspect, a process mostly governed by bilateral treaties.

The principle of territoriality also governs **immigration law.** When people cross a border into a new country, the decision about whether they can remain there, and under what conditions, is up to the new state. The state of origin cannot compel their return. National laws establish conditions for foreigners to travel and visit on a state's territory, to work there, and sometimes to become citizens (*naturalization*). Many other

FIGURE 6.1   World Court Case of Argentina v. Uruguay

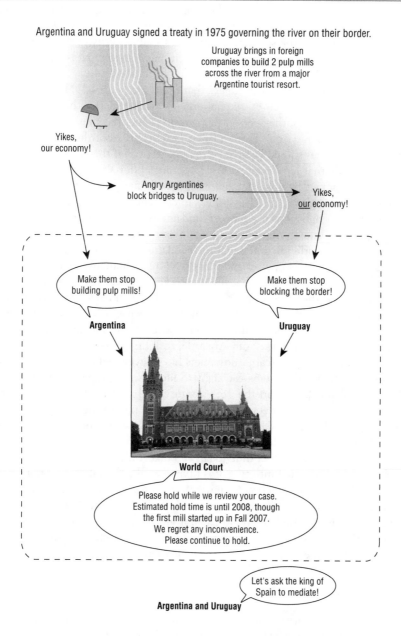

legal issues are raised by people traveling or living outside their own country—passports and visas, babies born in foreign countries, marriages to foreign nationals, bank accounts, businesses, taxes, and so forth. Practices vary from country to country, but the general principle is that national laws prevail on the territory of a state.

HUMAN RIGHTS

A relatively new area of international law concerns **human rights**—the rights of human beings against certain abuses of their *own* governments.[13] The very idea of human rights flies in the face of the sovereignty and territorial integrity of states. Sovereignty gives states the right to do as they please in their own territory: Nobody can tell them how to treat their own citizens.

One approach to human rights argues that rights are *universal*. No matter where a person resides, no matter their ethnic nationality, and no matter their local religious, ethnic, or clan traditions, that person has certain rights that must be respected. The other approach to human rights is often labeled *relativism*. According to this idea, local traditions and histories should be given due respect, even if this means limiting rights that others outside that local context find important. Efforts to promote human rights are routinely criticized by governments with poor human-rights records by Western standards (including China and Russia) as "interference in our internal affairs." This charge puts human-rights law on shaky ground and reflects a more relativist stance.

The concept of human rights arises from at least three sources. The first is religion. Nearly every major world religion has at its foundation the idea that humans were created in an image of a higher power and that therefore all humans are to be afforded the dignity and respect that are due that higher power. Nowhere is this idea more clearly spelled out than in the American Declaration of Independence, written by Thomas Jefferson, that all people are "endowed by their creator with certain unalienable rights." Second, political and legal philosophy for centuries has discussed the idea of natural law and natural rights. From Aristotle, to John Locke, to Immanuel Kant, to Jean-Jacques Rousseau, political philosophers have developed the idea that a natural law exists that grants all humans the right to life, liberty, property, and happiness.[14] Finally, political revolutions in the 18th century, such as the American and French revolutions, translated the theory of natural law and natural rights into practice. In America, the Declaration of Independence, and in France, the Declaration of the Rights of Man and Citizen, created laws that solidified the idea that humans have certain rights that no state or other individuals can take away.

Rights are often divided into two broad types: civil-political and economic-social. Civil-political rights are sometimes referred to as "negative rights" and include what are considered traditional Western rights such as free speech, freedom of religion, equal protection under the law, and freedom from arbitrary imprisonment. Economic-social rights are referred to as "positive rights" and include rights to good living conditions, food, health care, social security, and education.[15]

---

[13] Donnelly, Jack. *Universal Human Rights in Theory and Practice*. 2nd ed. Cornell, 2003. Donnelly, Jack. *International Human Rights*. 3rd ed. Westview, 2006. Falk, Richard A. *Human Rights Horizons*. Routledge, 2000. Thomas, Daniel. *The Helsinki Effect: International Norms, Human Rights, and the Demise of Communism*. Princeton, 2001. Cohen, Cynthia Price, ed. *Human Rights of Indigenous Peoples*. Transnational, 1998. Cronin, Bruce. *Institutions for the Common Good: International Protection Regimes in International Society*. Cambridge, 2003.

[14] Hayden, Patrick, ed. *The Philosophy of Human Rights*. Paragon, 2001.

[15] Forsythe, David. *Human Rights in International Relations*. Cambridge, 2000.

No state has a perfect record on any type of human rights, and states differ as to which areas they respect or violate. When the United States criticizes China for prohibiting free speech, using prison labor, and torturing political dissidents (civil-political rights), China notes that the United States has 40 million poor people, the highest ratio of prison inmates in the world, and a history of racism and violence (economic-social rights).[16]

Overall, despite the poor record of the world's states on some points, progress has been made on others. For example, slavery—once considered normal worldwide—has been largely abandoned in the past 150 years. Historically, a significant global shift in human rights occurred at the end of World War II. Horrified by Nazi Germany's attempt to exterminate the Jewish population and by Japanese abuses of Chinese citizens, many scholars and practitioners began to suggest that there were limits to state sovereignty. States could not claim to be sovereign and above interference if they attempted to massacre their own people. In the aftermath of World War II and the creation of the United Nations, some of the most significant international attempts to codify and enforce human rights began.

In 1948, the UN General Assembly adopted what is considered the core international document concerning human rights: the **Universal Declaration of Human Rights (UDHR).**[17] The UDHR does not have the force of international law, but it sets forth (hoped-for) international norms regarding behavior by governments toward their own citizens and foreigners alike. The declaration roots itself in the principle that violations of human rights upset international order (causing outrage, sparking rebellion, etc.) and in the fact that the UN Charter commits states to respect fundamental freedoms. The declaration proclaims that "all human beings are born free and equal" without regard to race, sex, language, religion, political affiliation, or the status of the territory in which they were born. It goes on to promote norms in a wide variety of areas, including banning torture, guaranteeing religious and political freedom, and ensuring the right of economic well-being.

Since the adoption of the UDHR, the UN has opened seven treaties for state signature to further define protections of human rights. Unlike the UDHR, these treaties are legally binding contracts signed by states. Of course, international law is only as good as the enforcement mechanisms behind it. Yet these seven treaties are important in outlining the basic protections for individuals expected by the international community.

Today, NGOs play a key role in efforts to win basic political rights in authoritarian countries—including a halt to the torture, execution, and imprisonment of those expressing political or religious beliefs.[18] The leading organization pressing this struggle is **Amnesty International,** an NGO that operates globally to monitor and try to rectify

---

[16] People's Republic of China, State Council. America's "Abominable" Human Rights Conditions. *The Washington Post,* Feb. 16, 1997: C3.

[17] Morsink, Johannes. *The Universal Declaration of Human Rights: Origins, Drafting, and Intent.* Pennsylvania, 1999.

[18] Keck, Margaret, and Kathryn Sikkink. *Activists Beyond Borders: Advocacy Networks in International Politics.* Cornell, 1998. Risse, Thomas, Stephen C. Ropp, and Kathryn Sikkink, eds. *The Power of Human Rights: International Norms and Domestic Change.* Cambridge, 1999.

glaring abuses of human rights.[19] Amnesty International has a reputation for impartiality and has criticized abuses in many countries, including the United States. Other groups, such as Human Rights Watch, work in a similar way but often with a more regional or national focus. NGOs often provide information and advocacy for the UN and other organizations that attempt to promote human rights. They essentially serve as a bridge between the global or regional organizations and efforts to promote human rights "on the ground."[20]

Enforcing norms of human rights is difficult, because it involves interfering in a state's internal affairs. Cutting off trade or contact with a government that violates human rights tends to hurt the citizens whose rights are being violated by further isolating them. The most effective method yet discovered is a combination of *publicity* and *pressure*. Rarer are humanitarian interventions using military force to overcome armed resistance by local authorities or warlords and bring help to civilian victims of wars and disasters.[21]

The U.S. State Department has actively pursued human rights since the late 1970s. An annual U.S. government report assesses human rights in states around the world. In states where abuses are severe or becoming worse, U.S. foreign aid has been withheld from these states or their armed forces. (But in other cases, CIA funding supported the abusers.)[22]

WAR CRIMES

Large-scale abuses of human rights often occur during war. Serious violations of this kind are considered **war crimes.**[23] In wartime, international law is especially difficult to enforce, but extensive norms of legal conduct in war as well as international treaties are widely followed. After a war, losers can be punished for violations of the laws of war, as Germans were in the Nuremberg trials after World War II.

In the 1990s, for the first time since World War II, the UN Security Council authorized an international war crimes tribunal, directed against war crimes in the former Yugoslavia. Similar tribunals were later established for genocide in Rwanda and Sierra Leone.[24] All continue in operation. In 1998 most of the world's states signed a treaty to create a permanent **International Criminal Court (ICC).**[25] It hears cases of

---

[19] Hopgood, Stephen. *Keepers of the Flame: Understanding Amnesty International.* Cornell, 2006.

[20] Clark, Ann Marie. *Diplomacy of Conscience: Amnesty International and Changing Human Rights Norms.* Princeton, 2000.

[21] Weiss, Thomas G. *Military-Civilian Interactions: Humanitarian Crises and the Responsibility to Protect.* 2nd ed. Rowman & Littlefield, 2005. Welsh, Jennifer M., ed. *Humanitarian Intervention and International Relations.* Oxford, 2004. Wheeler, Nicholas J. *Saving Strangers: Humanitarian Intervention in International Society.* Oxford, 2001.

[22] Liang-Fenton, Debra, ed. *Implementing U.S. Human Rights Policy: Agendas, Policies, and Practices.* U.S. Institute of Peace Press, 2004.

[23] Falk, Richard, Irene Gendzier, and Robert Jay Lifton, eds. *Crimes of War: Iraq.* Nation, 2006. Howard, Michael, George J. Andreopoulos, and Mark R. Shulman, eds. *The Laws of War: Constraints on Warfare in the Western World.* Yale, 1994.

[24] Bass, Gary Jonathan. *Stay the Hand of Vengeance: The Politics of War Crimes Tribunals.* Princeton, 2000. Neier, Aryeh. *War Crimes: Brutality, Genocide, Terror, and the Struggle for Justice.* Times, 1998.

[25] Schabas, William A. *An Introduction to the International Criminal Court.* 2nd ed. Cambridge, 2004.

genocide, war crimes, and crimes against humanity from anywhere in the world. The ICC opened for business in 2003 in The Hague, with 18 judges sworn in from around the world (but not the United States, a nonparticipant). The ICC issued its first arrest warrants, arising from the long civil war in Uganda, in 2005, and began its first trial, of a Congolese militia leader, in 2008. What makes the ICC different (and controversial) is the idea of *universal jurisdiction*—that the court has the ability to prosecute individuals of any nation. This makes the ICC different from the World Court, which has only states as complainants and defendants. Under the ICC, individuals can be prosecuted for their roles in violations of human rights. Three mechanisms can trigger an ICC trial. First, a state can turn over an individual for trial if the state agrees to do so. Second, against the wishes of a state, a special prosecutor at the ICC can begin a trial if the crimes occurred in the territory of a signatory to the ICC. Third, the UN Security Council can begin proceedings even against individuals from nonsignatory states.

The most important principle in the laws of war is the effort to limit warfare to the combatants and to protect civilians when possible. It is illegal to target civilians in a war unless there is a compelling military utility to do so. Even then, the amount of force used must be *proportional* to the military gain, and only the *necessary* amount of force can be used. To help separate combatants from civilians, soldiers must wear uniforms and insignia, such as a shoulder patch with a national flag. This provision is frequently violated in guerrilla warfare, making that form of warfare particularly brutal and destructive of civilian life. If one cannot tell the difference between a bystander and a combatant, one is likely to kill both when in doubt. By contrast, in a large-scale conventional war it is much easier to distinguish civilians from soldiers, although the effort is never completely successful.

Soldiers have the right under the laws of war to surrender, which is to abandon their status as combatants and become **prisoners of war (POWs).** They give up their weapons and their right to fight, and earn instead the right (like civilians) not to be targeted. POWs may not be killed, mistreated, or forced to disclose information beyond their name, rank, and serial number. The laws of war reserve a special role for the **International Committee of the Red Cross (ICRC).** The ICRC provides practical support—such as medical care, food, and letters from home—to civilians caught in wars and to POWs. Exchanges of POWs are usually negotiated through the ICRC. Armed forces must respect the neutrality of the Red Cross, and usually do so (again, guerrilla war is problematical). In the current war on terrorism, the United States does not consider the "enemy combatants" it detains to be POWs, but has granted the ICRC access to most (though not all) of them. More controversial is the U.S. policy called "extraordinary rendition," which lets terrorist suspects captured overseas be transferred to other countries, including some that use torture, for questioning.

The laws of warfare impose moral responsibility on individuals in wartime, as well as on states. The Nuremberg tribunal established that participants can be held accountable for war crimes they commit. German officers defended their actions as "just following orders," but this was rejected; the officers were punished, and some executed, for their war crimes.

The laws of warfare have been undermined by the changing nature of war. Conventional wars by defined armed forces on defined battlegrounds are giving way to irregular and "low-intensity" wars fought by guerrillas and death squads in cities or jungles. The lines between civilians and soldiers blur in these situations, and war crimes become more commonplace.[26] Although violence against civilians is outlawed in war, norms regarding such actions remain contested in the context of asymmetrical warfare including today's radical Islamist movements. In a 2006 poll in six Muslim countries (see Figure 6.2), the number justifying violence against civilians ranged from 13 percent in Morocco (where the context implicitly was al Qaeda actions) to an actual majority in Jordan (where the context was Palestinian actions against Israel).

THE EVOLUTION OF WORLD ORDER

The most powerful states, especially hegemons, have great influence on the rules and values that have become embedded over time in a body of international law.[27] For example, the principle of free passage on the open seas is now formally established in international law. But at one time warships from one state did not hesitate to seize the ships of other states and make off with their cargoes. This practice was profitable to the state that pulled off such raids, but of course their own ships could be raided in return. Such behavior made long-distance trade itself more dangerous, less predictable, and less profitable. The trading states could benefit more by getting rid of the practice. So, over time, a norm developed around the concept of freedom of navigation on the high seas. It became one of the first areas of international law developed by the Dutch legal scholar Hugo Grotius in the mid-1600s—a time when the Dutch dominated world trade and could benefit most from free navigation.

FIGURE 6.2   Public Opinion on Violence against Civilians in Six Muslim Countries, 2005

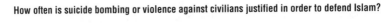

How often is suicide bombing or violence against civilians justified in order to defend Islam?

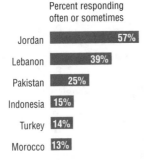

Percent responding
often or sometimes

Jordan   57%
Lebanon   39%
Pakistan   25%
Indonesia   15%
Turkey   14%
Morocco   13%

Source: Pew Global Attitudes Survey.

---

[26] Wippman, David, and Matthew Evangelista, eds. *New Wars, New Laws? Applying the Laws of War in 21st Century Conflicts.* Transnational, 2005.
[27] Ikenberry, G. John. *After Victory: Institutions, Strategic Restraint, and the Rebuilding of Order after Major Wars.* Princeton, 2001.

Dutch power, then, provided the backbone for the international legal concept of freedom of the seas. Later, when Britain was dominant, it enforced the principle of free seas through the cannons of its warships. As the world's main trading state, Britain benefited from a worldwide norm of free shipping and trade. And with the world's most powerful navy, it was in a position to define and enforce the rules for the world's oceans.

Likewise, 20th-century world order depended heavily on the power of the United States (and, for a few decades, on the division of power between the United States and the Soviet Union). The United States at times came close to adopting the explicit role of "world police force." But in truth the world is too large for any single state—even a hegemon—to police effectively. Rather, the world's states usually go along with the rules established by the most powerful state without constant policing. Meanwhile, they try to influence the rules by working through international institutions (to which the hegemon cedes some of its power). In this way, although states do not yield their sovereignty, they vest some power and authority in international institutions and laws and generally work within that framework.

The various theories discussed in this chapter, then, have in common their emphasis on the identity principle and the flexible, evolving nature of national interests. States do not only promote international norms that advance state interests, but also redefine their interests in light of international norms.

CHAPTER 7

CRITICAL THEORIES

MARXISM

Marxist approaches to IR, historically most important among social theories, hold that both IR and domestic politics arise from unequal relationships between **economic classes.** This emphasis on classes—implying that the domestic and economic attributes of societies shape the society's external relations with other states—contrasts with the realist approach to IR with its separation of domestic and international politics.

Marxism is a branch of socialism, a theory that holds that the more powerful classes oppress and exploit the less powerful by denying them their fair share of the surplus they create. The oppressed classes try to gain power in order to seize more of the wealth for themselves. This process, called *class struggle*, is one way of looking at the political relationships between richer and poorer people, and ultimately between richer and poorer world regions.

Socialism is more concerned with the distribution of wealth than with the absolute creation of wealth. It sees the global North-South divide, like any division between the rich and poor, as a zero-sum game in which the creation of wealth in the North most often comes at the expense of the South. It also gives politics (the state) more of a role in redistributing wealth and managing the economy than does capitalism. For socialists, international exchange is shaped by capitalists' exploitation of cheap labor and cheap resources—using states to help create the political conditions for this exploitation. (Some socialists focus on workers in poor countries, some on workers in richer industrialized countries, and some on both.) Socialism favors the *redistribution of wealth* toward the workers who produce that wealth. Because such redistribution does not happen naturally under capitalism, socialism generally endorses the use of the state for this purpose. It favors *governmental planning* to manage a national economy rather than leaving such management to market forces. Often, socialists advocate *state ownership* of capital, rather than private ownership, so that the accumulation of wealth is controlled by the state, which can distribute it equitably. But after decades of experimentation, it is clear that whatever its benefits in equity, state ownership is inefficient. China now calls its economic system "market socialism"—a combination of continuing state ownership of many large industries, capitalism at the local level, and openness to international investment and trade.

Marxism includes both communism and other approaches. In the mid-19th century, *Karl Marx* emphasized labor as the source of economic surplus. At that time, the Industrial Revolution was accompanied by particular hardship among industrial workers (including children) in Europe. Marxists still believe that the surplus created by labor should be recaptured by workers through political struggle. Today, Marxism is most influential in countries of the global South, where capital is scarce and labor conditions are wretched.

Marx's theories of class struggle were oriented toward *domestic* society in the industrializing countries of his time, not toward poor countries or international relations. Traditional Marxists looked to the advanced industrialized countries for revolution and socialism, which would grow out of capitalism. In their view, the poor countries would have to develop through their own stages of accumulation from feudalism to capitalism before taking the revolutionary step to socialism. What actually happened was the opposite. Proletarian workers in industrialized countries enjoyed rising standards of living and did not make revolutions. Meanwhile, in the backward poor countries, oppressed workers and peasants staged a series of revolutions, successful and failed. Indeed, contrary to Marx's expectations, *peasants* have played a key role in revolutions.[1] Marxists traditionally consider peasants backward, ignorant, individualistic, and politically passive as compared to the better-educated and class-conscious proletariat. But in practice, the successful revolutions have been peasant rebellions (often led by Marxists talking about the proletariat). The largest was the Chinese revolution in the 1930s and 1940s.

Why did revolutions occur in poor rather than advanced countries? The answer largely shapes how one sees North-South relations today.[2] Marxists have mostly (but not exclusively) followed a line of argument developed by V. I. Lenin, founder of the Soviet Union, before the Russian Revolution of 1917.[3] Russia was then a relatively backward state, as the global South is today, and most Marxists considered a revolution there unlikely (looking instead to Germany).

Lenin's theory of imperialism argued that European capitalists invested in colonies where they could earn big profits, and then used part of these to *buy off* the working class at home. But Lenin saw that after the scramble for colonies in the 1890s, few areas of the world remained to be colonized. Imperialist expansion could occur only at the expense of other imperialist states, leading to interimperialist competition and wars such as World War I. Seizing on Russia's weakness during that war, Lenin led the first successful communist revolution there in 1917. Lenin's general idea still shapes a major approach to North-South relations—the idea that industrialized states exploit poor countries (through both formal and informal colonization) and buy off their own working classes with the profits. Through this *globalization of class relations*, world accumulation concentrates surplus toward the rich parts of the world and away from the poor ones. Revolutions, then, would be expected in poor regions.

Many revolutionaries in the global South sought to break loose from exploitation by the European colonizers, and later the dominance of the United States. Such an approach has not worked well. A policy of self-reliance does not foster growth (see p. 149). Not all Marxist approaches favor a policy of self-reliance after revolution,

---

[1] Moore, Barrington. *Social Origins of Dictatorship and Democracy: Lord and Peasant in the Making of the Modern World.* Beacon, 1993 [1966]. Scott, James C. *Weapons of the Weak: Everyday Forms of Peasant Resistance.* Yale, 1986.

[2] Brewer, Anthony. *Marxist Theories of Imperialism: A Critical Survey.* 2nd ed. Routledge, 1990.

[3] Lenin, V. I. *Imperialism, the Highest Stage of Capitalism.* 1916.

however. *Leon Trotsky*, a Russian revolutionary, believed that after the 1917 revolution, Russia would never be able to build socialism alone and should make its top priority the spreading of revolution to other countries to build a worldwide alliance. Trotsky's archrival Stalin wanted to build "socialism in one country," and he prevailed (and had Trotsky killed). Most revolutions since then, including China's, have had a strongly nationalist flavor.

Marxist theories in IR entered a low-visibility phase after the collapse of the Soviet Union and China's turn toward capitalism—events that seemed to discredit Marxist theories. However, in recent years Marxists and former Marxists have taken power in a number of Latin American countries. These events, along with China's continuing formal adherence to Marxism, suggest that Marxist theories of IR have ongoing importance in the post–Cold War era.

IMPERIALISM

Imperialism, especially in the 16th to mid-20th centuries, structured world order starkly around the dominance principle, with masters and slaves, conquerors and conquered peoples with their land, labor, and treasures. At the same time, imperialism depends on the identity principle to unite the global North around a common racial identity that defines nonwhite people as an out-group. (Although identity issues today are more complex, racism still affects North-South relations.)

European imperialism got its start in the 15th century with the development of oceangoing sailing ships in which a small crew could transport a sizable cargo over a long distance. Portugal pioneered the first voyages of exploration beyond Europe. Spain, France, and Britain soon followed. With superior military technology, Europeans gained control of coastal cities and of resupply outposts along major trade routes. Gradually this control extended farther inland, first in Latin America, then in North America, and later throughout Asia and Africa.

In the 16th century, Spain and Portugal had extensive empires in Central America and Brazil, respectively. Britain and France had colonies in North America and the Caribbean. The imperialists bought slaves in Africa and shipped them to Mexico and Brazil, where they worked in tropical agriculture and in mining silver and gold. The wealth produced was exported to Europe, where monarchs used it to buy armies and build states.

These empires decimated indigenous populations and cultures, causing immense suffering. Over time, the economies of colonies developed with the creation of basic transportation and communication infrastructure, factories, and so forth. But these economies were often molded to the needs of the colonizers, not the local populations.

Decolonization began with the British colonists in the United States, who declared independence in 1776. Most of Latin America gained independence a few decades later. The new states in North America and Latin America were, of course, still run by the descendants of Europeans, to the disadvantage of Native Americans and African slaves.

New colonies were still being acquired by Europe through the end of the 19th century, culminating in a scramble for colonies in Africa in the 1890s (resulting in arbitrary territorial divisions as competing European armies rushed inland from all sides). India became

FIGURE 7.1 Conquest of the World

Former colonial territories of European states.

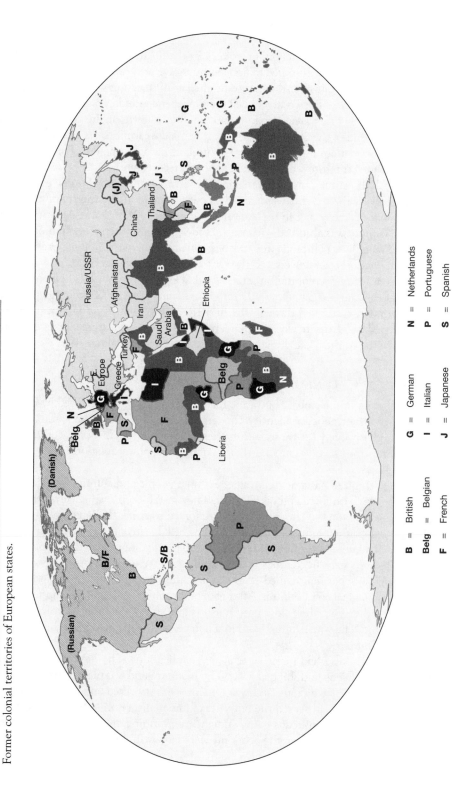

B = British	**G** = German	**N** = Netherlands
Belg = Belgian	**I** = Italian	**P** = Portuguese
F = French	**J** = Japanese	**S** = Spanish

Britain's largest and most important colony in the 19th century. Latecomers such as Germany and Italy were frustrated to find few attractive territories remaining in the world when they tried to build overseas empires in the late 19th century. Ultimately, only a few non-European areas of the world retained their independence: Japan, most of China, Iran, Turkey, and a few other areas. Japan began building its own empire, as did the United States, at the end of the 19th century. China became weaker and its coastal regions fell under the domination, if not the formal control, of European powers. Europe colonized most of the world's territory at one time or another (see Figure 7.1).

In the 20th century, the world regions formerly dominated by Europe gained independence, with their own sovereign states participating in the international system. Independence came earlier in the Americas (around 1800). In Latin America, most of the 19th century was absorbed with wars, border changes, the rise and fall of dictatorships and republics, a chronic foreign debt problem, revolutions, and recurrent military incursions by European powers and the United States to recover debts.

In the wave of decolonization after World War II, it was not local colonists (as in the Americas) but indigenous populations in Asia and Africa who won independence. Decolonization continued through the mid-1970s until almost no European colonies remained. Most of the newly independent states have faced tremendous challenges and difficulties in the postcolonial era because of their colonial histories.

EFFECTS OF COLONIALISM

For most states in the global South, the history of having been colonized by Europeans is central to their national identity, foreign policy, and place in the world. For these states—and especially for those within them who favor socialist perspectives—international relations revolves around their asymmetrical power relationships with industrialized states.

Being colonized has a devastating effect on a people and culture. Foreigners overrun a territory with force and take it over. They install their own government, staffed by their own nationals. The inhabitants are forced to speak the language of the colonizers, to adopt their cultural practices, and to be educated at schools run under their guidance. The inhabitants are told that they are racially inferior to the foreigners.

White Europeans in colonies in Africa and Asia were greatly outnumbered by native inhabitants but maintained power by a combination of force and (more important) psychological conditioning. After generations under colonialism, most native inhabitants either saw white domination as normal or believed that nothing could be done about it. The whites often lived in a bubble world separated from the lives of the local inhabitants.

Colonialism also had negative *economic* implications. The most easily accessible minerals were dug up and shipped away. The best farmland was planted in export crops rather than subsistence crops, and was sometimes overworked and eroded. The infrastructure that was built served the purposes of imperialism rather than the local population—for instance, railroads going straight from mining areas to ports. The education and skills needed to run the economy were largely limited to whites.

FIGURE 7.2   Areas of White Minority Rule in Africa, 1952–1994

Formal colonialism was swept away over 40 years. However, postcolonial dependency lingers on in many former colonies.

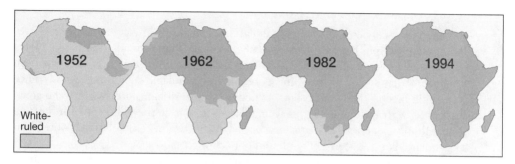

Source: Adapted from Andrew Boyd. *An Atlas of World Affairs.* 9th ed. NY: Routledge, 1992, p. 91.

The economic effects were not all negative, however. Colonialism often fostered local economic accumulation (although controlled by whites). Cities grew. Mines were dug and farms established. It was in the colonial administration's interest to foster local cycles of capital accumulation. Colonizers created much of the infrastructure that exists today in many poor countries. In some cases (though not all), colonization combined disparate communities into a cohesive political unit with a common religion, language, and culture, thus creating more opportunities for economic accumulation. In some cases, the local political cultures replaced by colonialism were themselves oppressive to the majority of the people.

Wherever there were colonizers, there were anticolonial movements. Independence movements throughout Africa and Asia gained momentum during and after World War II, when the European powers were weakened. Through the 1960s, a wave of successful independence movements swept from one country to the next, as people stopped accepting imperialism as normal or inevitable (see Figure 7.2).

Some colonies—for example, Algeria and Vietnam—won independence through warfare to oust their European masters; others won it peacefully by negotiating a transfer of power with weary Europeans. Some colonial liberation movements fought guerrilla wars based on communist ideology. The Soviet Union supported such movements, and the United States opposed them. But in most cases the appeal of liberation movements was the general theme of anticolonialism rather than any ideology.

Across the various methods and ideologies of liberation movements in the global South, one common feature was reliance on nationalism for strong popular support. Nationalism was only one idea that these movements took from Europe and used to undermine European control; others included democracy, freedom, progress, and Marxism. Leaders of liberation movements often had gone to European universities. Under European control many states also developed infrastructures, educational and religious institutions, health care, and military forces on the European model. Europe's conquest of the global South thus contributed tools to undo their conquest.[4]

POSTCOLONIAL DEPENDENCY

If imperialism concentrated the accumulation of wealth in the core and drained economic surplus from the periphery, one might expect that accumulation in the global South would take off once colonialism was overthrown. Generally this has not been the case. A few states, such as Singapore, have accumulated capital successfully since becoming independent. But others, including many African states, seem to be going backward, with little new capital accumulating to replace the old colonial infrastructure. Most former colonies are making only slow progress in accumulation. Political independence has not been a cure-all for poor countries.

One reason for these problems is that under colonialism, the training and experience needed to manage the economy were often limited to white Europeans, leaving a huge gap in technical and administrative skills after independence.

Another problem faced by newly independent states was that as colonies, their economies had been narrowly developed to serve the needs of the European home country. Many of these economies rested on the export of one or two products. It is not easy to restructure an economy away from the export of a few commodities. Nor do state leaders generally want to do so, because the leaders benefit from the imports that can be bought with hard currency (including weapons). In any case, coffee plantations and copper mines take time and capital to create, and they represent capital accumulation—they cannot just be abandoned. In addition, local inhabitants' skills and training are likely to be concentrated in the existing industries. Furthermore, infrastructure such as railroads most likely was set up to serve the export economy. For instance, in Angola and Namibia the major railroads lead from mining or plantation districts to ports (see Figure 7.3).

The newly independent states inherited borders that were drawn in European capitals by foreign officers looking at maps. As a result, especially in Africa, the internal rivalries of ethnic groups and regions made it very difficult for the new states to implement coherent economic plans. In a number of cases, ethnic conflicts within former colonies led to civil wars, which halted or reversed capital accumulation. Finally, governments of many postcolonial states did not function very effectively, creating another obstacle to accumulation. In some cases, corruption became much worse after independence (see p. 188). In other cases, governments tried to impose central control and planning on their national economy, based on nationalism, mercantilism, or socialism.

In sum, liberation from colonial control did not change underlying economic realities. The main trading partners of newly independent countries were usually their former colonial masters. The main products were usually those developed under colonialism. The administrative units and territorial borders were those created by Europeans. The state continued to occupy the same peripheral position in the world-system after

---

[4] Barraclough, Geoffrey. *An Introduction to Contemporary History.* Chapter 6. Penguin, 1964.

FIGURE 7.3   Borders, Railroads, and Resources in Angola and Namibia

Despite the independence of Angola and Namibia, colonial times shaped the borders and infra-structure in the region.

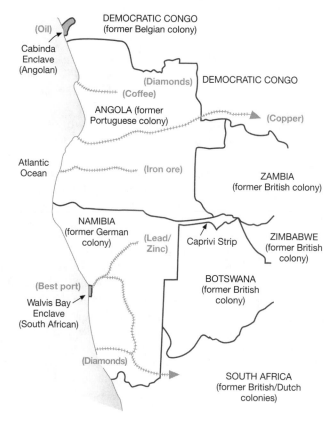

independence as it had before. And in some cases it continued to rely on its former colo-nizer for security.

For these reasons, the period after independence is sometimes called **neocolonialism—**the continuation of colonial exploitation without formal political control. This concept also covers the relationship of the global South with the United States, which (with a few exceptions) was not a formal colonizer. And it includes the North-South interna-tional relations of Latin American states, independent for almost two centuries.

Marxist IR scholars have developed **dependency theory** to explain the lack of ac-cumulation in the global South.[5] These scholars define dependency as a situation in

---

[5] Cardoso, Fernando Henrique, and Enzo Faletto. *Dependency and Development in Latin America*. Translated by Marjory Mattingly Urquidi. California, 1979. Packenham, Robert A. *The Dependency Movement: Scholarship and Politics in Dependency Studies*. Harvard, 1992. Evans, Peter. *Dependent Development: The Alliance of Multinational, State, and Local Capital in Brazil*. Princeton, 1979.

which accumulation of capital cannot sustain itself internally. A dependent country must borrow capital to produce goods; its debt payments then reduce the accumulation of surplus. (Dependency is a form of international interdependence—rich regions need to loan out their money just as poor ones need to borrow it—but it is an interdependence with an extreme power imbalance.)

Dependency theorists focus not on the overall structure of the world-system (center and periphery) but on how a peripheral state's own internal class relationships play out. The development (or lack of development) of a state depends on its local conditions and history, though it is affected by the same global conditions as other countries located in the periphery.

One historically important configuration of dependency is the **enclave economy,** in which foreign capital is invested in a poor country to extract a particular raw material in a particular place—usually a mine, oil well, or plantation. Here the cycle of capital accumulation is primed by foreign capital, is fueled by local resources, and completes itself with the sale of products on foreign markets. Such an arrangement leaves the country's economy largely untouched except to give employment to a few local workers in the enclave and to provide taxes to the state (or line the pockets of some state officials). Over time, it leaves the state's natural resources depleted.

A different historical pattern is that of nationally controlled production, in which a local capitalist class controls a cycle of accumulation based on producing export products. The cycle still depends on foreign markets, but the profits accrue to the local capitalists, building up a powerful class of rich owners within the country. This class—the local bourgeoisie—tends to behave in a manner consistent with the interests of rich industrialized countries (on whose markets the class depends). They are not unpatriotic, but their interests tend to converge with those of foreign capitalists. For instance, they want to keep local wages as low as possible, to produce cheap goods for consumers in the rich countries. The local capitalists, in alliance with political authorities, enforce a system of domination that ultimately serves the foreign capitalists. This is another form of dependency.

After World War II, a third form of dependency became more common—penetration of national economies by MNCs. Here the capital is provided externally (as with enclaves), but production is for local markets. For instance, a GM factory in Brazil produces cars mostly for sale within Brazil. To create local markets for such manufactured goods, income must be concentrated enough to create a middle class that can afford such goods. This sharpens disparities of income within the country (most people remain poor). The cycle of accumulation depends on local labor and local markets, but because MNCs provide the foreign capital, they take out much of the surplus as profit.

According to dependency theory, the particular constellation of forces within a country determines which coalitions form among the state, the military, big landowners, local capitalists, foreign capitalists (MNCs), foreign governments, and middle classes such as professionals and skilled industrial workers. On the other side, peasants, workers, and sometimes students and the church form alliances to work for more equal distribution of income, human and political rights, and local control of the economy. These class alliances and the resulting social relationships are not determined by any general rule but by concrete conditions and historical developments in each country.

Like other Marxist theories, dependency theory pays special attention to class struggle as a source of social change. Some people think that under conditions of dependency, economic development is almost impossible. Others think that development is possible under dependency, despite certain difficulties.

REVOLUTIONARY MOVEMENTS

Poverty and lack of access to basic human needs are prime causes of revolutions, especially when poor people see others living much better.[6] Most revolutionary movements espouse egalitarian ideals—a more equal distribution of wealth and power.

During the Cold War years, the classic third world revolutionary movement was a communist insurgency based in the countryside. Usually "U.S. imperialism" or another such foreign presence was viewed as a friend of the state and an enemy of the revolution. Sometimes the U.S. government gave direct military aid to governments facing such revolutionary movements; in a number of countries, U.S. military advisors and even combat troops were sent to help put down the revolutions and keep communists from taking power. For its part, the Soviet Union often armed and helped train the revolutionaries. Thus, the domestic politics of third world countries became intertwined with great-power politics in the context of the North-South gap.

By the early 1990s, these communist third world revolutions seemed to have played themselves out—winning in some places, losing in others, and coming to a stalemate in a few countries. The end of the Cold War removed superpower support from both sides, and the collapse of the Soviet Union and the adoption of capitalist-oriented economic reforms in China undercut the ideological appeal of communist revolutions. Several Marxist revolutionary movements linger, however, including in Colombia, Peru, India, and Nepal.

In foreign policy, revolutionary governments often start out planning radically different relationships with neighbors and great powers. The pattern of international alliances often shifts after revolutions, as when a Cold War client of one superpower shifted to the other after a change of government. But the new government usually discovers that, once it holds power, it has the same interest as other states in promoting national sovereignty and territorial integrity. The rules of the international system now work for the revolutionaries instead of against them, once they control a state. Their state also has the same geographical location as before, the same historical conflicts with its neighbors, and the same ethnic ties. So it is not unusual over time to find similar foreign policies emanating from a revolutionary government as from its predecessor.

Thus, although revolutions create short-term shifts in foreign policy, over the longer term the rules of international relations have tended to triumph over revolutionary challenges. Likewise, though revolutions promise great economic change, the overall state of economic conditions and relations—especially between North and South—has resisted change.

---

[6] Skocpol, Theda. *Social Revolutions in the Modern World*. Cambridge, 1994. Gurr, Ted Robert. *Why Men Rebel*. Princeton, 1970. McAdam, Doug, Sidney Tarrow, and Charles Tilly. *Dynamics of Contention*. Cambridge, 2001.

THE WORLD-SYSTEM

The global system of regional class divisions has been seen by some IR scholars as a **world-system** or a *capitalist world economy*.[7] This view is Marxist in orientation (focusing on economic classes) and relies on a global level of analysis. In the world-system, class divisions are regionalized. The global South mostly extracts raw materials (including agriculture)—work that uses much labor and little capital, and pays low wages. Industrialized regions mostly manufacture goods—work that uses more capital, requires more skilled labor, and pays workers higher wages. The manufacturing regions are called the **core** (or *center*) of the world-system; the extraction regions are called the **periphery.**

The most important class struggle today, in this view, is that between the core and the periphery of the world-system. The core uses its power (derived from its wealth) to concentrate surplus from the periphery, as it has done for about 500 years. Conflicts among great powers, including the two world wars and the Cold War, basically result from competition among core states over the right to exploit the periphery.

The core and periphery are not sharply delineated. Within the periphery, there are also centers and peripheries (for instance, the city of Rio de Janeiro compared to the Amazon rain forest) as there are within the core (such as New York City compared to the Mississippi Delta). The whole global structure is one of overlapping hierarchies. The concentration of capital and the scale of wages each form a continuum rather than a sharp division into two categories.[8]

In world-system theory, the **semiperiphery** is an area in which some manufacturing occurs and some capital concentrates, but not to the extent of the most advanced areas in the core. Eastern Europe and Russia are commonly considered semiperipheral, as are some of the newly industrializing countries (see pp. 182–183) such as Taiwan and Singapore. The semiperiphery acts as a kind of political buffer between the core and periphery because poor states can aspire to join the semiperiphery instead of aspiring to rebel against domination by the core.

Over time, membership in the core, the semiperiphery, and the periphery changes somewhat, but the overall global system of class relations remains. Areas that once were beyond the reach of Europeans, such as the interior of Latin America, become incorporated as periphery. Areas of the periphery can become semiperiphery and even join the core, as North America did. And core states can slip into the semiperiphery if they fall behind in accumulation, as Spain did in the late 16th to early 17th centuries. Because world-system theory provides only general concepts but not firm definitions of what constitutes the core, semiperiphery, and periphery, it is hard to say exactly which states belong to each category.[9]

---

[7] Wallerstein, Immanuel. *The Modern World-System*. 3 vols. Academic, 1974, 1980, 1989. Amin, Samir, Giovanni Arrighi, André Gunder Frank, and Immanuel Wallerstein. *Dynamics of Global Crisis*. Monthly Review Press, 1982. Frank, André Gunder. *World Accumulation, 1492–1789*. Monthly Review Press, 1978.
[8] Boswell, Terry, and Christopher Chase-Dunn. *The Spiral of Capitalism and Socialism: Toward Global Democracy*. Rienner, 2000.
[9] Hopkins, Terence K., and Immanuel Wallerstein. *The Age of Transition: Trajectory of the World-System, 1945–2025*. Zed, 1996.

The actual patterns of world trade support world-system theory to some extent. Table 7.1 shows the net exports (exports minus imports) of each world region for several types of goods. As the circled numbers indicate, different regions specialize in exporting different kinds of goods. In 1997, the industrialized West fit the profile of the core, exporting more than it imported in machinery, chemicals, and similar heavy manufactured goods. All the other regions imported more than they exported in such goods. But by 2002, as the table shows, manufacturing had shifted to Asia—here including China, Taiwan, Hong Kong, and South Korea (but not Japan)—which also became a net exporter of heavy manufactured goods. Asia also still has a niche in exporting light manufacturing including textile production. Such a pattern fits the semiperiphery category. The industrialized West imports these light manufactures. The shift of export-oriented manufacturing from the industrialized countries to Asia reflects globalization.

The industrialized West's net imports of energy are an enormously important type of trade and another indication of globalization. Asia now also imports energy. The Middle East specializes in exporting oil, and Russia, Latin America, and Africa all export energy on balance as well. This is an extraction role typical of the periphery. Latin America has net exports in food, agricultural products, and minerals—also typical of the periphery. These regions' patterns of specialization must be kept in perspective, however. All regions both import and export all these types of goods, and the net exports listed in the table amount to only a small part of the world's total trade.

Semiperiphery regions, which export manufactured products, are just those—China and South Asia—that have been growing very rapidly in recent years. The three regions that engage with the globalizing world economy primarily as raw-material exporters (Africa, the Middle East, and Latin America) are growing more slowly. Having exportable

TABLE 7.1 **Commodity Structure of World Trade by Region**

Net Exports (Exports Minus Imports) for 2002, in Billions of 2007 Dollars

| Region[a] | Manufactured Goods | | Raw Materials | |
	Machinery/Chemicals[b]	Textiles	Agriculture and Minerals	Energy
North America/Western Europe/Japan	133	−135	−4	−260
Russia and Eastern Europe	−21	0	3	38
Middle East	−80	3	−4	149
Latin America	−22	6	12	36
Asia	115	131	−6	−28
Africa	−49	1	1	580

[a]Regions do not exactly match those used elsewhere in this book. World total imports do not equal exports owing to discrepancies in data from national governments. China, Taiwan, Hong Kong, and South Korea are here included in Asia.

[b]Machinery, metal manufactures, and chemicals.

Source: Calculated from data in United Nations. *World Economic and Social Survey 2004*. United Nations, 2004, pp. 156–59.

natural resources would seem a big plus for an economy, but in fact the problems of basing economic growth on resource exports have been called the *resource curse*.[10]

Overall, North-South relations show how difficult it has become to separate political economy from international security. The original political relations contained in European imperialism led to economic conditions in the South—such as high population growth, urbanization, and concentrations of wealth—that in turn led to political movements for independence, and later to revolutions. Marxists emphasize that the economic realities of accumulation, or the lack of accumulation, lie beneath all the political struggles related to global North-South relations.

POSTMODERNISM

Like Marxism, **postmodernism** is a broad approach to scholarship that has left its mark on various academic disciplines. Because of their roots in literary criticism, postmodernists pay special attention to *texts* and to *discourses*—how people talk and write about their subject (IR).[11] Postmodern critiques of realism thus center on analyzing realists' words and arguments.[12] A central idea of postmodernism is that there is no single, objective reality but a multiplicity of experiences and perspectives that defy easy categorization. For this reason, postmodernism itself is difficult to present in a simple or categorical way.

From a postmodern perspective, realism cannot justify its claim that states are the central actors in IR and that states operate as unitary actors with coherent sets of objective interests (which they pursue through international power politics). Postmodern critics of realism see nothing objective about state interests, and certainly nothing universal (in that one set of values or interests applies to all states).

More fundamentally, postmodernism calls into question the whole notion of states as actors. States have no tangible reality; they are "fictions" that we (as scholars and citizens) construct to make sense of the actions of large numbers of individuals. For postmodernists, the stories told about the actions and policies of states are just that—stories. From this perspective, an arbitrary distinction leads bookstores to put spy novels on the fiction shelf whereas biographies and histories go on the nonfiction shelf. None of these is an objective reality, and all are filtered through an interpretive process that distorts the actual experiences of those involved.[13] Contrary to realism's claim that states are unitary actors, postmodernists see multiple realities and experiences lurking below the surface of the fictional entities that realists construct (states). The Soviet Union, for example, was treated by realists as a single actor with a single

---

[10] Auty, Richard M. *Sustaining Development in Mineral Economies: The Resource Curse Thesis*. Routledge, 1993.

[11] Rosenau, Pauline Marie. *Post-Modernism and the Social Sciences: Insights, Inroads, and Intrusions*. Princeton, 1992.

[12] Der Derian, James. *On Diplomacy: A Genealogy of Western Estrangement*. Blackwell, 1987.

[13] Shapiro, Michael J. Textualizing Global Politics. In Der Derian, James, and Michael J. Shapiro, eds. *International/Intertextual Relations: Postmodern Readings of World Politics*. Lexington, 1989, pp. 11–22. Shapiro, Michael J., and Hayward R. Alker, eds. *Challenging Boundaries: Global Flows, Territorial Identities*. Minnesota, 1996.

set of objective interests. Indeed, it was considered the second most important actor in the world. Realists were amazed when the Soviet Union split into 15 pieces, each containing its own fractious groups and elements. It became clear that the "unitary state" called the Soviet Union had masked (and let realists ignore) the divergent experiences of constituent republics, ethnic groups, and individuals.

Postmodernists seek to "deconstruct" such constructions as states, the international system, and the associated stories and arguments (texts and discourses) with which realists portray the nature of international relations. To *deconstruct* a text—a term borrowed from literary criticism—means to tease apart the words in order to reveal hidden meanings, looking for what might be omitted or included only implicitly. The hidden meanings not explicitly addressed in the text are often called the **subtext.**[14]

Omissions are an aspect of subtext, as when realist theories of IR omit women and gender, for example. In its emphasis on states, realism omits the roles of individuals, domestic politics, economic classes, MNCs, and other nonstate actors. In its focus on the great powers, realism omits the experiences of poor countries. In its attention to military forms of leverage, it omits the roles of various nonmilitary forms of leverage.

Realism focuses so narrowly because its aim is to reduce IR to a simple, coherent model. The model is claimed to be objective, universal, and accurate. To postmodernists, the realist model is none of these things; it is a biased model that creates a narrow and one-sided story for the purpose of promoting the interests of powerful actors. Postmodernists seek to destroy this model along with any other model (including neoliberalism) that tries to represent IR in simple objective categories. Postmodernists instead want to celebrate the diversity of experiences that make up IR without needing to make sense of them by simplifying and categorizing.[15]

PEACE STUDIES

Peace studies, like other critical theories, challenges fundamental concepts behind both realism and neoliberalism.[16] In particular, peace studies seeks to shift the focus of IR away from the interstate level of analysis and toward a broad conception of social relations at the individual, domestic, and global levels of analysis. Peace studies connects war and peace with individual responsibility, economic inequality, gender relations, cross-cultural understanding, and other aspects of social relationships. Peace studies seeks the potentials for peace not in the transactions of state leaders but in the transformation of entire societies (through social revolution) and in transnational communities (bypassing states and ignoring borders to connect people and groups

---

[14] Campbell, David. *Politics without Principle: Sovereignty, Ethics, and the Narratives of the Gulf War.* Rienner, 1993.
[15] Walker, R. B. J., and Saul H. Mendlovitz, eds. *Contending Sovereignties: Redefining Political Community.* Rienner, 1990. Walker, R. B. J. *Inside/Outside: International Relations as Political Theory.* Cambridge, 1993. Weber, Cynthia. *Simulating Sovereignty: Intervention, the State and Symbolic Exchange.* Cambridge, 1995.
[16] Barash, David P., and Charles P. Webel. *Peace and Conflict Studies.* Sage, 2002. Barash, David P., ed. *Approaches to Peace: A Reader in Peace Studies.* Oxford, 2000.

globally).[17] Another way in which peace studies seeks to broaden the focus of inquiry is to reject the supposed objectivity of traditional (realist and liberal) approaches. Most scholars of peace studies think that a good way to gain knowledge is to participate in action—not just to observe objectively. This lack of objectivity has been criticized as **normative bias** because scholars impose their personal norms and values on the subject. Scholars in peace studies respond, however, that realism itself has normative biases and makes policy prescriptions.

The development and implementation of peaceful strategies for settling conflicts—using alternatives to violent forms of leverage—are known by the general term **conflict resolution.** These methods are at work, competing with violent methods, in virtually all international conflicts. Recently the use of conflict resolution has been increasing, becoming more sophisticated, and succeeding more often.[18] Most conflict resolution uses a third party whose role is **mediation** between two conflicting parties.[19] Most of today's international conflicts have one or more mediating parties working regularly to resolve the conflict short of violence. No hard-and-fast rule states what kinds of third parties mediate what kinds of conflicts.[20] In some cases, discussion by private individuals and groups can ease tensions as well.[21]

If both sides agree in advance to abide by a solution devised by a mediator, the process is called *arbitration*. In that case, both sides present their arguments to the arbitrator, who decides on a "fair" solution. Arbitration often uses a panel of three people, one chosen by each side unilaterally and a third on whom both sides agree. Conflicting parties (and mediators) can also use *confidence-building* measures to gradually increase trust.

Peace studies scholars argue that war is not just a natural expression of power, but one closely tied to militarism in (some) cultures.[22] **Militarism** is the glorification of war, military force, and violence through TV, films, books, political speeches, toys, games, sports, and other such avenues. Militarism also refers to the structuring of society around war—for example, the dominant role of a military-industrial complex in a national economy, or the dominance of national security issues in domestic politics. Militarism may underlie the propensity of political leaders to use military force.

Because realism assumes the normalcy of military conflicts, it recognizes only a negative kind of peace—the temporary absence of war. By contrast, **positive peace** refers to a peace that resolves the underlying reasons for war—peace that is not just a cease-fire but also a transformation of relationships. Under positive peace, not only do state armies stop fighting each other, they stop arming, stop forming death squads against internal protest,

---

[17] Cancian, Francesca M., and James William Gibson. *Making War/Making Peace: The Social Foundations of Violent Conflict.* Wadsworth, 1990. Rapoport, Anatol. *Peace: An Idea Whose Time Has Come.* Michigan, 1992. Galtung, Johan. *Peace by Peaceful Means: Peace and Conflict, Development and Civilization.* Sage, 1996.
[18] Kurtz, Lester R., ed. *Encyclopedia of Violence, Peace, and Conflict.* 3 vols. Academic, 1999. Väyrynen, Raimo, ed. *New Directions in Conflict Theory: Conflict Resolution and Conflict Transformation.* Sage, 1991.
[19] Bercovitch, Jacob, ed. *Resolving International Conflicts: The Theory and Practice of Mediation.* Rienner, 1996.
[20] Kremenyuk, V. A., ed. *International Negotiation: Analysis, Approaches, Issues.* 2nd ed. Jossey-Bass, 2002.
[21] Agha, Hussein, Shai Feldman, Ahmad Khalidi, and Ze'ev Schiff. *Track II Diplomacy: Lessons from the Middle East.* MIT, 2003.
[22] Bacevich, Andrew J. *The New American Militarism: How Americans Are Seduced by War.* Oxford, 2005. Grossman, Dave. *On Killing: The Psychological Cost of Learning to Kill in War and Society.* Little, Brown, 1995.

and reverse the economic exploitation and political oppression that scholars in peace studies believe are responsible for social conflicts that lead to war.

Proponents of this approach see broad social and economic issues—assumed by realists to be relatively unimportant—as inextricably linked with positive peace. Some scholars define poverty, hunger, and oppression as forms of violence—which they call **structural violence** because it is caused by the structure of social relations rather than by direct actions such as shooting people. Structural violence in this definition kills and harms many more people each year than do war and other forms of direct political violence. Positive peace is usually defined to include the elimination of structural violence because it is considered a source of conflict and war.

The creation of a **world government** has long been debated by scholars and pursued by activists. Some scholars believe progress is being made (through the UN) toward the eventual emergence of a world government. Others think the idea is impractical or even undesirable (merely adding another layer of centralized control, when peace demands decentralization and freedom).

Scholars in peace studies also study **peace movements**—people taking to the streets in protest against war and militarism.[23] In the U.S. peace movement since World War I, an *internationalist* wing has seen international organizations (today, the UN) as the best hope for peace and has supported wars against aggression. A *pacifist* wing has opposed all wars, distrusted international organizations whose members are state governments, and favored more radical social change to achieve positive peace.[24] The philosophies of **nonviolence** and **pacifism** are based on a unilateral commitment to refrain from using any violent forms of leverage in bargaining.[25]

Peace studies, postmodernism, and the various Marxist approaches to IR all share an unwillingness to take for granted the nature of states as units analyzed by more conventional theories of IR. All these critical approaches dissect the state and seek to understand motivations and dynamics ignored by the traditional theories.

---

[23] Lynch, Cecelia. *Beyond Appeasement: Interpreting Interwar Peace Movements in World Politics.* Cornell, 1999. Carter, April. *Peace Movements: International Protest and World Politics Since 1945.* Longman, 1992.
[24] DeBenedetti, Charles. *Origins of the Modern American Peace Movement, 1915–1929.* KTO, 1978.
[25] Ackerman, Peter, and Jack DuVall. *A Force More Powerful: A Century of Nonviolent Conflict.* St. Martin's, 2001.

CHAPTER 8

GENDER THEORIES

Scholarship on gender has cut a broad swath across academic disciplines, from literature to psychology to history. In recent years, it has made inroads in international relations, once considered one of the fields most resistant to gendered arguments.[1]

WHY GENDER MATTERS

Gender scholarship encompasses a variety of strands of work, but all have in common the insight that gender matters in understanding how IR works—especially in issues relating to war and international security. *Feminist scholarship* in various disciplines seeks to uncover hidden assumptions about gender in how we study a subject. What scholars traditionally claim to be universal often turns out to be true only of males. Some feminist IR scholars argue that the core assumptions of realism—especially of anarchy and sovereignty—reflect the ways in which *males* tend to interact and to see the world. In this view, the realist approach simply assumes male participants when discussing foreign policy decision making, state sovereignty, or the use of military force.

This critique is somewhat complex. Because the vast majority of heads of state, diplomats, and soldiers *are* male, it may be realistic to study them as males. What the feminist critics then ask is that scholars explicitly recognize the gendered nature of their subject (rather than implicitly assuming all actors are male). In this view, our understanding of male actors in IR can be increased by considering how their gender identity affects their views and decision processes. And females also influence IR (more often through nonstate channels than males do)—influences often ignored by realism. Some feel that women scholars tend to be more interested in these roles and effects than are their male colleagues. Yet when a survey in 2005 listed the 25 most influential IR scholars, all 25 were male. In a 2007 update, two women made the list, near the bottom.[2]

---

[1] Tickner, J. Ann. *Gendering World Politics: Issues and Approaches in the Post–Cold War Era.* Columbia, 2001. Peterson, V. Spike, and Anne Sisson Runyan. *Global Gender Issues.* 2nd ed. Westview, 1999. Steans, Jill. *Gender and International Relations: An Introduction.* Rutgers, 1998. Whitworth, Sandra. *Feminism and International Relations.* St. Martin's, 1994. Tickner, J. Ann. *Gender in International Relations: Feminist Perspectives on Achieving Global Security.* Columbia, 1992.
[2] Peterson, Susan, Michael J. Tierney, and Daniel Maliniak. Inside the Ivory Tower. *Foreign Policy* 151, Nov./Dec. 2005: 58–64. Maliniak, Daniel, et al. Inside the Ivory Tower. *Foreign Policy* 153, Mar./Apr. 2007.

Beyond revealing the hidden assumptions about gender in a field of scholarship, feminist scholars often *challenge traditional concepts of gender* as well. In IR, these traditional concepts revolve around the assumptions that males fight wars and run states, whereas females are basically irrelevant to IR. Such gender roles are based in the broader construction of masculinity as suitable to *public* and political spaces, whereas femininity is associated with the sphere of the *private* and domestic.

Like realists (see pp. 19–20), gender theorists follow a long line of tradition.[3] Not long before Thucydides, the ancient Greek woman poet Sappho wrote love poems to women on the island of Lesbos. Just before Machiavelli, the Italian-born writer Christine de Pisan praised women's abilities to make peace. A century after Hobbes, Mary Wollstonecraft in Britain argued for equal rights for women. And a century before Morgenthau founded American realism, the American Susan B. Anthony worked tirelessly for pacifism, abolitionism, and suffragism.

Beyond a basic agreement that gender is important, there is no such thing as "the feminist approach" to IR but several such approaches—*strands* of scholarship and theory. Although they are interwoven (all paying attention to gender and to the status of women), they often run in different directions. On some core issues, the different strands of feminism have conflicting views, creating interesting debates *within* feminism.

One strand, **difference feminism,** focuses on valorizing the feminine—that is, valuing the unique contributions of women *as* women. Difference feminists do not think women do all things as well as men or vice versa. Because of their greater experience with nurturing and human relations, women are seen as potentially more effective than men (on average) in conflict resolution as well as in group decision making. Difference feminists believe there are real differences between the genders that are not just social constructions and cultural indoctrination (although these contribute to gender roles, too). Some difference feminists believe there is a core biological essence to being male or female (sometimes called *essentialism*), but most think women's difference is more culturally than biologically determined. In either case, feminine perspectives create a *standpoint* from which to observe, analyze, and criticize the traditional perspectives on IR.

Another strand, **liberal feminism,** rejects these claims as being based on stereotyped gender roles. Liberal feminists see the "essential" differences in men's and women's abilities or perspectives as trivial or nonexistent—men and women are equal. They deplore the exclusion of women from positions of power in IR but do not believe that including women would change the nature of the international system. Liberal feminists seek to include women more often as subjects of study—such as women state leaders, women soldiers, and other women operating outside the traditional gender roles in IR.

A third approach combines feminism with postmodernism (see Chapter 7). **Postmodern feminism** tends to reject the assumptions about gender made by both difference and liberal feminists. Where difference feminists consider gender differences important and fixed, and liberal feminists consider those differences trivial, postmodern feminists find them important but arbitrary and flexible.

---

[3] Thanks to Francine D'Amico for these comparisons.

THE MASCULINITY OF REALISM

Difference feminism provides a perspective from which to reexamine the core assumptions of realism—especially the assumption of autonomy, from which flow the key realist concepts of sovereignty and anarchy. To realists, the international system consists of autonomous actors (states) that control their own territory and have no right to infringe on another's territory. Some difference feminists have argued that realism emphasizes autonomy and separation because men find separation easier to deal with than interconnection.

This view rests on a psychological theory that boys and girls grow up from a young age with different views of separateness and connection.[4] In this theory, because a child's primary caretaker is almost always female in the early years, girls form their gender identity around the perception of *similarity* with their caretaker (and by extension the environment in which they live), but boys perceive their *difference* from the caretaker. From this experience, boys develop social relations based on individual *autonomy*, but girls' relations are based on *connection*. As a result, women are held to be more likely than men to fear abandonment, whereas men are more likely to fear intimacy.

In *moral* reasoning, according to this theory, boys tend to apply abstract rules and stress individual rights, but girls pay more attention to the concrete contexts of different situations and to the responsibility of group members for each other. In playing *games*, boys resolve disputes through arguments about the rules and then keep playing, but girls are more likely to abandon a game rather than argue over the rules and risk the social cohesion of their group. In *social relations*, boys form and dissolve friendships more readily than girls, who are more likely to stick loyally with friends. (The empirical evidence in psychological research for these theorized gender differences is mixed at best.)

Realism, of course, rests on the concept of states as separate, autonomous actors that make and break alliances freely while pursuing their own interests (but not interfering in each other's internal affairs). Such a conception of autonomy parallels the masculine psyche just described. Thus, some feminist scholars find in realism a hidden assumption of masculinity. Furthermore, the sharp distinction that realists draw between international politics (anarchic) and domestic politics (ordered) parallels the distinction in gender roles between the public (masculine) and private (feminine) spheres. Thus, realism constructs IR as a man's world.

By contrast, an international system based on *feminine* principles might give greater importance to the *interdependence* of states than to their autonomy, stressing the responsibility of people to care for each other with less regard for states and borders. In the struggle between the principles of human rights and of sovereignty (noninterference in internal affairs), human rights would receive priority. In the choice of forms of leverage when conflicts arise between states, violence might be less prevalent.

The realist preoccupation with the interstate level of analysis presumes that the logic of war itself is autonomous and can be separated from other social relationships such as economics, domestic politics, sexism, and racism. Difference feminism, however, reveals the *connections* of these phenomena with war. It suggests new avenues for understanding

---

[4] Gilligan, Carol. *In a Different Voice: Psychological Theory and Women's Development.* Harvard, 1982. Chodorow, Nancy. *The Reproduction of Mothering.* California, 1978.

war at the domestic and individual levels of analysis—underlying causes that realists largely ignore.

From this difference-feminist perspective, neoliberalism (p. 54) has gone backward from traditional liberalism, by accepting the realist assumption of separate unitary states as the important actors and downplaying substate and transnational actors including women.[5] Neoliberalism's conception of cooperation as rule-based interactions among autonomous actors also reflects masculinist assumptions.

GENDER IN WAR AND PEACE

In addition to its emphasis on autonomy and anarchy, realism stresses military force as the key form of leverage in IR. Here, too, many difference feminists see in realism a hidden assumption of masculinity. They see war as not only a male occupation, but also the quintessentially male occupation. In this view, men are inherently the more warlike gender, and women the more peaceful.[6] Thus, although realism may accurately portray the importance of war and military force in IR as we now know it, this merely reflects the male domination of the international sphere to date—not a necessary, eternal, or inescapable logic of relations among states.[7]

Difference feminists find plenty of evidence to support the idea of war as a masculine pursuit. Anthropologists have found that in all known cultures, males are the primary (and usually the only) combatants in warfare, despite the enormous diversity of those cultures in so many other ways. (Of course, voting and political leadership were also male domains for most of history, yet feminist scholars would hardly call those activities essentially masculine.)

One supposed link between war and masculinity is the male sex hormone testosterone (along with related hormones), which some biologists have connected with aggressive behavior in animals. However, testosterone does not *cause* aggression. Rather, social interactions "feed back" to affect testosterone levels (winners' testosterone levels rise while losers' levels fall). Thus testosterone is a link in a complex system of relationships between the organism and the social environment. Complex behaviors such as aggression and war cannot be said to be biologically *driven* or predetermined, because humanity's most striking biological capability is flexibility. Even some feminist scholars who see gender differences as strictly cultural, and not biological at all, view war as a masculine construction.[8]

Both biologically and anthropologically, no firm evidence connects women's caregiving functions (pregnancy and nursing) with any particular kinds of behavior such as

---

[5] Moghadam, Valentine M. *Globalizing Women: Transnational Feminist Networks*. Johns Hopkins, 2005. Meyer, Mary K., and Elisabeth Prügl, eds. *Gender Politics in Global Governance*. Rowman & Littlefield, 1999.
[6] Woolf, Virginia. *Three Guineas*. Hogarth, 1977 [1938]. Reardon, Betty. *Sexism and the War System*. Teachers College, 1985.
[7] Goldstein, Joshua S. *War and Gender: How Gender Shapes the War System and Vice Versa*. Cambridge, 2001. Lorentzen, Lois Ann, and Jennifer Turpin, eds. *The Women and War Reader*. New York University, 1998.
[8] Hartsock, Nancy C. M. Masculinity, Heroism, and the Making of War. In Harris, Adrienne, and Ynestra King, eds. *Rocking the Ship of State: Toward a Feminist Peace Politics*. Westview, 1989, pp. 133–52.

reconciliation or nonviolence—although females have been studied less than males. The role of women varies considerably from one society to another. Although they rarely take part in combat, women sometimes provide logistical support to male warriors and sometimes help drive the men into a war frenzy by dancing, shaming nonparticipating males, and other activities supportive of war. Yet in other cultures, women restrain the men from war or play special roles as mediators in bringing wars to an end.

The idea of women as peacemakers has a long history. In ancient Athens, the (male) playwright Aristophanes speculated about how women might end the unpopular Peloponnesian War with Sparta, then in progress. In his play *Lysistrata*, a young woman organizes the Athenian and Spartan women to withhold sex from the men until the latter stop the war (the women also make off with the war treasury). In short order, the men come to their senses and make peace.[9] Women have formed their own organizations to work for peace on many occasions. In 1852, *Sisterly Voices* was published as a newsletter for women's peace societies. Bertha von Suttner in 1892 persuaded Alfred Nobel to create the Nobel Peace Prize (which Suttner won in 1905). During World War I, in 1915, Jane Addams and other feminists convened an international women's peace conference at The Hague. They founded the Women's Peace Party (now called the Women's International League for Peace and Freedom).[10] After World War I, the *suffrage* movement won the right for women to vote. Difference feminists thought that women would vote for peace and against war, changing the nature of foreign policy, but women generally voted as their husbands did. Similarly, decades later when women participated in liberation struggles against colonialism in the global South, some feminists thought such participation would change foreign policies in the newly independent countries, but in general such changes did not materialize (partly because women were often pushed aside from political power after the revolution).

Nonetheless, U.S. public opinion on foreign policy issues since the 1930s partially vindicates difference feminists. A **gender gap** in polls shows that women are about 10 percentage points lower than men on average in their support for military actions. This gender gap shrinks, however, when broad consensus on a military action exists, as when U.S. forces attacked terrorist supporters in Afghanistan in late 2001.

Meanwhile, feminists in recent decades have continued to organize women's peace organizations.[11] In the 1980s, Women's Action for Nuclear Disarmament (WAND) opposed the nuclear arms buildup, and women encamped for years at Britain's Greenham Common air base. In 1995, the UN-sponsored Beijing conference on women brought together women activists from around the world, and helped deepen feminists' engagement with global issues such as North-South inequality. In Bahrain, women won the right to vote and to run for office in 2002, but none were elected.

In 2000, the UN Security Council passed Resolution 1325, mandating greater inclusion of women and attention to gender in UN peacekeeping and reconstruction.

---

[9] Aristophanes. *Lysistrata*. Edited by Jeffrey Henderson. Oxford, 1987.

[10] Degen, Marie Louise. *The History of the Woman's Peace Party*. Burt Franklin Reprints, 1974 [1939].

[11] Stephenson, Carolyn M. Feminism, Pacifism, Nationalism, and the United Nations Decade for Women. In Stiehm, Judith, ed. *Women and Men's Wars*. Oxford: Pergamon, 1983, pp. 341–48.

But in several locations UN peacekeepers participated in local prostitution, rape, and even sex trafficking. In 2004, Secretary-General Annan called "shameful" the reported behavior of UN troops from several countries serving in Democratic Congo. Investigators there found hundreds of cases of sexual crimes by UN personnel.

As a result of Resolution 1325, "gender advisors" have begun to accompany international peacekeeping and relief operations to provide practical advice on more effective operations in the context of local cultures' gender relations. For example, the head of a group of Swedish men sent to build a bridge in Sri Lanka initially said, "Our task is to build a bridge, we don't need to worry about gender issues." When asked how it would be used, he replied, "By car mostly," but when asked, "The women too?" he said, "No, they'll probably walk." As a result of this gender perspective the bridge was redesigned to include a pedestrian walkway.[12]

WOMEN IN IR

Liberal feminists are skeptical of difference-feminist critiques of realism. They believe that when women are allowed to participate in IR, they play the game basically the same way men do, with similar results. They think that women can practice realism—based on autonomy, sovereignty, anarchy, territory, military force, and all the rest—just as well as men can. Liberal feminists therefore tend to reject the critique of realism as masculine. (In practice, many feminist scholars draw on both difference feminists' and liberal feminists' views in various proportions.)[13]

Liberal feminism focuses on the integration of women into the overwhelmingly male preserves of foreign policy making and the military. In most states, these occupations are typically at least 90 percent male. The U.S. military, with one of the highest proportions of women anywhere in the world or in history, is still 85 percent male.[14] For liberal feminists, the main effect of this gender imbalance on the nature of IR—that is, apart from effects on the status of women—is to waste talent. Liberal feminists think that women have the same capabilities as men, so the inclusion of women in traditionally male occupations (from state leader to foot soldier) would bring additional capable individuals into those areas. Gender equality would thus increase national capabilities by giving the state a better overall pool of diplomats, generals, soldiers, and politicians.

In support of their argument that, on average, women handle power just as men do, liberal feminists point to the many examples of women who have served in such positions. No distinctly feminine feature of their behavior in office distinguishes these leaders from their male counterparts. Rather, they have been diverse in character and policy. Of course, women in traditionally male roles may have been selected (or self-selected) on the basis of their suitability to such roles: they may not act the way "average" women would act. Still, they do show that individuals cannot be judged accurately using group characteristics alone.

---

[12] Genderforce: Sweden. *From Words to Action*. Booklet, circa 2006.

[13] Kelly, Rita Mae, et al., eds. *Gender, Globalization, and Democratization*. Rowman & Littlefield, 2001.

[14] Seager, Joni. *The Penguin Atlas of Women in the World*. Penguin, 2003.

Female state leaders do not appear to be any more peaceful, or any less committed to state sovereignty and territorial integrity, than are male leaders (see Table 8.1). Some have even suggested that women in power tend to be more warlike to compensate for being females in traditionally male roles. Overall, women state leaders, like men, seem capable of leading in war or in peace as circumstances demand.[15]

Liberal feminists also believe that women soldiers, like women politicians, have a range of skills and abilities comparable to men's. Again, the main effect of including more women would be to improve the overall quality of military forces.[16] About 200,000

TABLE 8.1 Notable Women State Leaders of Recent Decades

Leader	Country	Record in Office	Time Frame
Angela Merkel	Germany	Only current woman leader of a great power; put limits on German troops with NATO forces in Afghanistan	2005–
Ellen Johnson-Sirleaf	Liberia	Struggling to keep country calm after civil war	2006–
Margaret Thatcher	Britain	First woman to lead a great power in a century; went to war to recover Falkland Islands from Argentina	1982
Indira Gandhi	India	Led war against Pakistan	1971
Golda Meir	Israel	Led war against Egypt and Syria	1973
Benazir Bhutto	Pakistan	Struggled to control own military	late 1980s
Corazon Aquino	Philippines	Struggled to control own military	late 1980s
Tansu Çiller	Turkey	Led a harsh war to suppress Kurdish rebels	mid-1990s
Violetta Chamorro	Nicaragua	Kept the peace between factions after civil war	1980s
Chandrika Kumaratunga	Sri Lanka	Tried to make peace with separatists, but returned to war	1990s and since
Megawati Sukarnoputri	Indonesia	Struggled to keep country calm; lost re-election after one term	2004

Note: Other states, such as Finland, Norway, New Zealand, Iceland, and Chile have had women leaders when war and peace were not major political issues in those countries.

---

[15] D'Amico, Francine, and Peter R. Beckman, eds. *Women in World Politics: An Introduction*. Bergin & Garvey, 1995. Nelson, Barbara J., and Najma Chowdhury, eds. *Women and Politics Worldwide*. Yale, 1994. McGlen, Nancy E., and Meredith Reid Sarkees. *Women in Foreign Policy: The Insiders*. Routledge, 1993.
[16] De Pauw, Linda Grant. *Battle Cries and Lullabies: Women in War from Prehistory to the Present*. Oklahoma, 1998. Fraser, Antonia. *The Warrior Queens*. Knopf, 1989.

women soldiers serve in the U.S. military (15 percent of the total) and more than 1 million women are veterans. Women perform well in a variety of military roles, including logistical and medical support, training, and command. Women have had success in other countries that have allowed them into the military (or, in a few cases, drafted them).

Although women have served with distinction in military forces, they have been excluded from combat roles in almost all those forces. In some countries, military women are limited to traditional female roles such as nurses and typists. Even when women may hold nontraditional positions such as mechanics and pilots (as in the United States), most women remain in the traditional roles. And certain jobs still remain off-limits; for instance, women cannot serve on U.S. submarines or in combat infantry. Thus relatively few cases exist to judge women's abilities in combat.

Those cases include historical examples of individual women who served in combat (sometimes disguised as men, sometimes not). In the 15th century, Joan of Arc rallied French soldiers to defeat England, turning the tide of the Hundred Years' War. (The English burned her at the stake as a witch after capturing her.) Women have often participated in combat in rebel forces fighting guerrilla wars in Vietnam, Nicaragua, and elsewhere, as well as in terrorist or paramilitary units in countries such as Peru, Germany, Italy, and Palestine. Women in Eritrea's guerrilla forces became part of that country's regular army after independence and then served in frontline combat units during Eritrea and Ethiopia's trench warfare in the late 1990s.

In recent years, U.S. women soldiers have found themselves in combat (today's mobile tactics and fluid front lines make it hard to separate combat from support roles). During the 1991 Gulf War, tens of thousands of U.S. women served, 13 were killed, and 2 were captured as prisoners of war. In the late 1990s, women began serving on some U.S. combat ships and airplanes, but not in ground combat units. In the Iraq War, women flew all types of airplanes and helicopters, and one woman was in the first group of U.S. POWs captured early in the war. During the subsequent years of war in Iraq, U.S. women military police have acquitted themselves well in numerous firefights. All these cases suggest that (at least some) women are able to hold their own in combat.

The main reason that military forces exclude women from combat seems to be fear about what effect their presence might have on the male soldiers, whose discipline and loyalty have traditionally been thought to depend on male bonding and single-minded focus. Liberal feminists reject such arguments and argue that group bonding in military units does not depend on gender segregation. (After all, similar rationales were once given for racial segregation in U.S. military forces.)[17]

The effect of war on noncombatant women has also received growing attention.[18] Attacks on women in Algeria, Rwanda, Bosnia, Afghanistan, Democratic Congo, and Sudan pointed to a possible new trend toward women as military targets. Systematic rape was used as a terror tactic in Bosnia and Rwanda, and the Japanese army in World

---

[17] Katzenstein, Mary Fainsod, and Judith Reppy, eds. *Beyond Zero Tolerance: Discrimination in Military Culture*. Rowman & Littlefield, 1999.

[18] Giles, Wenona, and Jennifer Hyndman, eds. *Sites of Violence: Gender and Conflict Zones*. California, 2004. Carpenter, R. Charli. *Innocent Women and Children: Gender, Norms, and the Protection of Civilians*. Ashgate, 2006. Enloe, Cynthia. *Maneuvers: The International Politics of Militarizing Women's Lives*. California, 2000.

War II operated an international network of sex slaves known as "comfort women." Rape has long been treated as a normal if regrettable by-product of war, but recently certain instances of rape were declared war crimes (see pp. 94–96).

In sum, liberal feminists reject the argument that women bring uniquely feminine assets or liabilities to foreign and military affairs. They do not critique realism as essentially masculine in nature but do criticize state practices that exclude women from participation in international politics and war.

DIFFERENCE FEMINISM VERSUS LIBERAL FEMINISM?

The arguments of difference feminists and liberal feminists may seem totally at odds. Difference feminists argue that realism reflects a masculine perception of social relations, whereas liberal feminists think that women can be just as realist as men. Liberal feminists believe that female participation in foreign policy and the military will enhance state capabilities, but difference feminists think women's unique abilities can be put to better use in transforming (feminizing) the entire system of international relations rather than in trying to play men's games.

The evidence in favor of both positions can be reconciled to some extent by bearing in mind that the character and ability of an individual are not the same as that of his or her group. Rather, the qualities of individuals follow a bell curve distribution, with many people clustered in the middle and fewer people very high or low on a given capability.

Gender differences posited by difference feminists mean that one bell curve is shifted from the other, even though the two may still overlap quite a bit (see Figure 8.1). To take a simple example, a few women are physically larger than almost all men, and a few men

FIGURE 8.1   Overlapping Bell Curves

Bell curves show that individuals differ in capabilities such as physical strength or peacemaking ability. Although the genders differ on average, for most individuals (in the area of overlap) such differences do not come into play. Liberal feminists emphasize the area where the curves overlap; difference feminists emphasize the overall group differences.

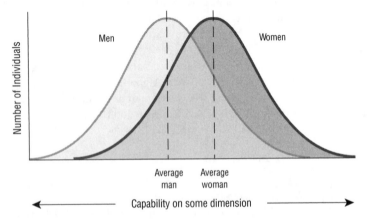

are smaller than almost all women. But on average men are somewhat larger than women. On various dimensions of capability, the women's curve is above or below the men's on average, but there is still much overlap.

Liberal feminist arguments emphasize the overlap of the two bell curves. They say that individual women—*most* women on most relevant dimensions—are well within the male curve and thus can perform equally with the men. Indeed, women in nontraditional gender roles may well perform better than their male counterparts, because presumably women who self-select into such roles (such as joining the military) are near the high end of the female bell curve, whereas the men are closer to the middle of the male curve (because more of them join). Similarly, women who become state leaders are presumably more adept at foreign policy making than most women (or men), because political processes tend to select women at the high end of the curve in terms of their affinity for realism.

Difference feminists are more interested in the shift in the two bell curves, not their overlap. On average, in this perspective, women tend to see international relations in a somewhat different way from that of men. So although *individuals* selected to participate in foreign policy and the military may not differ from their male counterparts, women as a group differ. Women voters display different concerns regarding IR than men (as shown by the gender gap in opinion polls and voting patterns).

By this logic, then, profound differences in IR—and a shift away from the utility of realism in explaining state behavior—would occur only if many women participated in key foreign policy positions. That is, a *few* women politicians or women soldiers do not change the masculine foundations of IR. Women foreign policy makers today are surrounded by males (advisors, military officers, political leaders, and foreign state leaders). But a world in which *most* politicians or soldiers were female might be a different story. Then, instead of the selection of women for their ability to fit into men's games, the rules of the game might themselves change to reflect the fact that "average" women would be the main actors in the traditionally important IR roles. Of course, these theories of difference feminists have never been tested, because women have never attained predominance in foreign policy making in any country—much less in the international system as a whole.

In addition to the liberal and difference strands of feminism, the third strand, postmodern feminism, is connected with the rise of postmodernism in the social sciences.

POSTMODERN FEMINISM

One line of criticism directed at realism combines feminism and postmodernism.[19] *Postmodern feminism* seeks to deconstruct realism with the specific aim of uncovering the pervasive hidden influences of gender in IR while showing how arbitrary the construction of gender roles is. Feminist postmodernists agree with difference feminists that realism carries hidden meanings about gender roles but deny that there is any

---

[19] Sylvester, Christine. *Feminist Theory and International Relations in a Postmodern Era.* Cambridge, 1994.
Peterson, V. Spike, ed. *Gendered States: Feminist (Re)Visions of International Relations Theory.* Rienner, 1992.

fixed inherent meaning in either male or female genders. Rather, feminist postmodernists look at the interplay of gender and power in a more open-ended way. Postmodern feminists criticize liberal feminists for trying merely to integrate women into traditional structures of war and foreign policy. They criticize difference feminists as well, for glorifying traditional feminine virtues.

In studying war, postmodern feminists have challenged the archetypes of the (male) "just warrior" and the (female) "beautiful soul." They argue that women are not just passive bystanders or victims in war, but active participants in a system of warfare tied to both genders. Women act not only as nurses and journalists at the "front" but as mothers, wives, and girlfriends on the "home front."[20] These scholars believe that stories of military forces should not omit the roles of prostitutes at military bases, nor should stories of diplomacy omit the roles of diplomats' wives.[21]

Postmodern feminists reject not only realism but also some of the alternative approaches that emphasize the protection of women and other noncombatants. Just-war doctrine (see pp. 88–89) is considered too abstract—a set of concepts and rules that does not do justice to the richness of each historical context and the varied roles of individual men and women within it.[22]

Postmodern feminists have tried to deconstruct the language of realism, especially when it reflects influences of gender and sex. For instance, the first atomic bombs had male gender (they were named "Fat Man" and "Little Boy"); the coded telegram informing Washington, D.C., that the first hydrogen bomb had worked said simply, "It's a boy" (presumably being born a girl would have indicated a failure). The plane that dropped the atomic bomb on Hiroshima (the *Enola Gay*) had female gender; it was named after the pilot's mother. Likewise the French atom-bomb test sites in the South Pacific were all given women's names.[23] Similarly, pilots have pasted pinup photos of nude women onto conventional bombs before dropping them. In all these cases, postmodern feminists would note that the feminine gender of vehicles, targets, or decorations amplifies the masculinity of the weapon itself.

These efforts find sex and gender throughout the subtext of realism. For example, the terms *power* and *potency* refer to both state capability and male virility. Military force depends on phallic objects—weapons designed to shoot projectiles, penetrate targets, and explode. Nuclear weapons are also repeatedly spoken of in sexual terms, perhaps due to their great "potency." Female models are hired to market tanks, helicopter missiles, and other "potent" weapons to male procurement officers at international military trade shows. The phallic character of weapons has seemingly persisted even as technology has evolved from spears to guns to missiles.[24]

---

[20] Elshtain, Jean Bethke. *Women and War*. 2nd ed. Chicago, 1995.

[21] Enloe, Cynthia. *Bananas, Beaches, and Bases: Making Feminist Sense of International Politics*. California, 1989. Pettman, Jan Jindy. *Worlding Women: A Feminist International Politics*. Routledge, 1996. Moon, Katherine H. S. *Sex among Allies: Military Prostitution in U.S.-Korea Relations*. Columbia, 1997.

[22] Elshtain, *Women and War*. 2nd ed. Chicago, 1995. Ruddick, Sara. *Maternal Thinking: Towards a Politics of Peace*. Women's Press, 1989.

[23] Cohn, Carol. Sex and Death in the Rational World of Defense Intellectuals. *Signs* 12 (4), 1987: 687–718.

[24] Trexler, Richard C. *Sex and Conquest: Gendered Violence, Political Order, and the European Conquest of the Americas*. Cornell, 1995.

All three strands of feminist theories provide explanations that often differ from both realist and liberal theories. In the case of response to aggression, feminists might call attention to the importance of gender roles such as the need for state leaders to prove their manhood by standing up to the bad guys. This is connected with the male role as protector of the orderly domestic sphere (home, family, country) against the dangerous and anarchic outside world. Since 2001, gender roles have become increasingly visible on both sides of the "war on terror," with both women's positions in society and men's concepts of masculinity becoming contested territory between the West and armed Islamist groups. Traditional theories of IR that ignore these issues may lack explanatory power as a result.

CHAPTER 9

THEORIES OF CONFLICT

NATIONALISM

International conflicts have many sources, which are not mutually exclusive and often operate simultaneously. Before considering conflicts over tangible benefits such as territory and money, we will discuss the difficult conflicts in which intangible elements such as ethnic hatred, religious fervor, or ideology come into play—conflicts of ideas. These identity-based sources of international conflict today have been shaped historically by nationalism as the link between identity and internationally recognized statehood.

Nationalism—devotion to the interests of one's own nation over others—may be the most important force in world politics in the past two centuries. A nation is a population that shares an identity, usually including a language and culture. But nationality is a difficult concept to define precisely. To some degree, the extension of political control over large territories created the commonality necessary for nationhood—states created nations, as was the case with France. At the same time, however, the perceived existence of a nation has often led to the creation of a corresponding state as a people win sovereignty over their own affairs—nations created states.[1]

The principle of *self-determination* implies that people who identify as a nation should have the right to form a state and exercise sovereignty over their affairs. Self-determination is a widely praised principle in international affairs today (not historically). But it is generally secondary to the principles of sovereignty (noninterference in other states' internal affairs) and territorial integrity, with which it frequently conflicts. Self-determination does not give groups the right to change international borders, even those imposed arbitrarily by colonialism, in order to unify a group with a common national identity. Generally, though not always, self-determination has been achieved by violence. When the borders of (perceived) nations do not match those of states, conflicts almost inevitably arise. Today such conflicts are widespread—in Northern Ireland, Quebec, Israel-Palestine, India-Pakistan, Sri Lanka, Tibet, Sudan, and many other places.

The Netherlands helped establish the principle of self-determination when it broke free of Spanish ownership around 1600 and set up a self-governing Dutch republic. The struggle over control of the Netherlands was a leading cause of the Thirty Years' War

---

[1] Gellner, Ernest. *Nations and Nationalism*. Cornell, 1983. Tilly, Charles. *Coercion, Capital and European States, A.D. 990–1990*. Blackwell, 1990. Hobsbawm, E. J. *Nations and Nationalism Since 1780: Programme, Myth, Reality*. Cambridge, 1990.

(1618–1648), and in that war states mobilized their populations for war in new ways. This process of popular mobilization intensified greatly in the French Revolution and the subsequent Napoleonic Wars (1803–1815), when France instituted a universal draft and a centrally run "command" economy. Its citizen army was composed for the first time of Frenchmen rather than mercenaries. People participated in part because they were patriotic. Their nation-state embodied their aspirations, and brought them together in a common national identity. Independence struggles in the United States and Latin America, and later Germany and Italy, drew on similar motivations.

ETHNIC CONFLICT

Ethnic conflict is quite possibly the most important source of conflict in the numerous wars now occurring throughout the world.[2] **Ethnic groups** are large groups of people who share ancestral, language, cultural, or religious ties and a common *identity* (individuals identify with the group).[3] Although conflicts between ethnic groups often have material aspects—notably over territory and government control—ethnic conflict itself is based not on tangible causes (what someone does) but on intangible ones (who someone is).

Ethnic groups often form the basis for nationalist sentiments. Not all ethnic groups identify as nations; for instance, within the United States various ethnic groups coexist (sometimes uneasily) with a common *national* identity as Americans. But in locations where millions of members of a single ethnic group live as the majority population in their ancestors' land, they usually think of themselves as a nation. In most such cases they aspire to have their own state.

Territorial control is closely tied to the aspirations of ethnic groups for statehood. Any state's borders deviate to some extent (sometimes substantially) from the actual location of ethnic communities. Members of the ethnic group are left outside its state's borders, and members of other ethnic groups are located within the state's borders. The resulting situation can be dangerous, with part of an ethnic group controlling a state and another part living as a minority within another state controlled by a rival ethnic group. Frequently the members of the minority group suffer discrimination in the other state, and the "home" state tries to rescue or avenge them.

An ethnic group may lack any home state. Kurds share a culture, and many of them aspire to create a state of Kurdistan. But Kurds reside in four states—Turkey, Iraq, Iran, and Syria—all of which strongly oppose giving up control of part of their own territory to create a Kurdish state (see Figure 9.1). Kurds enjoyed autonomy in part of

---

[2] Gurr, Ted Robert. *Peoples versus States: Minorities at Risk in the New Century*. U.S. Institute of Peace Press, 2000. Saideman, Stephen M. *The Ties That Divide*. Columbia, 2001. Horowitz, Donald L. *Ethnic Groups in Conflict*. 2nd ed. California, 2000. Rothchild, Donald. *Managing Ethnic Conflict in Africa: Pressures and Incentives for Cooperation*. Brookings, 1997. Chua, Amy. *World on Fire: How Exporting Free Market Democracy Breeds Ethnic Hatred and Global Instability*. Doubleday, 2003. Williams, Robin M. *The Wars Within: Peoples and States in Conflict*. Cornell, 2003.
[3] Krause, Jill, and Neil Renwick, eds. *Identities in International Relations*. St. Martin's, 1996.

FIGURE 9.1 **Kurdish Area**

Ethnic populations often span international borders. Shaded region shows the approximate area of Kurdish settlements.

northern Iraq under U.S. protection in the 1990s and maintained a quasi-autonomous status in post-Saddam Iraq.[4]

Ethnic conflicts often create pressures to redraw borders by force. When ethnic populations are minorities in territories controlled by rival ethnic groups, they may even be driven from their land or (in rare cases) systematically exterminated. By driving out the minority ethnic group, a majority group can assemble a more unified, more contiguous, and larger territory for its nation-state, as ethnic Serbs tried to do through "ethnic cleansing" after the breakup of Yugoslavia. Outside states often worry about the fate of "their people" living as minorities in neighboring states.

In extreme cases, governments use **genocide**—systematic extermination of ethnic or religious groups in whole or in part—to try to destroy scapegoated groups or political rivals. Under its fanatical policies of racial purity, Nazi Germany exterminated 6 million Jews and millions of others, including homosexuals, Gypsies, and communists. The pledges of world leaders after that experience to "never again" allow genocide have been found wanting as genocide recurred in the 1990s in Bosnia and Rwanda, and most recently in Darfur, Sudan.[5] In cases of both genocide and less extreme scapegoating, ethnic hatreds do not merely bubble up naturally, but are provoked and channeled by politicians to strengthen their own power.

Why do ethnic groups frequently dislike each other? Often there are long-standing historical conflicts over specific territories or natural resources, or over one ethnic group's economic exploitation or political domination of another. These tangible grievances are amplified by intergroup psychology.[6] The ethnic group is a kind of ex-

---

[4] McDowall, David. *A Modern History of the Kurds.* 3rd ed. Tauris, 2004.
[5] Power, Samantha. *The Problem from Hell: America and the Age of Genocide.* Basic Books, 2002. Barnett, Michael. *Eyewitness to a Genocide: The United Nations and Rwanda.* Cornell, 2003. Straus, Scott. *The Order of Genocide: Race, Power, and War in Rwanda.* Cornell, 2006.
[6] Glad, Betty, ed. *Psychological Dimensions of War.* Sage, 1990.

tended *kinship* group—a group of related individuals sharing some ancestors. Even when kinship relations are not very close, a *group identity* makes a person act as though the other members of the ethnic group were family. Perhaps as technology allows far-flung groups to congregate in cyberspace, there will be less psychological pressure to gather ethnic groups physically in a territorial nation-state.

Ethnocentrism, or *in-group bias*, is the tendency to see one's own group in favorable terms and an *out-group* in unfavorable terms. Some scholars believe that ethnocentrism has roots in a biological propensity to protect closely related individuals, though this idea is controversial.[7] More often in-group bias is understood in terms of social psychology. No *minimum criterion* of similarity or kin relationship is needed to evoke the group identity process, including in-group bias. In psychological experiments, even trivial differentiations can evoke these processes. If people are assigned to groups based on a known but unimportant characteristic (such as preferring circles or triangles), before long the people in each group show in-group bias and hostility to the other group's members.[8]

In-group biases are far stronger when the other group looks different, speaks a different language, or worships in a different way (or all three). All too easily, an out-group can be dehumanized and stripped of all human rights. This **dehumanization** includes the common use of animal names—"pigs," "dogs," and so forth—for members of the out-group. Especially in wartime, when people see members of an out-group killing members of their in-group, dehumanization can be extreme. The restraints on war that have evolved in regular interstate warfare, such as not massacring civilians (see pp. 94–96), are easily discarded in interethnic warfare.

Ethnic groups are only one point along a spectrum of kinship relations—from nuclear families through extended families, villages, provinces, and nations, up to the entire human race. Loyalties fall at different points along the spectrum. It is unclear why people identify most strongly at one level of group identity. States reinforce their citizens' identification with the state through flags, anthems, pledges of allegiance, patriotic speeches, and so forth. Perhaps someday people will shift loyalties even further, developing a *global identity* as humans first and members of states and ethnic groups second.

RELIGIOUS CONFLICT

One reason ethnic conflicts often transcend material grievances is that they find expression as *religious* conflicts. Because religion is the core of a community's value system in much of the world, people whose religious practices differ are easily disdained and treated as unworthy or even inhuman. When overlaid on ethnic and territorial conflicts, religion often surfaces as the central and most visible division between groups.

Nothing inherent in religion mandates conflicts—in many places members of different religious groups coexist peacefully. But religious differences hold the potential for conflict, and for making existing conflicts more intractable, because religions

---

[7] Shaw, Paul, and Yuwa Wong. *Genetic Seeds of Warfare: Evolution, Nationalism, and Patriotism*. Unwin Hyman, 1989.
[8] Tajfel, H., and J. C. Turner. The Social Identity Theory of Intergroup Behavior. In Worchel, S., and W. Austin, eds. *Psychology of Intergroup Relations*. 2nd ed. Nelson-Hall, 1986, pp. 7–24.

involve core values, which are held as absolute truth.[9] This is increasingly true as *fundamentalist* movements have gained strength in recent decades. (The reasons for fundamentalism are disputed, but it is clearly a global-level phenomenon.) Members of these movements organize their lives and communities around their religious beliefs; many are willing to sacrifice and even die for those beliefs. Fundamentalist movements challenge the values and practices of **secular** political organizations—those created apart from religious establishments (the separation of religion and state). Among the secular practices threatened by fundamentalist movements are the rules of the international system, whereby states are treated as formally equal and sovereign whether they are "believers" or "infidels." As transnational belief systems, religions often serve as a higher law than state laws and international treaties.

Some have suggested that international conflicts in the coming years may be generated by a clash of civilizations—based on the differences between the world's major cultural groupings, which overlap quite a bit with religious communities.[10] The idea has been criticized for being overly general, and for assuming that cultural differences naturally create conflict. In fact, although religious and ethnic conflicts receive tremendous attention in the media, *most* ethnic and religious groups living in states do not fight.

Islamist groups advocate basing government and society on Islamic law. These groups vary greatly in the means they employ to pursue this goal. Most are nonviolent—charities and political parties. Some are violent—militias and terrorist networks.[11] Although Islamist movements seek changes primarily in domestic policies, they have also become a transnational force affecting world order and global North-South relations. The areas of the world that are predominantly Islamic stretch from Nigeria to Indonesia, centered historically in the Middle East (see Figure 9.2). Many international conflicts around this zone involve Muslims on one side and non-Muslims (or secular authorities) on the other, as a result of geographical and historical circumstances including colonialism and oil. In many cases, Islamist movements reflect long-standing *anti-Western* sentiment in these countries—against the old European colonizers who were Christian—and are in some ways *nationalist* movements expressed through religious channels. In some Middle Eastern countries with authoritarian governments, mosques provide the only available avenue for political opposition. Religion thus becomes a means to express opposition to the status quo in politics and culture.

The more radical Islamist movements not only threaten some existing governments—especially those tied to the West—but also undermine traditional norms of state sovereignty. They reject Western political conceptions of the state (based on individual autonomy) in favor of a more traditional Islamic orientation based on community. Some aspire to create a single political state encompassing most of the Middle East, as existed

---

[9] Appleby, R. Scott. *The Ambivalence of the Sacred: Religion, Violence, and Reconciliation*. Rowman & Littlefield, 2000.
[10] Huntington, Samuel P. *The Clash of Civilizations and the Remaking of World Order*. Simon & Schuster, 1996.
[11] Esposito, John L. *Unholy War: Terror in the Name of Islam*. Oxford, 2002. Lewis, Bernard. *The Crisis of Islam: Holy War and Unholy Terror*. Modern Library, 2003.

FIGURE 9.2 **Members of the Islamic Conference and Areas of Conflict**

Shaded countries are members of the conference; numbered regions are areas of conflict between Muslims and non-Muslims or secular authorities.

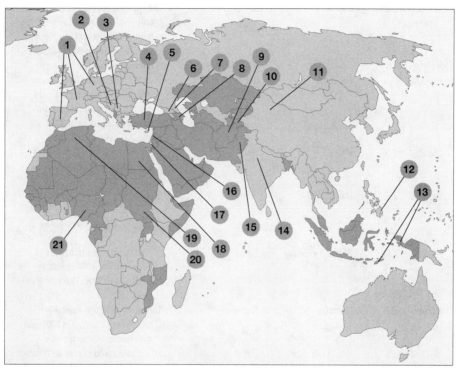

1	Germany, France, Spain	8	Armenia/Azerbaijan	15	Pakistan
2	Bosnia-Herzegovina	9	Afghanistan	16	Lebanon
3	Serbia/Kosovo	10	Tajikistan	17	Israel/Palestine
4	Turkey	11	Western China	18	Egypt
5	Cyprus	12	Philippines	19	Algeria
6	Georgia	13	East Timor/Indonesia	20	Sudan
7	Southern Russia/Chechnya	14	India	21	Nigeria

in the *caliphate* of A.D. 600–1200.[12] Such a development would create a profound challenge to the present international system—particularly to its current status quo powers—and would therefore be opposed at every turn by the world's most powerful states. Armed Islamist groups vary tremendously, and in some cases violently disagree with each other (see Table 9.1). In particular, Sunni and Shi'ite groups generally do not cooperate. Overall, conflicts involving Islamist movements are more complex than simply religious

---

[12] Lawrence Wright. *The Looming Tower: Al Qaeda and the Road to 9/11*. Knopf, 2006.

TABLE 9.1 Major Armed Islamist Groups

Group	Country	Branch of Islam	Actions
Islamic Republic of Iran	Iran	Shi'ite	Only Islamic revolution to successfully control a state (since 1979); held off secular Iraq in 1980s war; now attempting to build nuclear weapons.
Hezbollah	Lebanon	Shi'ite	Fought well against Israeli army in 2006 war. Previously claimed credit for driving Israel from southern Lebanon in 2000. Popular even with Sunnis.
Mahdi Army	Iraq	Shi'ite	Has clashed with U.S. forces in Iraq; major faction in Iraqi government.
Various	Iraq	Sunni	Insurgent forces have inflicted many casualties on U.S. forces in Iraq. Foreign fighters active in Iraq.
Hamas	Palestine (Gaza)	Sunni	Forces have killed hundreds of Israeli civilians. Won Palestinian elections in 2006. Controls Gaza Strip.
Islamic Courts	Somalia	Sunni	Took control of the capital and most of the country in 2006, but was ousted within months.
al Qaeda	World (Pakistan?)	Sunni	9/11 attacks and European bombings. Is among major insurgent groups in Iraq.
Taliban	Afghanistan	Sunni	Controlled Afghanistan and gave sanctuary to al Qaeda until ousted after 9/11. Regrouped in remote Pakistan and staged many attacks in 2006–2008.

Islamist guerrilla fighters/terrorists are also active in conflicts in Chechnya (Russia), Kashmir (India), Central Asia, the Philippines, Indonesia, and Europe.

conflicts; they concern power, economic relations, ethnic chauvinism, and historical empires as well.

TERRITORIAL DISPUTES

If conflicts of ideas can be intractable because of psychological and emotional factors, conflicts about material interests are somewhat easier to settle based on the reciprocity principle. Among the international conflicts that concern tangible "goods," those about territory have special importance because of the territorial nature of the state (see p. 25). Historically, military means have been the most effective way to control territory, and wars have redrawn the borders of many states. Since World War II, however, a strong norm has developed in the international system *against* trying to alter borders by force.

Because states value home territory with an almost fanatical devotion, states seldom yield territory in exchange for money or any other positive reward. Nor do states quickly forget territory that they lose involuntarily. The goal of regaining territory lost to another state is called **irredentism.** This form of nationalism often leads directly to serious interstate conflicts.[13] Because of their association with the integrity of states, territories are valued far beyond any inherent economic or strategic value they hold.

The value states place on home territory seems undiminished despite the apparent reduction in the inherent value of territory as technology has developed. Historically, territory was the basis of economic production—agriculture and the extraction of raw materials. Winning and losing wars meant gaining or losing territory, which meant increasing wealth and hence long-term power. Today, however, much more wealth derives from trade and technology than from agriculture. The costs of most territorial disputes appear to outweigh any economic benefits that the territory in question could provide. Exceptions exist, however, such as the fighting over lucrative diamond-mining areas in several African countries.

Secession efforts by a province or region to break away from an existing state are a special type of conflict over borders. Dozens of secession movements exist around the world, of varying sizes and political effectiveness, but they succeed in seceding only rarely. The existing state almost always tries to hold on to the area in question.

Wars of secession can be large and deadly, and can easily spill over international borders or draw in other countries. This spillover is particularly likely if members of an ethnic or a religious group span two sides of a border, constituting the majority group in one state and a majority in a nearby region of another state, but a minority in the other state as a whole. This pattern occurs in Bosnia-Serbia, Moldova-Russia, and India-Pakistan, for example. In some cases, secessionists want to merge their territories with the neighboring state, which amounts to redrawing the international border. International norms frown on such an outcome.

The strong international norms of sovereignty and territorial integrity treat secession movements as domestic problems that are of little concern to other states. When secession conflicts do spill over international borders, the international community tends to side with existing governments. The general principle seems to be this: "We existing states all have our own domestic problems and disaffected groups or regions, so we must stick together behind sovereignty and territorial integrity." (An exception was Kosovo's 2008 declaration of independence from Serbia, recognized by the United States and the largest EU states over the objections of Serbia, Russia, and China.) Increasingly, autonomy for a region has become a realistic compromise between secession and full control by a central government.

---

[13] Diehl, Paul F., ed. *A Road Map to War: Territorial Dimensions of International Conflict.* Vanderbilt, 1999. Diehl, Paul F., and Gary Goertz. *Territorial Changes and International Conflict.* Routledge, 1992. Ambrosio, Thomas. *Irredentism: Ethnic Conflict and International Politics.* Praeger, 2001.

Border disputes between existing states are taken more seriously by the international community, but are less common than secessionist conflicts. Because of the norm of territorial integrity, few important border conflicts remain among long-established states. At one time, huge chunks of territory were passed between states at the stroke of a pen (on a peace treaty or marriage contract). However, since the end of World War II only a minuscule amount of territory has changed hands between established states through force (this does not apply to the formation of new states and the fragmenting of old ones). Furthermore, when territorial disputes do occur between established states, they can sometimes be settled peacefully, especially when the involved territory is small. Today, only a few of the world's interstate borders are disputed. Nonetheless, those that persist are important sources of international conflict.

Several of the world's remaining interstate territorial disputes concern the control of small islands, which often provide strategic advantages, natural resources (such as offshore oil), or fishing rights. For instance, the tiny disputed *Spratly Islands* in the South China Sea, whose surrounding waters may hold substantial oil reserves, are claimed in part or in full by China, Taiwan, Vietnam, the Philippines, Malaysia, and Brunei (see Figure 9.3). All of those states except Brunei have resorted to military oc-

FIGURE 9.3   Disputed Islands

The Spratly Islands exemplify contemporary conflicts over territory and natural resources around islands. All or part of the Spratlys are claimed by China, Vietnam, Malaysia, Brunei, the Philippines, and Taiwan.

cupation at times to stake their claims, but in 2002 the countries agreed to avoid conflicts over the islands, and they remain calm.

States treat **territorial waters** near their shores as part of their national territory. Definitions of such waters are not universally agreed upon, but norms have developed in recent years, especially since the *UN Convention on the Law of the Sea (UNCLOS)* (see p. 172). Waters within three miles of shore have traditionally been recognized as territorial, but beyond that there are disputes about how far out national sovereignty extends and for what purposes. UNCLOS generally allows a 12-mile limit for shipping, and a 200-mile *exclusive economic zone (EEZ)* covering fishing and mineral rights (but allowing for free navigation by all). The EEZs together cover a third of the world's oceans (see Figure 9.4). Because of the EEZs, sovereignty over a single tiny island can now bring with it rights to as much as 100,000 square miles of surrounding ocean. But these zones overlap greatly, and shorelines do not run in straight lines; thus numerous questions of interpretation arise about how to delineate territorial and economic waters.

Airspace above a state is considered the territory of the state. To fly over a state's territory, an airplane must have the state's permission. *Outer space,* by contrast, is considered international territory like the oceans. International law does not define exactly where airspace ends and outer space begins. However, orbiting satellites fly higher than airplanes, move very fast, and cannot easily change direction to avoid overflying a country. Also, very few states can shoot down satellites. Because satellites have become useful to all the great powers as intelligence-gathering tools, and because all satellites are extremely vulnerable to attack, a norm of demilitarization of outer space has developed. No state has ever attacked the satellite of another.

Despite the many minor border disputes that continue to plague the world, most struggles to control territory do not involve changing borders. Rather, they are conflicts over which governments will control entire states. In theory, states do not interfere in each other's governance, because of the norm of sovereignty. In practice, states often have strong interests in the governments of other states and use a variety of means to influence who holds power in those states. Sometimes a state merely exerts subtle influences on another state's elections; at other times, a state supports rebel elements seeking to overthrow the second state's government. Occasionally, one state invades another in order to change its government, as the United States did in Iraq in 2003. People generally resent having foreigners choose their government for them—even if they did not like the old government—and the international community frowns on such overt violations of national sovereignty. Nonetheless, international conflicts over the control of governments—along with territorial disputes—involve core issues of the status and integrity of states, with high stakes on the line.

ECONOMIC CONFLICT

Economic competition is the most pervasive form of conflict in international relations because every sale made and every deal reached across international borders entails a resolution of conflicting interests (mainly over prices). However, such economic

Figure 9.4   State-Controlled Waters

Overfishing and similar problems of managing the "commons" of world oceans have been addressed by enclosing the most important ocean areas under the exclusive control of states. Shaded areas are within the 200-mile economic zones controlled by states under terms of the UNCLOS treaty.

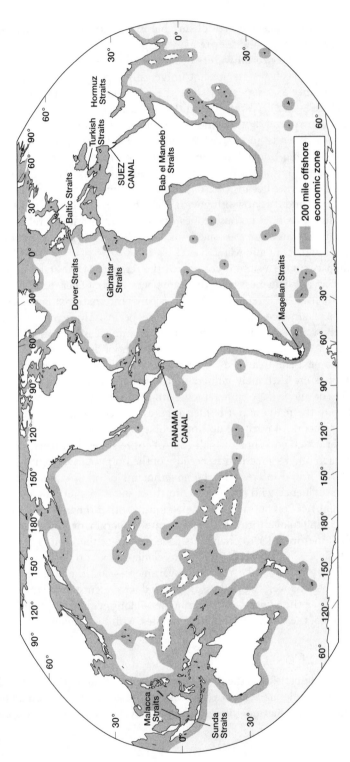

Source: Adapted from Andrew Boyd, *An Atlas of World Affairs*, 9th ed. New York: Routledge, 1992.

transactions also contain a strong element of mutual economic gain in addition to the element of conflict. Thus, economic conflicts do not usually lead to military force and war. But economic conflicts do still bear on international security in some ways.[14]

First, many states' foreign policies are influenced by *mercantilism*—a practice of centuries past in which trade and foreign economic policies were manipulated to build up a monetary surplus that could be used to finance war (see pp. 144–147). Because a trade surplus confers an advantage in international security affairs over the long run, trade conflicts have implications for international security relations. Second, the theory of **lateral pressure** holds that the economic growth of states leads to geographic expansion as they seek natural resources beyond their borders (by various means, peaceful and violent). As great powers expand their economic activities outward, their competition leads to conflicts and sometimes to war.[15] Third, *military industry*—especially for high-technology weapons such as fighter aircraft or missiles—draws governments into the middle of economic trading. Economic competition (over who profits from such sales) is interwoven with security concerns (over who gets access to the weapons). Fourth, economic competition also becomes a security issue when it concerns trade in *strategic materials* needed for military purposes, such as special minerals or alloys for aircraft production and uranium for atomic weapons. Finally, drug trafficking has become linked with security concerns because military forces participate regularly in operations against the heavily armed drug traffickers.[16] Conflicts over drugs generally concern states on one side and nonstate actors on the other, but other states can be drawn in as well.

THE WANING OF WAR

Although various kinds of conflicts remain widespread in the world, a strong trend toward fewer wars has become evident in recent years.[17] The United States is embroiled in war, but for the world as a whole the current period is one of the least warlike ever, with fewer and smaller wars than in the past.

First consider the long-term trend. In the first half of the 20th century, world wars killed tens of millions and left whole continents in ruin. In the second half of that century, during the Cold War, proxy wars killed millions, and the world feared a nuclear war that could have wiped out our species. Now, in the early 21st century, wars like those in Iraq and Sudan kill hundreds of thousands. We fear terrorist attacks that could destroy a city, but not life on the planet. Generation by generation, the world has moved forward, unevenly but inexorably, from tens of millions killed, to millions, to hundreds of thousands. This is still a large number and the impacts of war are still catastrophic.

Events in the post–Cold War era continue this long-term trend toward smaller wars. The late 1990s and early 21st century saw the termination of lingering Cold

---

[14] Mansfield, Edward D., and Brian M. Pollins. *Economic Interdependence and International Conflict: New Perspectives on an Enduring Debate*. Michigan, 2003.

[15] Choucri, Nazli, and Robert C. North. *Nations in Conflict: National Growth and International Violence*. Freeman, 1975. Choucri, Nazli, Robert C. North, and Susumu Yamakage. *The Challenge of Japan: Before World War II and After*. Routledge, 1993.

[16] Kopp, Pierre. *Political Economy of Illegal Drugs*. Routledge, 2004.

[17] Human Security Centre. *Human Security Report 2005: War and Peace in the 21st Century*. Oxford, 2006. Hewitt, J. Joseph, Jonathan Wilkenfeld, and Ted Robert Gurr, *Peace and Conflict 2008*. Paradigm, 2007.

FIGURE 9.5 Wars in Progress, June 2008

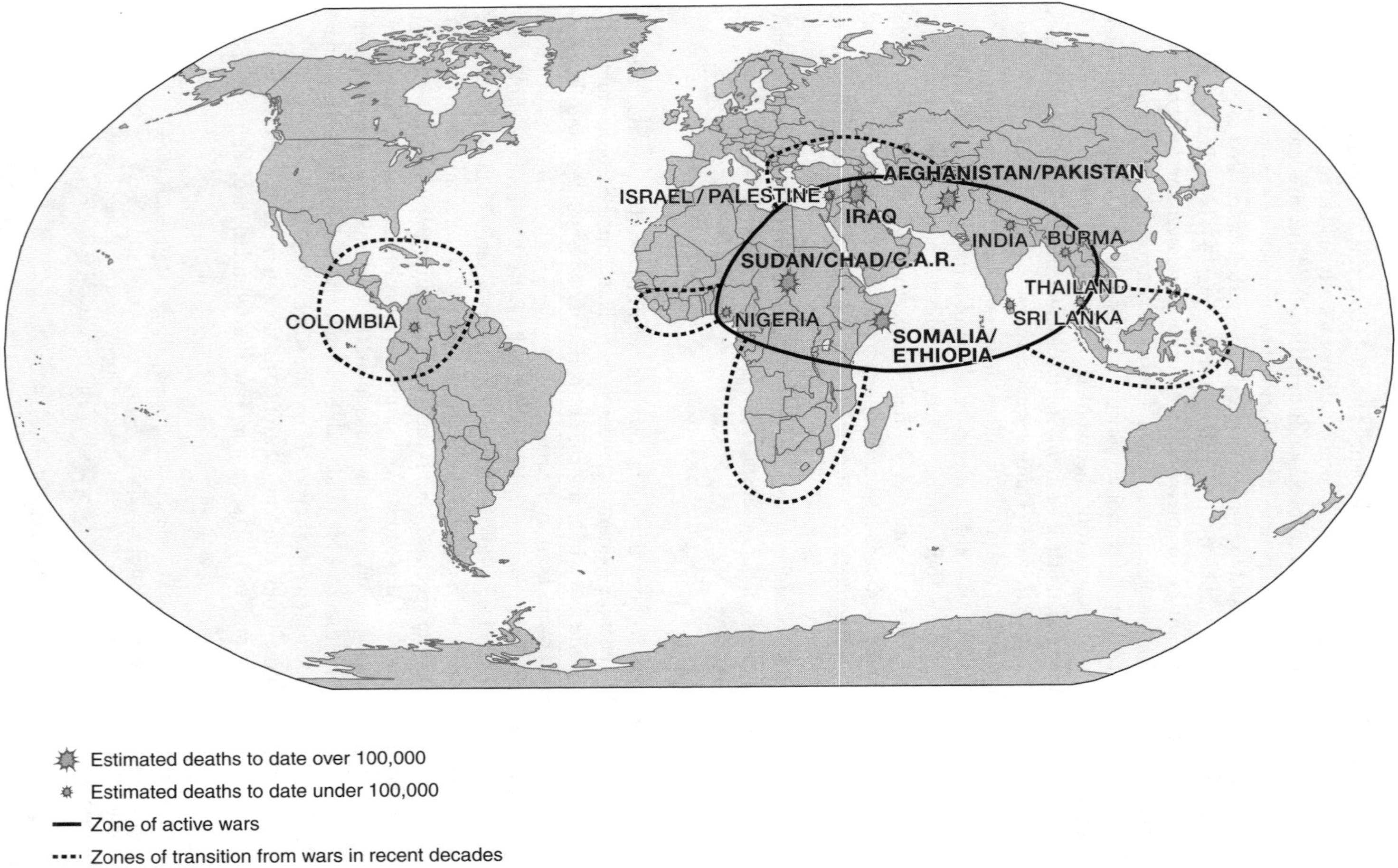
AFGHANISTAN/PAKISTAN
ISRAEL / PALESTINE
IRAQ
INDIA
BURMA
SUDAN/CHAD/C.A.R.
THAILAND
COLOMBIA
NIGERIA
SRI LANKA
SOMALIA/
ETHIOPIA
Estimated deaths to date over 100,000
Estimated deaths to date under 100,000
Zone of active wars
Zones of transition from wars in recent decades

War–era conflicts such as in Angola, Northern Ireland, Guatemala, and southern Sudan. Most of the wars that flared up after the Cold War ended, such as in Bosnia, Kosovo, Algeria, Rwanda, Burundi, and Uganda, have also come to an end. The post–Cold War era may seem a conflict-prone period in which savage wars flare up with unexpected intensity around the world, but in fact the post–Cold War era has been more peaceful than the Cold War. Latin America and Russia/Eastern Europe have nearly extinguished wars in their regions, joining a zone of peace already encompassing North America, Western Europe, Japan/Pacific, and China.

Today's most serious conflicts consist mainly of skirmishing rather than all-out battles. The last battle between heavily armed forces on both sides (with, for example, artillery, tanks, and airplanes) was the 2003 invasion of Iraq, a short and one-sided affair. Aside from Iraq, the last interstate war, between Ethiopia and Eritrea, ended in 2000. The last great-power war (with great powers fighting each other) ended more than 50 years ago. As recently as the early 1990s around a million people died in wars every year, but that rate has fallen by more than 80 percent.

Figure 9.5 shows the 11 wars in progress in 2008. The largest are in Iraq, western Sudan (Darfur), and Afghanistan. All are in the global South. All but Colombia are in a zone of active fighting (outlined on the map) spanning parts of Africa, South Asia, and the Middle East. In five smaller zones (dotted lines on the map), dozens of wars of recent decades have ended. Some of the countries in these zones still face difficult postwar years with the possibility of sliding back into larger-scale violence.[18]

CAUSES OF WAR

The Roman writer Seneca said nearly 2,000 years ago: "Of war men ask the outcome, not the cause."[19] This is not true of political scientists. They want to know why countries fight. The question of why war breaks out can be approached in different ways. Descriptive approaches, favored by historians, tend to focus narrowly on specific direct causes of the outbreak of war, which vary from one war to another.[20] For example, one could say that the assassination of Archduke Franz Ferdinand in 1914 "caused" World War I. More theoretical approaches, favored by many political scientists, tend to focus on the search for general explanations, applicable to a variety of contexts, about why wars break out.[21] For example, one can see World War I as caused by shifts in the balance of power among European states, with the assassination being only a catalyst. Broad generalizations about the causes of war have been elusive. Wars do not have a single or simple cause. Many theories about war have been put forward, but few have universal validity.

---

[18] Fortna, Virginia Page. *Peace Time: Cease-Fire Agreements and the Durability of Peace*. Princeton, 2004.

[19] Seneca, Hercules Furens. In *Seneca's Tragedies*. Vol. 1. Translated by Frank Justus Miller. Heinemann, 1917.

[20] Howard, Michael. *The Invention of Peace: Reflections on War and the International Order*. Yale, 2001. Rotberg, Robert I., and Theodore K. Rabb, eds. *The Origin and Prevention of Major Wars*. Cambridge, 1989. Blainey, Geoffrey. *Causes of War*. 3rd ed. Free Press, 1988.

[21] Vasquez, John A., ed. *What Do We Know about War?* Rowman & Littlefield, 2000. Maoz, Zeev, and Azar Gat, eds. *War in a Changing World*. Michigan, 2001. Copeland, Dale C. *The Origins of Major War*. Cornell, 2001. Van Evera, Stephen. *Causes of War: Power and the Roots of Conflict*. Cornell, 1999. Holsti, Kalevi J. *Peace and War: Armed Conflicts and International Order*. Cambridge, 1991.

Some political scientists study war from a statistical perspective, analyzing data on types of wars and the circumstances under which they occurred.[22] Current research focuses on the effects of democracy, government structure, trade, international organizations, and related factors in explaining the escalation or settlement of "militarized interstate disputes."[23]

Wars are very diverse. They arise from different situations and play different sorts of roles in bargaining over conflicts. Starting from the largest wars, we may distinguish several main categories. **Hegemonic war** is a war over control of the entire *world order*—the rules of the international system as a whole, including the role of world hegemony (see pp. 31–34). This class of wars (with variations in definition and conception) is also known as *world war*, *global war*, *general war*, or *systemic war*. The last hegemonic war was World War II. **Total war** is warfare by one state waged to conquer and occupy another. The goal is to reach the capital city and force the surrender of the government, which can then be replaced with one of the victor's choosing. **Limited war** includes military actions carried out to gain some objective short of the surrender and occupation of the enemy. Many border wars have this character: after occupying the land it wants, a state may stop short and defend its gains. *Raids* are limited wars that consist of a single action—a bombing run or a quick incursion by land. Raiding that is repeated or fuels a cycle of retaliation usually becomes a limited war or what is sometimes called *low-intensity conflict*.

Civil war refers to war between factions within a state trying to create, or prevent, a new government for the entire state or some territorial part of it.[24] (The aim may be to change the entire system of government, to merely replace the people in it, or to split a region off as a new state.) **Guerrilla war**, which includes certain kinds of civil wars, is warfare without front lines. Irregular forces operate in the midst of, and often hidden or protected by, civilian populations. The purpose is not to directly confront an enemy army but rather to harass and punish it so as to gradually limit its operation and effectively liberate territory from its control. Efforts to combat a guerrilla army—counterinsurgency—often mix military operations with political or humanitarian ones. Guerrilla wars, without fixed front lines, are extremely painful for civilians. Conventional armies fighting against guerrillas often cannot distinguish them from civilians and punish both together. Currently, all the world's wars are guerrilla (counterinsurgency) wars with a regular state army on one side and irregular, local rebels on the other.

Scholars and policy makers are paying increasing attention to the difficult transitions from war to peace in these guerrilla wars around the world—postwar reconciliation, conflict resolution, transitional governments representing opposing factions, economic reconstruction, and so forth. UN peacekeepers and NGOs focus on the linked tasks of disarmament, demobilization, and reintegration (DDR for short) of armed groups in postwar

---

[22] Wright, Quincy. *A Study of War*. Chicago, 1965 [1942]. Richardson, Lewis F. *Arms and Insecurity*. Boxwood, 1960. Midlarsky, Manus I., ed. *Handbook of War Studies II*. Michigan, 2000.

[23] Bremer, Stuart A., and Thomas R. Cusack. *The Process of War: Advancing the Scientific Study of War*. Gordon & Breach, 1995. Singer, J. David, and Paul F. Diehl, eds. *Measuring the Correlates of War*. Michigan, 1990.

[24] Collier, Paul, and Nicholas Sambanis, eds. *Understanding Civil War: Evidence and Analysis* [2 volumes]. World Bank, 2005. Walter, Barbara F., and Jack Snyder, eds. *Civil Wars, Insecurity, and Intervention*. Columbia, 1999. Walter, Barbara. *Committing to Peace: The Successful Settlement of Civil Wars*. Princeton, 2002.

society. In several countries where long internal wars in the 1990s had led to dehumanization and atrocities—notably in South Africa—new governments used **truth commissions** to help the society heal and move forward. The commission's role was to hear honest testimony from the period, to bring to light what really happened during these wars, and in exchange to offer most of the participants asylum from punishment. Sometimes international NGOs helped facilitate the process.[25]

TERRORISM

Terrorism refers to political violence that targets civilians deliberately and indiscriminately. Beyond this basic definition other criteria can be applied, but the definitions become politically motivated: one person's freedom fighter is another's terrorist. More than guerrilla warfare, terrorism is a shadowy world of faceless enemies and irregular tactics marked by extreme brutality.[26]

Traditionally, the purpose of terrorism is to demoralize a civilian population in order to use its discontent as a means of pressure for political change. Related to this is the aim of creating drama in order to gain media attention for a cause. Motives and means of terrorism vary widely, but terrorism is seldom mindless; it is usually a calculated use of violence. The primary effect of terrorism is psychological. In part the effectiveness of terrorism in capturing attention is due to the dramatic nature of the incidents, especially as shown on television news. Terrorism also gains attention because of the randomness of victims. Although only a few dozen people may be injured by a bomb left in a market, millions of people realize "it could have been me," because they, too, shop in markets. Attacks on airplanes augment this fear because many people already fear flying. Terrorism thus amplifies a small amount of power by its psychological effect on large populations; this is why it is usually a tool of the powerless.

In typical acts of terrorism, a *nonstate* actor uses attacks against *civilians* by secret *nonuniformed* forces, operating *across international borders*, as a leverage against *state* actors. In recent years, suicide bombings have become widespread, offering tactical advantage to terrorist groups and promising a direct trip to heaven for the bomber. Terrorism is often a tactic of desperation, and it almost always reflects weakness in the power position of the attacker. Attacks in recent years by al Qaeda and related organizations follow a somewhat different pattern, planned less to create fear among Western infidels than simply to kill as many of them as possible—and ultimately to touch off apocalyptic violence that al Qaeda's followers believe will bring about God's intervention. The psychological effect is aimed at Muslim populations worldwide.

Terrorists are more willing than states are to violate the norms of the international system because, unlike states, they do not have a stake in that system.[27] Conversely, when a political group gains some power or legitimacy, its use of terrorism usually diminishes. States themselves carry out acts designed to terrorize their own populations

[25] Wilson, Richard A. *The Politics of Truth and Reconciliation in South Africa: Legitimizing the Post-Apartheid State*. Cambridge, 2001.

[26] Lutz, James M. *Global Terrorism*. Routledge, 2004. Benjamin, Daniel, and Steven Simon. *The Age of Sacred Terror*. Random, 2002. Kushner, Harvey W. *Encyclopedia of Terrorism*. Sage, 2003.

[27] Booth, Ken, and Tim Dunne, eds. *Worlds in Collision: Terror and the Future of Global Order*. Palgrave, 2002.

or those of other states, but scholars tend to avoid the label "terrorism" for such acts, preferring to call it repression or war. But in today's world of undeclared war, guerrilla war, civil war, and ethnic violence, a large gray zone surrounds clear cases of terrorism.[28] Disagreements about whether terrorism included Palestinian attacks on Israel, and Pakistani attacks in Kashmir, scuttled efforts to pass a UN treaty on terrorism in 2001.

State-sponsored terrorism refers to the use of terrorist groups by states—usually under control of the state's intelligence agency—to achieve political aims. Often, state involvement in terrorism is very difficult to trace. Counterterrorism has become a sophisticated operation as well as a big business—a trend that accelerated after September 2001.[29] Lately, many private companies have expanded the business of providing security services, including antiterrorist equipment and forces, to companies and individuals doing business internationally.[30] These companies have been very busy since September 2001, as governments, companies, and individuals worldwide adapt to the new security environment that comes from a global terrorist threat.

PROLIFERATION

Proliferation is the spread of weapons of mass destruction—nuclear weapons, ballistic missiles, and chemical or biological weapons—into the hands of more actors. The implications of proliferation for international relations are difficult to predict but profound. Ballistic missiles with weapons of mass destruction remove the territorial protection offered by state borders and make each state vulnerable to others. Some realists, who believe in the basic rationality of state actions, are not so upset by this prospect, and some even welcome it. They reason that in a world where the use of military force could lead to mutual annihilation, there would be fewer wars—just as during the arms race of the Cold War, the superpowers avoided war. Other IR scholars who put less faith in the rationality of state leaders are much more alarmed by proliferation. They fear that with more and more nuclear (or chemical/biological) actors, miscalculation or accident—or fanatical terrorism—could lead to the use of weapons of mass destruction on a scale unseen since 1945.[31]

The leaders of great powers tend to side with the second group.[32] They have tried to restrict the most destructive weapons to the great powers. Proliferation erodes the great powers' advantage relative to middle powers. There is also a widespread fear that these weapons may fall into the hands of terrorists or other nonstate actors who would be immune from threats of retaliation (with no territory or cities to defend). Evidence

[28] Stern, Jessica. *Terror in the Name of God: Why Religious Militants Kill*. HarperCollins, 2003. Pape, Robert A. *Dying to Win: The Strategic Logic of Suicide Terrorism*. Random House, 2005. Bloom, Mia. *Dying to Kill: The Allure of Suicide Terror*. Columbia, 2005. Ross, Jeffrey Ian. *Political Terrorism: An Interdisciplinary Approach*. Lang, 2006.

[29] Young, Mitchell, ed. *The War on Terrorism*. Greenhaven, 2003.

[30] Avant, Deborah. *The Market for Force: The Consequences of Privatizing Security*. Cambridge, 2005.

[31] Sagan, Scott D., and Kenneth N. Waltz. *The Spread of Nuclear Weapons: A Debate*. Norton, 1995.

[32] Schrafstetter, Susanna, and Stephen Twigge. *Avoiding Armageddon: Europe, the United States, and the Struggle for Nuclear Nonproliferation, 1945–1970*. Praeger, 2004.

captured during the 2001 war in Afghanistan showed that the al Qaeda organization was trying to obtain weapons of mass destruction and would be willing to use them. In 2007, two teams of armed assailants broke into the South African nuclear facility where atomic bombs had once been designed and produced. Lax security at the vast, far-flung former Soviet nuclear complex increased fears that fissionable materials could reach terrorists.[33] However, states that sell technology with proliferation potential can make money doing so. This is another international collective goods problem.

Nuclear proliferation could occur simply by a state or nonstate actor's buying (or stealing) one or more nuclear weapons or the components to build one. The means to prevent this include covert intelligence, tight security measures, and safeguards to prevent a stolen weapon from being used. A larger-scale but more limited form of nuclear proliferation is states' development of nuclear complexes to produce their own nuclear weapons on an ongoing basis.[34] Here larger numbers of weapons are involved and strong potentials exist for arms races in regional conflicts and rivalries—between Israel and the Arab states,[35] Iran and its Arab neighbors, India and Pakistan, the two Koreas,[36] and possibly Taiwan and China.

The **Non-Proliferation Treaty (NPT)** of 1968 created a framework for controlling the spread of nuclear materials and expertise. The International Atomic Energy Agency (IAEA), a UN agency based in Vienna, is charged with inspecting the nuclear power industry in member states to prevent secret military diversions of nuclear materials. However, in the 1990s, Pakistan's top nuclear scientist sold bomb kits with low-grade uranium, enrichment centrifuges, and bomb designs to Libya, Iran, and North Korea. A number of potential nuclear states (such as Israel) have not signed the NPT, and even states that have signed may sneak around its provisions by keeping some facilities secret (as Iraq and Iran did). In 2006, the UN Security Council imposed mild sanctions on Iran for its uranium enrichment program. Iran insisted on its right to enrich uranium for what it called peaceful purposes.

A number of middle powers and two great powers (Japan and Germany) have the potential to make nuclear weapons but have chosen not to do so. The reasons for deciding against "going nuclear" include norms against using nuclear weapons, fears of retaliation, and practical constraints including cost. At present, nuclear states are the "big five," Israel, India, and Pakistan (with dozens of warheads each, and growing), and North Korea (with perhaps a half dozen).

Overall, the emerging problems of proliferation and terrorism add to the enduring list of more conventional means by which international actors pursue their interests in situations of conflict.

---

[33] Allison, Graham. *Nuclear Terrorism: The Ultimate Preventable Catastrophe*. Times, 2004.

[34] Perkovich, George. *India's Nuclear Bomb: The Impact on Global Proliferation*. California, 1999. Lewis, John Wilson, and Xus Litai. *China Builds the Bomb*. Stanford, 1988.

[35] Cohen, Avner. *Israel and the Bomb*. Columbia, 1998. Maoz, Zeev. *Defending the Holy Land: A Critical Analysis of Israel's Security and Foreign Policy*. Michigan, 2006.

[36] Sigal, Leon V. *Disarming Strangers: Nuclear Diplomacy with North Korea*. Princeton, 1999. Cha, Victor D., and David C. Kang. *Nuclear North Korea: A Debate on Engagement Strategies*. Columbia, 2003.

CHAPTER 10

THEORIES OF TRADE

LIBERALISM AND MERCANTILISM

International trade amounts to about a sixth of the total economic activity in the world. More than $11 trillion worth of trade crosses international borders each year. This is a very large number, nearly 10 times the world's military spending, for example. The great volume of international trade reflects the fact that trade is profitable. The role of trade in the economy varies somewhat from one nation to another, but overall, it is at least as important in the global South as in the industrialized North. Trade is not just economic but also political. It crosses state-defined borders, is regulated by states that are pressured by interest groups, and occurs within trade regimes maintained by and negotiated among states. Scholars of *international political economy (IPE)* study the politics of international economic activities.[1]

Two major approaches within IPE differ on their views of trade.[2] One approach, called **mercantilism,** generally shares with realism the belief that each state must protect its own interests at the expense of others—not relying on international organizations to create a framework for mutual gains. Mercantilists therefore emphasize relative power (as do realists): what matters is not so much a state's absolute amount of well-being as its position relative to rival states.[3]

In addition, mercantilism (like realism) holds that the importance of economic transactions lies in their implications for the military. States worry about relative wealth and trade because these can be translated directly into military power. Thus, although military power may not necessarily be an effective source of leverage in economic negotiations, mercantilists believe that the outcome of economic negotiations matters for military power.

Liberalism, an alternative approach, generally shares the assumption of anarchy but does not see this condition as precluding extensive cooperation to realize common

---

[1] Gilpin, Robert. *Global Political Economy: Understanding the International Economic Order.* Princeton, 2001. Frieden, Jeffry A., and David A. Lake. *International Political Economy: Perspectives on Global Power and Wealth.* 4th ed. St. Martin's, 2000. Lipson, Charles, and Benjamin J. Cohen, eds. *Theory and Structure in International Political Economy.* MIT, 1999. Peterson, V. Spike. *A Critical Rewriting of Global Political Economy: Integrating Reproductive, Productive, and Virtual Economies.* Routledge, 2003. Yarbrough, Beth V., and Robert M. Yarbrough. *The World Economy: Trade and Finance.* 7th ed. South-Western, 2006.

[2] Crane, George T., and Abla M. Amawi, eds. *The Theoretical Evolution of International Political Economy: A Reader.* 2nd ed. Oxford, 1997.

[3] Grieco, Joseph, and John Ikenberry. *State Power and World Markets: The International Political Economy.* Norton, 2002.

gains.[4] It holds that by building international organizations, institutions, and norms, states can mutually benefit from economic exchanges. It matters little to liberals whether one state gains more or less than another—just whether the state's wealth is increasing in *absolute* terms. This concept parallels the general liberal idea that IOs allow states to relax their narrow, short-term pursuit of self-interest in order to realize longer-term mutual interests (see pp. 53–55). Liberalism is the dominant approach in Western economics, though more so in *microeconomics* (the study of firms and households) than in *macroeconomics* (the study of national economies). Marxism is often treated as a third theoretical/ideological approach to IPE (see Chapter 7).

Most international economic exchanges (as well as security relationships) contain some element of mutual interests—joint gains that can be realized through cooperation—and some element of conflicting interests. Game theorists call this a "mixed interest" game. For example, in the game of Chicken (see p. 41), the two drivers share an interest in avoiding a head-on collision, yet their interests diverge in that one can be a hero only if the other is a chicken. In international trade, even when two states both benefit from a trade (a shared interest), one or the other will benefit more (a conflicting interest). Liberalism emphasizes the shared interests in economic exchanges, whereas mercantilism emphasizes the conflicting interests. For liberals, the most important goal of economic policy is to create a maximum of total wealth by achieving optimal *efficiency* (maximizing output, minimizing waste). For mercantilists, the most important goal is to create the most favorable possible *distribution* of wealth (see Figure 10.1).

FIGURE 10.1   Joint and Individual Benefits

Any deal struck, such as at point A, yields certain benefits to each actor (dotted lines). Joint benefits are maximized at the Pareto-optimal frontier, but the distribution of those benefits, as between points B and C (both of which are better than A for both actors), is a matter for bargaining. Liberalism is more concerned with joint benefits, mercantilism more with the relative distribution.

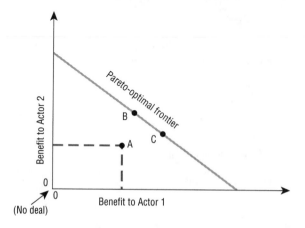

[4] Neff, Stephen C. *Friends but No Allies: Economic Liberalism and the Law of Nations.* Columbia, 1990. Ward, Benjamin. *The Ideal Worlds of Economics: Liberal, Radical, and Conservative Economic World Views.* Basic, 1979.

Liberalism views government's most useful role as one of noninterference in economics except to regulate markets in order to help them function efficiently (and to create infrastructure such as roads). Politics, in this view, should serve the interests of economic efficiency. For example, governments should support free trade, which allows global markets to maximize wealth. For mercantilists, by contrast, economics should serve politics: the creation of wealth underlies state power. Because power is relative, trade is desirable only when the distribution of benefits favors one's own state over rivals.[5] Mercantilism achieved prominence several hundred years ago, and Britain used trade to rise in relative power in the international system around the 18th century. At that time mercantilism meant specifically the creation of a trade surplus in order to stockpile money in the form of precious metal (gold and silver), which could then be used to buy military capabilities (mercenary armies and weapons) in time of war.[6] Mercantilism declined in the 19th century as Britain decided it had more to gain from free trade than from protectionism. It returned as a major approach in the period between World Wars I and II, when liberal global trading relations broke down.

Mercantilists favor creating a positive balance of trade (trade surplus). The **balance of trade** is the value of a state's imports relative to its exports (see Figure 10.2). The balance of trade must ultimately be reconciled, one way or another. In the short term, a state can trade for a few years at a deficit and then a few years at a surplus. The imbalances are carried on the national accounts as a kind of loan. But a trade deficit that persists for years becomes a problem for the state. With a trade surplus, rather than be-

FIGURE 10.2 **Balance of Trade**

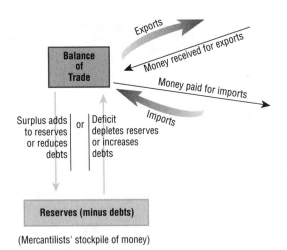

(Mercantilists' stockpile of money)

---

[5] Grieco, Joseph M. *Cooperation among Nations: Europe, America, and Non-Tariff Barriers to Trade*. Cornell, 1990. Gowa, Joanne. *Allies, Adversaries, and International Trade*. Princeton, 1993. Hirschman, Albert O. *National Power and the Structure of Foreign Trade*. California, 1945.
[6] Coulomb, Fanny. *Economic Theories of Peace and War*. Routledge, 2004.

ing unable to find the money it might need to cope with a crisis or fight a war, the state sits on a pile of money representing potential power. Such a strategy is attuned to realism's emphasis on relative power and is an example of the dominance principle. For one state to have a trade surplus, another must have a deficit.

COMPARATIVE ADVANTAGE

The overall success of liberal economics is due to the substantial gains that can be realized through trade.[7] These gains result from the **comparative advantage** that different states enjoy in producing different goods (a concept pioneered by economists Adam Smith and David Ricardo 200 years ago). States differ in their abilities to produce certain goods because of differences in natural resources, labor force characteristics, technology, and other such factors. In order to maximize the overall creation of wealth, each state should specialize in producing the goods for which it has a comparative advantage and then trade for goods that another state is better at producing. Of course, the costs of transportation and of processing the information in the trade (called *transaction costs*) must be included in the costs of producing an item. But frequently both of these are low relative to the differences in the cost of producing items in different locations.

Two commodities of great importance in the world are oil and cars. It is much cheaper to produce oil (or another energy source) in Saudi Arabia than in Japan, and much cheaper to produce cars in Japan than in Saudi Arabia. Japan needs oil to run its industry (including its car industry), and Saudi Arabia needs cars to travel its vast territory (including reaching its remote oil wells). Even with shipping and transaction costs, shipping Japanese cars to Saudi Arabia and Saudi oil to Japan saves a huge amount of money, compared to the costs if each were self-sufficient.

A state need not have an absolute advantage (that is, be the most efficient producer in the world) in producing one kind of good in order to make specialization pay. It need only specialize in producing goods that are lower in cost than other goods relative to world market prices. Imagine that Japan discovered a way to produce synthetic oil using the same mix of labor and capital that it now uses to produce cars, and that this synthetic oil could be produced a bit more cheaply than what it costs Saudi Arabia to produce oil, but that Japan could still produce cars *much* more cheaply than can Saudi Arabia. From a strictly economic point of view, Japan should keep producing cars (its comparative advantage) and not divert capital and labor to make synthetic oil (where it has only a slight advantage). The extra profits Japan would make from exporting more cars would more than compensate for the slightly higher price it would pay to import oil.

Thus, international trade generally expands the Pareto-optimal frontier (see Figure 10.1 on p. 145) by increasing the overall efficiency of production. Free trade allocates global resources to states that have the greatest comparative advantage in producing

[7] Lake, David A., ed. *The International Political Economy of Trade*. Elgar, 1993. Odell, John S., and Thomas D. Willett, eds. *International Trade Policies: Gains from Exchange between Economics and Political Science*. Michigan, 1990. Irwin, Douglas. *Against the Tide: An Intellectual History of Free Trade*. Princeton, 1996.

each kind of commodity. As a result, prices are both lower overall and more consistent worldwide. Increasingly, production is oriented to the world market.

Trade is not without drawbacks, however, especially when seen from a political rather than purely economic vantage point. First, long-term benefits may incur short-term costs. When a state begins to import goods that it had been producing domestically, its economy may be disrupted; workers may need to retrain and find new jobs, and capital may not be easy to convert to new uses. Furthermore, the benefits and costs of trade tend not to be evenly distributed *within* a state. Some industries or communities may benefit at the expense of others. For example, if a U.S. manufacturing company moves its factory to Mexico to take advantage of cheaper labor there and exports its goods back to the United States, the workers at the old U.S. factory lose their jobs, but U.S. consumers enjoy cheaper goods. The costs of such a move fall heavily on a few workers, but the benefits are spread thinly across many consumers. This kind of unequal distribution of costs and benefits often creates political problems for free trade even when the *overall* economic benefits outweigh the costs. One is far more likely to find worker or industry interest groups (see p. 156) forming to fight the concentrated costs (losing jobs) rather than consumer groups forming to promote diffuse benefits (slightly cheaper goods).

Workers in industrialized countries, in industries that face increasing competition from low-wage countries in the global South—such as steel, automobiles, electronics, and clothing—are among those adversely affected by free trade. Not surprisingly, labor unions have been among the strongest political opponents of unfettered trade expansion. Human-rights NGOs have joined labor unions in pushing for trade agreements to include requirements for improving working conditions in low-wage countries; these could include laws regarding a minimum wage, child labor, and worker safety. Environmental groups also have actively opposed the unrestricted expansion of trade, which they see as undermining environmental laws in industrialized countries and promoting environmentally harmful practices worldwide.

POLITICAL INTERFERENCE IN MARKETS

A free and efficient market requires a fairly large number of buyers looking for the same item and a large number of sellers supplying it. It also requires that participants have fairly complete information about the other participants and transactions in the market. Also, the willingness of participants to deal with each other should not be distorted by personal (or political) preferences but should be governed only by price and quality considerations. Failures to meet these various conditions are called *market imperfections:* they reduce efficiency (to the dismay of liberal economists). Most political intrusions into economic transactions are market imperfections. International trade occurs more often at world market prices than does domestic economic exchange. No world government owns industries, provides subsidies, or regulates prices.

Nonetheless, world markets are often affected by politics. When states are the principal actors in international economic affairs, the number of participants is often small. When there is just one supplier of an item—a *monopoly*—the supplier can set the price quite high. An *oligopoly* is a monopoly shared by just a few large sellers—often allowing for tacit or explicit coordination to force the price up. For example,

OPEC members agree to limit oil production to keep prices up. *Foreign* governments have little power to break up monopolies. Another common market imperfection in international trade is *corruption* (see p. 188). *Taxation* is yet another political influence. For instance, a government may keep taxes low on foreign companies in hopes of attracting them to locate and invest in the country. Taxes applied to international trade itself, called *tariffs*, are a frequent source of international conflict (see p. 150).

Political interference in free markets is most explicit when governments apply *sanctions* against economic interactions of certain kinds or between certain actors. Enforcing sanctions is always a difficult task, because actors have a financial incentive to break the sanctions through black markets or other means.[8] Without broad multilateral support for international sanctions, they generally fail. Refusing to participate in mutually profitable economic trade often harms oneself more than the target of one's actions, unless nearly all other states follow suit (note that sanctions enforcement is a collective goods problem).

One obvious way to avoid becoming dependent on other states, especially for a weak state whose trading partners would tend to be more powerful, is to avoid trading and instead to try to produce everything it needs by itself. Such a strategy is called *self-reliance* or **autarky.** But it has proven ineffective. A self-reliant state pays a very high cost to produce goods for which it does not have a comparative advantage. As other states cooperate among themselves to maximize their joint creation of wealth, the relative power of the autarkic state in the international system tends to fall.

During the Cold War, the economies of the Soviet Union and Eastern Europe stood apart from the capitalist world economy. As **centrally planned** (or *command*) economies, they banned private property in favor of state ownership. Political authorities set prices and decided on quotas for production and consumption of each commodity according to a long-term plan. The Soviet economy had some notable successes in rapidly industrializing in the 1930s, surviving the German assault in the 1940s, and developing world-class aerospace and military production capabilities in the 1950s and 1960s. But it stagnated under the weight of bureaucracy, ideological rigidity, environmental destruction, corruption, and high military spending. Now the former Soviet republics and Eastern Europe are **transitional economies,** trying to make the change to a market-based economy connected to the world capitalist economy.[9]

PROTECTIONISM

Although few states pursue strategies of autarky, many states try to manipulate international trade to strengthen one or more domestic industries and shelter them from world markets. Such policies are broadly known as **protectionism**—that is, protection of

---

[8] Drezner, Daniel W. *The Sanctions Paradox: Economic Statecraft and International Relations*. Cambridge, 1999. O'Sullivan, Meghan L. *Shrewd Sanctions: Statecraft and State Sponsors of Terrorism*. Brookings, 2003. Lopez, George A., and David Cortwright. *Smart Sanctions: Targeting Economic Statecraft*. Rowman & Littlefield, 2002. Martin, Lisa L. *Coercive Cooperation: Explaining Multilateral Economic Sanctions*. Princeton, 1992.
[9] Gustafson, Thane. *Capitalism Russian-Style*. Cambridge, 1999. Frye, Timothy. *Brokers and Bureaucrats: Building Market Institutions in Russia*. Michigan, 2000.

domestic industries from international competition. Although this term encompasses a variety of trade policies arising from various motivations, all are contrary to economic liberalism.

A state's *motivation* to protect domestic industry can arise from several sources. Often governments simply cater to the political demands of important domestic industries and interests, regardless of the overall national interest. An industry may lobby or give campaign contributions in order to win special tax breaks, subsidies, or restrictions on competing imports (see pp. 75–76). States often attempt to protect an *infant industry* as it starts up in the state for the first time, until it can compete on world markets (considered a relatively legitimate reason for temporary protection). In a number of poor states, the *textile* trade has been a protected infant industry (adding value without heavy capital requirements), although textile tariffs have now been eliminated.[10] Another motivation for protection is to give a domestic industry breathing room when market conditions shift or new competitors arrive on the scene. Sometimes domestic industry requires time to adapt and can emerge a few years later in a healthy condition. Yet another motivation is the protection of industry considered vital to national security, such as weapons production.

Finally, protection may be motivated by a defensive effort to ward off predatory practices by foreign companies or states. *Predatory* generally refers to efforts to unfairly capture a large share of world markets, or even a near-monopoly, so that eventually the predator can raise prices without fearing competition. Most often these efforts entail **dumping** products in foreign markets at prices below the minimum level necessary to make a profit. Dumping loses money in the short term but can lead to dominance of a market, with higher profits in the long run.

Just as there are several motivations for protectionism, so too governments use several tools to implement this goal. The simplest is a **tariff** or *duty*—a tax imposed on certain types of imported goods (usually as a percentage of their value) as they enter the country. Tariffs not only restrict imports but also can be an important source of state revenues. If a state is going to engage in protectionism, international norms favor tariffs as the preferred method of protection because they are straightforward and not hidden (see pp. 151–152). Most states maintain a long and complex schedule of tariffs, based on thousands of categories and subcategories of goods organized by industry.

Other means to discourage imports are **nontariff barriers** to trade. *Quotas* are ceilings on how many goods of a certain kind can be imported. The extreme version is a flat prohibition against importing a certain type of good (or goods from a certain country). Third (after tariffs and quotas), *subsidies* to a domestic industry allow it to lower its prices without losing money. Such subsidies are extensive in, but not limited to, state-owned industries. Subsidies can be funneled to industries in a variety of ways. A state can give tax breaks to an industry struggling to get established or facing strong foreign competition. It can make loans (or guarantee private loans) on favorable terms to companies in a favored industry. Sometimes governments buy goods from domestic producers at high guaranteed prices and resell them on world markets at lower prices. Fourth, *restrictions* and *regulations* make it hard to distribute and market a product even when it

---

[10] Aggarwal, Vinod K. *Liberal Protectionism: The International Politics of Organized Textile Trade*. California, 1985.

can be imported. Environmental and labor regulations can function as nontariff barriers as well. This is a significant source of controversy in the WTO. Fifth, when a state *nationalizes* an entire industry, such as oil production or banking, foreign competition is shut out.

Protectionism has both positive and negative effects on an economy, most often helping producers but hurting consumers. Even producers can be hurt if domestic industry uses protection to avoid needed improvements and therefore remains inefficient and uncompetitive—especially if protection continues over many years. But although it violates liberal principles, temporary protectionism can have a stabilizing effect under certain conditions.

THE WORLD TRADE ORGANIZATION

The **World Trade Organization (WTO)** is a global, multilateral IGO that promotes, monitors, and adjudicates international trade.[11] The WTO is the successor organization to the **General Agreement on Tariffs and Trade (GATT),** which was created in 1947 to facilitate freer trade on a multilateral basis. The GATT was more of a negotiating framework than an administrative institution. It did not actually regulate trade. Before the GATT, proposals for a stronger institutional agency had been rejected because of U.S. fears that overregulation would stifle free trade. Although the GATT was a regime with little institutional infrastructure until the mid-1990s, it did help arbitrate trade disputes, clarifying the rules and helping states observe them. In 1995, the GATT became the WTO. The GATT agreements on manufactured goods were subsumed into the WTO framework and then extended to include trade in services and intellectual property.

The WTO has some powers of enforcement and an international bureaucracy (more than 600 people), which monitors trade policies and practices in each member state and adjudicates disputes among members. However, as with most international institutions, the WTO's power over states is limited. A growing public backlash against free trade reflects uneasiness about the potential power of a foreign and secretive organization to force changes in democratically enacted national laws. But the WTO is the central international institution governing trade and therefore one that almost all countries want to participate in and develop.

Over time, the membership of the WTO has grown. By 2008, it had 152 member states—almost all of the world's major trading states except Russia (expected to join soon). After more than a decade of negotiations, China joined in 2001. The current members demand, as a condition of membership, liberalization of the trading practices of would-be members. These new practices have had major effects on China's economic and political development (see pp. 183–186).

The WTO framework is based on the principle of reciprocity—that one state's lowering of trade barriers to another should be matched in return. It also uses the concept of nondiscrimination, embodied in the **most-favored nation (MFN)** concept,

---

[11] Hoekman, Bernard, and Michel Kostecki. *The Political Economy of the World Trading System: From GATT to WTO.* 2nd ed. Oxford, 1999.

which says that trade restrictions imposed by a WTO member on its most-favored trading partner must be applied equally to all WTO members. If Australia applies a 20 percent tariff on French auto parts, it must not apply a 40 percent tariff on Japanese auto parts. Thus, the WTO does not get rid of barriers to trade altogether but equalizes them in a global framework to create a level playing field for all member states. States can still protect their industries but cannot play favorites among their trading partners. States may also extend MFN status to others that are not WTO members, as the United States did with China before it joined the WTO.

An exception to the MFN system is the **Generalized System of Preferences (GSP),** dating from the 1970s, by which industrialized states give trade concessions to poor countries to help economic development. Preferences amount to a promise by rich states to allow imports from poor ones under lower tariffs than those imposed under MFN.[12]

The WTO continues the GATT's role as a negotiating forum for multilateral trade agreements that lower trade barriers on a fair and reciprocal basis. These detailed and complex agreements specify the commitments of various states and regions to lower certain trade barriers by certain amounts on fixed schedules. Almost every commitment entails domestic political costs, because domestic industries lose protection against foreign competition. Even when other states agree to make similar commitments in other areas, lowering of trade barriers is often hard for national governments. As a result, negotiations on these multilateral agreements are long and difficult. Typically they stretch on for several years or more in a *round of negotiations*; after it is completed, the members begin a new round. Among the five rounds of GATT negotiations from 1947 to 1995, the **Uruguay Round** that started in 1986 was most difficult. As the round dragged on year after year, participants said the GATT should be renamed the "General Agreement to Talk and Talk." A successful conclusion to the round would add more than $100 billion to the world economy annually. But that money was a collective good, to be enjoyed both by states that made concessions in the final negotiations and by states that did not. Agreement was finally reached in late 1994.

Agricultural trade is politically more sensitive than trade in manufactured goods and was seriously addressed only in the Uruguay Round.[13] Trade in services, such as banking and insurance, is another current major focus of the WTO. Such trade approached one-quarter of the total value of world trade in the 1990s. Trade in telecommunications is a related area of interest. In 1997, 70 states (negotiating through the WTO) agreed on a treaty to allow telecommunications companies to enter each other's markets.

In 2001, trade ministers meeting in Doha, Qatar, agreed to launch a new round of trade negotiations, the **Doha Round.** The issues under negotiation included agriculture, services, industrial products, intellectual property, WTO rules (including how to handle antidumping cases), dispute settlement, and some trade and environmental questions.

---

[12] Hirata, Akira, and Ippei Yamazawa, eds. *Trade Policies towards Developing Countries*. St. Martin's, 1993. Glover, David J., and Diana Tussie, eds. *The Developing Countries in World Trade: Policies and Bargaining Strategies*. Rienner, 1993.

[13] Avery, William P., ed. *World Agriculture and the GATT*. Rienner, 1992.

The major sticking point has been the resistance of industrialized countries to cutting their agricultural subsidies, which shut out poor countries' agricultural exports. WTO members failed to conclude the Doha Round before President Bush's congressional "fast-track" authorization (which commits Congress to vote on trade deals in full without amending them) expired in 2007. Nonetheless, efforts to reach a deal continued in 2008.

In general, states continue to participate in the WTO because the benefits, in terms of global wealth creation, outweigh the costs, in terms of harm to domestic industries or painful adjustments in national economies. States try to change the rules in their favor during the rounds of negotiations (never with complete success), and between rounds they try to evade the rules in minor ways. But the overall benefits are too great to jeopardize by nonparticipation or by allowing frequent trade wars to occur.

BILATERAL AND REGIONAL AGREEMENTS

Although the WTO provides an overall framework for multilateral trade in a world-wide market, most international trade is governed by more specific agreements—bilateral trade agreements and regional free-trade areas.

Bilateral treaties covering trade are reciprocal arrangements to lower barriers to trade between two states. Usually they are fairly specific, dealing with particular products and trade barriers. Part of the idea behind the GATT/WTO was to strip away the maze of bilateral agreements on trade and simplify the system of tariffs and preferences. This effort has only partially succeeded. Bilateral trade agreements continue to play an important role. They have the advantages of reducing the collective goods problem inherent in multilateral negotiations and facilitating reciprocity as a means to achieve cooperation.[14] When WTO negotiations bog down, bilateral agreements can keep trade momentum going. Because most states have only a few most-important trading partners, a few bilateral agreements can go a long way.

In regional free-trade areas, groups of neighboring states agree to remove the entire structure of trade barriers (or most of it) within their area. The creation of a regional trade agreement allows a group of states to cooperate in increasing their wealth without waiting for the rest of the world. In fact, from an economic nationalist perspective, a free-trade area can enhance a region's power at the expense of other areas of the world. The most important free-trade area is connected with the European Union but with a somewhat larger membership. Because Europe contains a number of small industrialized states living close together, the creation of a single integrated market allows these states to gain the economic advantages that come inherently to a large state such as the United States. The European free-trade experiment has been a great success overall.

The United States, Canada, and Mexico signed the **North American Free Trade Agreement (NAFTA)** in 1994, following a 1988 U.S.-Canadian free-trade agreement.[15] In NAFTA's first decade, U.S. imports from both Mexico and Canada more than doubled. Initially, Mexico's currency dropped drastically relative to the dollar in 1994–1995. U.S.

---

[14] Oye, Kenneth A. *Economic Discrimination and Political Exchange: World Political Economy in the 1930s and 1980s.* Princeton, 1992.

[15] Hakim, Peter, and Robert E. Litan, eds. *The Future of North American Integration: Beyond NAFTA.* Brookings, 2002.

opponents of NAFTA, including various U.S. labor unions, criticized the low wages and poor labor laws in Mexico, which they feared would drag down U.S. labor standards. Environmentalists similarly criticized Mexico's lax environmental laws (relative to the United States) and saw NAFTA as giving U.S. corporations license to pollute by moving south of the border. But over the long run, neither the great benefits predicted by NAFTA supporters nor the disasters predicted by opponents materialized.

Politicians in North and South America have long spoken of creating a single free-trade area in the Western Hemisphere, from Alaska to Argentina—the *Free Trade Area of the Americas (FTAA)*. FTAA negotiations began in 2003 with a target date of 2005 but the talks stalled. Similarly, efforts to create a free-trade area in Asia began in the late 1980s but moved slowly. Unlike the European and North American arrangements, an Asian bloc would include very different kinds of states—rich and poor, democracies, dictatorships, and communist states. If the concept succeeds, it will form a third great regional trading bloc after the European Union and the North American (potentially all-American) free-trade area.

If regional free-trade areas gain strength, the WTO may be weakened. The more that states are able to meet the political requirements of economic growth through bilateral and regional agreements, the less they may depend on the worldwide agreements developed through the WTO. Indeed, the industrialized countries could potentially divide into three competing trading blocs, each internally integrated but not very open to the other two blocs. Regional free-trade areas in Europe and North America, and perhaps in Asia in the future, raise the possibility of trading zones practicing liberalism inwardly and mercantilism outwardly. However, as information technologies link the world across space, the integration of global markets seems likely to gain the upper hand.

INDUSTRIES AND INTEREST GROUPS

Not all international trade organizations exist to promote free trade. A **cartel** is an association of producers or consumers, or both, of a certain product—formed to manipulate its price on the world market. It is an unusual but interesting form of trade regime. Most often producers and not consumers form cartels, because there are usually fewer producers than consumers, and it seems possible for them to coordinate their actions so as to keep prices high. Cartels can use a variety of means to affect prices; the most effective is to coordinate limits on production by each member so as to lower the supply, relative to demand, of the good.

The most prominent cartel in the international economy is the **Organization of Petroleum Exporting Countries (OPEC)**. Its member states together control about 40 percent of the world's oil production, enough to significantly affect the price. (A cartel need not hold a monopoly on production of a good to influence its price.) At OPEC's peak of strength in the 1970s, the proportion was even higher. As Table 10.1 shows, Saudi Arabia is by far the largest oil exporter and therefore can single-handedly influence the price of oil worldwide, giving it a unique position in the world economy. OPEC illustrates the potential that a cartel creates for serious collective goods problems. Individual members of OPEC can (and do) cheat a bit by exceeding their production quotas while still enjoying the collective good of high oil prices. The collective good breaks down when too many members exceed their quotas, as has happened repeatedly to OPEC. Then world oil prices drop. Saudi Arabia's dominant position provides a form of hegemonic stability within the cartel. Saudi Arabia can take up the slack from some cheating in OPEC (cutting back its own production) and keep prices up. Or if too many OPEC members cheat on their quotas, it can punish them by flooding the market with oil and driving prices down until the other OPEC members collectively come to their senses.

TABLE 10.1 OPEC Members and Oil Production, February 2008

Member State	Millions of Barrels/Day
Saudi Arabia	9.2
Iran	3.9
Kuwait	2.6
United Arab Emirates	2.6
Venezuela	2.4
Iraq	2.4
Nigeria	2.1
Angola	1.9
Libya	1.8
Algeria	1.4
Indonesia	0.9
Qatar	0.8
Ecuador[a]	0.5
Total OPEC	32.2
Percent of World	40%

[a]Ecuador re-joined OPEC in 2007 after suspending its membership in 1992.

Note: Major oil exporters not in OPEC include Russia, Kazakhstan, Mexico, China, Britain, and Norway. Gabon left OPEC in 1995. The United States, until several decades ago a major oil exporter, is now a major importer.

Source: Data adapted from Middle East Economic Survey. www.mees.com/Energy_Tables/crude-oil.htm.

Consumers usually do not form cartels. However, for a few commodities that are subject to large price fluctuations on world markets—detrimental to both producers and consumers—joint producer-consumer cartels have been formed. In order to keep prices stable, producing and consuming states use the cartel to coordinate the overall supply and demand globally. Such cartels exist for coffee, several minerals, and some other products.[16]

In general, the idea of cartels runs counter to liberal economics because cartels are deliberate efforts to distort free markets. However, in occasional cases in which free markets create large fluctuations in price, the creation of a cartel can bring some order to chaos and result in greater efficiency. Cartels usually are not as powerful as market forces in determining overall world price levels: too many producers and suppliers

---

[16] Bates, Robert H. *Open-Economy Politics: The Political Economy of the World Coffee Trade.* Princeton, 1997.

exist, and too many substitute goods can replace ones that become too expensive, for a cartel to corner the market.

Although cartels operate in only a few industries, domestic industries and other domestic political actors often seek to influence a state's foreign economic policies (see pp. 75–76).[17] These pressures do not always favor protectionism. Industries that are advanced and competitive in world markets often try to get their governments to adopt free-trade policies. Means to influence foreign economic policy include lobbying, forming interest groups, paying bribes, and even encouraging coups. Actors include industry-sponsored groups, companies, labor unions, and individuals. Within an industry, such efforts usually work in a common direction because, despite competition among companies and between management and labor, all share common interests regarding the trade policies. However, a different industry may be pushing in a different direction. In many countries, government not only responds to industry influence, but also works actively with industries to promote their growth and tailor trade policy to their needs.[18] Such **industrial policy** is especially common in states where one or two industries are crucial to the entire economy (and of course where states own industries directly).[19] Interest groups not organized along industry lines, such as environmentalists for example, also have particular interests in state trade policies.

Intellectual property rights are a contentious area of trade negotiations. These are the rights of creators of books, films, computer software, and similar products to receive royalties when their products are sold. It is technically easy and cheap to copy such works and sell them in violation of the copyright, patent, or trademark. Infringement of intellectual property rights is widespread in many poor countries, on products such as DVDs and prescription drugs. In response, an IGO with 181 member states, the World Intellectual Property Organization (WIPO), tries to regularize patent and copyright law across borders. The WTO oversees the world's most important multilateral agreement on intellectual property, called TRIPS (Trade-Related aspects of Intellectual Property Rights). Most industrialized countries prefer to use TRIPS rules because these rules are stronger than WIPO safeguards and can be relaxed only if all WTO members agree. WIPO rules require only a majority vote to change. The 2001 WTO meeting at Doha led to a declaration that states could exempt certain drugs from TRIPS rules to deal with serious domestic health crises, such as an HIV/AIDS epidemic. But disputes slowed the effective distribution of medicines to millions of Africans with AIDS for several years, though progress picked up after 2004.

Companies trying to protect intellectual property in an international context cannot rely on the same enforcement of rules as in domestic contexts. They need to bring their own state's government to bear, as well as using their own resources. Because of

---

[17] Destler, I. M., and Peter J. Balint. *The New Politics of American Trade: Trade, Labor, and the Environment.* Institute for International Economics, 1999. Verdier, Daniel. *Democracy and International Trade: Britain, France, and the United States, 1860–1990.* Princeton, 1994.

[18] Strange, Susan. *States and Markets: An Introduction to International Political Economy.* 2nd ed. St. Martin's, 1994.

[19] Skalnes, Lars S. *Politics, Markets, and Grand Strategy: Foreign Economic Policies as Strategic Instruments.* Michigan, 2000. Busch, Marc L. *Trade Warriors: States, Firms, and Strategic Policy in High Technology Competition.* Cambridge, 1999. Hart, Jeffrey A. *Technology, Television, and Competition: The Politics of Digital TV.* Cambridge, 2004.

state sovereignty in legal matters, private international economic conflicts easily become government-to-government issues.[20]

Enforcement of Trade Rules

As with international law generally, economic agreements between states depend strongly on the reciprocity principle for enforcement. If one state protects its industries, or puts tariffs on the goods of other states, or violates the copyright on works produced in other countries, the main resort that other states have is to apply similar measures against the offending state. The use of reciprocity to enforce equal terms of exchange is especially important in international trade, in which states often negotiate complex agreements— commodity by commodity, industry by industry—based on reciprocity.[21]

Enforcement of equal terms of trade is complicated by differing interpretations of what is "fair." States generally decide which practices of other states they consider unfair (often prodded by affected domestic industries) and then take (or threaten) retaliatory actions to punish those practices. A U.S. law, the Super 301 provision, mandates retaliation against states that restrict access of U.S. goods to their markets. However, if the other state does not agree that its practices were unfair, the retaliatory actions may themselves seem unfair and call for counterretaliation. One disadvantage of reciprocity is that it can lead to a downward spiral of noncooperation, popularly called a trade war. To prevent this, states often negotiate agreements regarding what practices they consider unfair. In some cases, third-party arbitration can also be used to resolve trade disputes. Currently, the WTO hears complaints and sets levels of acceptable retaliation. In some cases, regional trade agreements establish mechanisms to hear and resolve complaints as well.

Retaliation for unfair trade practices usually is based on an attempt to match the violation in type and extent. Under WTO rules, a state may impose retaliatory tariffs equivalent to the losses caused by another state's unfair trade practices (as determined by WTO hearings). Usually, at the last minute, negotiators agree to avert large-scale retaliatory sanctions or trade wars.

Trade cooperation is easier to achieve under hegemony (see pp. 31–34). The efficient operation of markets depends on a stable political framework such as hegemony can provide. A hegemon can provide a world currency in which value can be universally calculated. It can punish the use of violence and can enforce norms of fair trade. Because its economy is so large and dominating, the hegemon has a potent leverage in the threat to break off trade ties, even without resort to military force. U.S. hegemony helped create the major norms and institutions of international trade in the post-1945 era.

States have found it worthwhile to expand trade steadily, using a variety of regimes and institutions to do so. Overall, despite a loss of state sovereignty as a result of growing interdependence, these efforts have benefited participating states. Stable political rules governing trade allow states to realize the great economic gains that can result from international exchange.

---

[20] Marlin-Bennett, Renée. *Knowledge Power: Intellectual Property, Information, and Privacy*. Rienner, 2004.
[21] Bhagwati, Jagdish, ed. *Going Alone: The Case for Relaxed Reciprocity in Freeing Trade*. MIT, 2002.

CHAPTER 11

THEORIES OF GLOBALIZATION

GLOBALIZATION

Globalization encompasses many trends, including expanded international trade, monetary coordination, multinational corporations, telecommunications, technical and scientific cooperation, cultural exchanges of new types and scales, migration and refugee flows, and relations between the world's rich and poor countries and between human beings and the natural environment. Although globalization clearly is very important, it is also rather vaguely defined and not well explained by any one theory. One popular conception of globalization is as "the widening, deepening and speeding up of worldwide interconnectedness in all aspects of contemporary social life...."[1] But at least three conceptions of this process compete.[2]

One view sees globalization as the fruition of liberal economic principles. A global marketplace has brought growth and prosperity (not to all countries but to those most integrated with the global market). This economic process has made traditional states obsolete as economic units. States are thus losing authority to supranational institutions such as the International Monetary Fund (IMF) and the European Union (EU), and to transnational actors such as MNCs and NGOs. The values of technocrats and elite educated citizens in liberal democracies are becoming global values, reflecting an emerging global civilization. The old North-South division is seen as less important, because the global South is moving in divergent directions depending on countries' and regions' integration with world markets.

A second perspective is skeptical of these claims about globalization. These skeptics note that the world's major economies are no more integrated today than before World War I (when British hegemony provided a common set of expectations and institutions). The skeptics also doubt that regional and geographic distinctions such as the North-South divide are disappearing in favor of a single global market. Rather, they see the North-South gap as increasing with globalization. Also, the economic integration of states may be leading not to a single world free-trade zone, but to distinct

---

[1] Held, David, Anthony McGrew, David Goldblatt, and Jonathan Perraton. *Global Transformations: Politics, Economics and Culture*. Stanford, 1999: 2.

[2] Friedman, Thomas L. *The World Is Flat: A Brief History of the Twenty-First Century*. Rev. Ed. Farrar, Straus & Giroux, 2006. Steger, Manfred B., ed. *Rethinking Globalism*. Rowman & Littlefield, 2004. Stiglitz, Joseph E. *Globalization and Its Discontents*. Norton, 2002. Kirton, John J., Joseph P. Daniels, and Andreas Freytag, eds. *Guiding Global Order: G8 Governance in the Twenty-First Century*. Ashgate, 2001. Cusimano, Maryann K. *Beyond Sovereignty: Issues for a Global Agenda*. Palgrave, 1999.

and rival regional blocs in America, Europe, and Asia. The supposed emerging world civilization is disproved by the fragmenting of larger units (such as the Soviet Union) into smaller ones along lines of language, religion, and other such cultural factors.

A third school of thought sees globalization as more profound than the skeptics believe, yet more uncertain than the view of supporters of liberal economics.[3] These "transformationalists" see state sovereignty as being eroded by the EU, the WTO, and other new institutions, so that sovereignty is no longer an absolute but just one of a spectrum of bargaining leverages held by states. The bargaining itself increasingly involves nonstate actors. Thus globalization diffuses authority. State power is not so much strengthened or weakened by globalization, but transformed to operate in new contexts with new tools.

While scholars debate these conceptions of globalization, popular debates focus on the growing power of large corporations operating globally, the disruptive costs associated with joining world markets (for example, job loss and environmental impacts), the perception of growing disparities between the rich and the poor, and the collusion of national governments in these wrongs through their participation in IOs such as the WTO and the IMF.[4] The globalization of the world economy has created a backlash in many parts of the world. Global-level integration has fueled a countercurrent of growing nationalism in several world regions where people believe their identities and communities to be threatened by the penetration of foreign influences. But just as scholars disagree on conceptions of globalization, so do protesters disagree on their goals and tactics.

The expansion of trade is a central aspect of globalization in the international political economy, but hardly the only one. Today's accelerating pace of economic activity grows out of a long history of world economic expansion, which serves as the foundation for globalization.[5] Globalization is transforming not only trade but money, business, integration, communication, environmental management, and the economic development of poor countries.

Interdependence is a political and not just an economic phenomenon. States that trade become mutually dependent on each other's *political* cooperation in order to realize economic gains through trade. In IPE, interdependence refers less often to a *bilateral* mutual dependence than to a *multilateral* dependence in which each state depends on the political cooperation of most or all of the others to keep world markets operating efficiently. Many IR scholars argue that interdependence inherently promotes peace.[6]

The mutual dependence of two or more states does not mean that their degree of dependence is equal or symmetrical. World markets vary in their openness and efficiency from one commodity and region to another. The degree of a state's *short-term*

[3] Rosenau, James N. *Distant Proximities: Dynamics beyond Globalization*. Princeton, 2003.

[4] Broad, Robin. *Citizen Backlash to Economic Globalization*. Rowman & Littlefield, 2002. Drainville, André C. *Contesting Globalization: Space and Place in the World Economy*. Routledge, 2004.

[5] North, Douglass C., and Robert Paul Thomas. *The Rise of the Western World: A New Economic History*. Cambridge, 1973. Hobsbawm, E. J. *Industry and Empire: From 1750 to the Present Day*. Penguin-Pelican, 1969. Tracy, James D., ed. *The Political Economy of Merchant Empires: State Power and World Trade, 1350–1750*. Cambridge, 1991.

[6] Mansfield, Edward D., ed. *International Conflict and the Global Economy*. Elgar, 2004.

dependence on another may differ from its *long-term* dependence. The short-term dislocation that is caused by disrupting exchange with another country is the *sensitivity* of supply. A state that cannot adjust its policies to cope with disrupted trade, even over the long run, suffers from *vulnerability* of supply.[7] For example, Japan before World War II could not adjust after the United States cut off its exports of oil to Japan.

Over time, as the world economy develops and technology advances, states are becoming *increasingly interdependent*. Some IR scholars point out that this is not entirely new. The great powers were very interdependent before World War I; for instance, international trade was about the same percentage of GDP then as now. But several other dimensions of interdependence show dramatic change. One is the extent to which individual *firms*, which used to be nationally based, now are international in their holdings and interests (becoming MNCs), and thus dependent on the well-being of other states in addition to their home state (making them tend to favor free trade).[8] Another key aspect of interdependence is the tight integration of world markets through the ever-expanding flow of *information* and communication worldwide (see pp. 166–169). This facilitates the free competition of goods and services in global markets as well as the expanding volume of money (capital) that moves around the world every day.[9] Yet another dimension of change is the expansion of *scope* in the global economy, from one based in Europe to a more diffuse network encompassing the world.

THE CURRENCY SYSTEM

The world monetary system is another aspect of globalization, part of the political environment that governments create to shape the rules for international business and the actions of multinational corporations (MNCs).

Because of the nature of state sovereignty, the international economy is based on national currencies (and one regional currency, the euro), not a world currency. One of the main powers of a national government is to create its own currency as the sole legal currency in the territory it controls. The national currencies are of no inherent value in another country, but can be exchanged one for another.[10] Traditionally, for centuries, the European state system used *precious metals*, gold in particular, as a global currency, valued in all countries. States held bars of gold as a kind of bank account denominated in an international currency. These piles of gold, the object of mercantilist trade policies, could buy armies or other power capabilities.

In recent decades the world has not used such a **gold standard** but has developed an international monetary system divorced from any tangible medium such as precious metals. Today, each state's currency can be exchanged for another's according to an **exchange rate.** (Not all states have **convertible currencies** but the important ones do;

---

[7] Keohane, Robert O., and Joseph S. Nye. *Power and Interdependence*. 3rd ed. Longman, 2001.

[8] Milner, Helen V. *Resisting Protectionism: Global Industries and the Politics of International Trade*. Princeton, 1988.

[9] Rosencrance, Richard. *The Rise of the Virtual State: Wealth and Power in the Coming Century*. Basic, 2000.

[10] Solomon, Robert. *Money on the Move: The Revolution in International Finance Since 1980*. Princeton, 1999. Cohen, Benjamin J. *The Future of Money*. Princeton, 2004. Aliber, Robert Z. *The New International Money Game*. U of Chicago, 2002.

their money is called **hard currency.** States maintain **reserves** of hard currency, which are the equivalent of the stockpiles of gold.) Exchange rates affect almost every international economic transaction—trade, investment, tourism, and so forth. In particular, currency policies directly affect trade issues, but are not governed by the WTO regime.

The relative values of currencies at a given point in time are arbitrary; only the *changes* in values over time are meaningful. For instance, the euro happens to be fairly close to the U.S. dollar in value, whereas the Japanese yen is denominated in units closer to the U.S. penny. In itself this disparity says nothing about the desirability of these currencies or the financial positions of their states. However, when the value of the euro rises *relative* to the dollar, because euros are considered more valuable than before, the euro is said to be strong. Inflation reduces a currency's value relative to others. The industrialized West has kept inflation relatively low—mostly below 5 percent annually—since 1980. And inflation in the rest of the world has come down dramatically in the past 15 years. Extremely high, uncontrolled inflation—more than 50 percent per month—is called **hyperinflation** and is ruinous to an economy.

One form of currency exchange uses **fixed exchange rates.** Here governments decide, individually or jointly, to establish official rates of exchange for their currencies. States have various means for trying to maintain, or modify, such fixed rates in the face of changing economic conditions. However, **floating exchange rates** are now more commonly used for the world's major currencies. Rates are determined by global currency markets in which private investors and governments alike buy and sell currencies. There is a supply and demand for each state's currency, with prices constantly adjusting in response to market conditions. These international currency markets involve huge amounts of money—a trillion and a half dollars every day—moving around the world. They are private markets, not as strongly regulated by governments as are stock markets.

National governments periodically *intervene* in financial markets, buying and selling currencies in order to manipulate their value. (These interventions may also involve changing interest rates paid by the government.) Such government intervention to manage the otherwise free-floating currency rates is called a **managed float** system. The leading industrialized states often, but not always, work together in such interventions.[11] In their interventions in international currency markets, governments are at a disadvantage because even acting together they control only a small fraction of the money moving on such markets; most of it is privately owned.

China's currency does not float freely but is "pegged" to the dollar—more recently to a basket of leading currencies—at a fixed rate set by the Chinese government. Thus it does not adjust much to different economic conditions in China and the United States. China runs a big trade surplus (see p. 146) while the United States runs a big trade deficit. Because of underlying U.S. economic problems, the value of the U.S. dollar has dropped against the European currency in recent years, but the dollar-yuan ratio was held steady (with incremental changes starting in 2006). This made China's exports to the United States cheaper and contributed to the trade imbalance and the loss of U.S. manufacturing jobs—an issue in U.S. domestic politics.

---

[11] Kirshner, Jonathan. *Currency and Coercion: The Political Economy of International Monetary Power.* Princeton, 1997.

Over the long term, the value of a state's currency tends to rise or fall relative to others because of changes in the long-term supply and demand for the currency. *Supply* is determined by the amount of money a government puts into circulation. Printing money is a quick way to generate revenue for the government, but fuels inflation. *Demand* for a currency depends on the state's economic health and political stability, reflecting that state's monetary policy and economic growth rate. Investors seek a currency that will not be watered down by inflation and that can be profitably invested in a growing economy. To some extent, exchange rates and trade surpluses or deficits tend to adjust automatically toward equilibrium (the preferred outcome for liberals). Economic liberals are not bothered by exchange rate changes over time, which allow the world economy to work out inefficiencies and maximize overall growth.

A unilateral move to reduce the value of one's own currency by changing a fixed or official exchange rate is called a **devaluation.** Generally, devaluation is a quick fix for financial problems in the short term, but it can create new problems. It causes losses to foreigners who hold one's currency, reducing investors' trust. As a result, demand for the currency drops, even at the new lower rate. Any weakening of a currency, whether through devaluation or a free market adjustment, encourages exports but carries dangers. Imported goods rise in price, foreign loans become more expensive to repay, and corporate profits may drop as a result. In general, any sharp or artificial change in exchange rates tends to disrupt smooth international trade and interfere with the creation of wealth.

BANKS AND DEBT

Governments control the printing of money. (In practice the decision is not one of "printing" but rather setting interest rates at which the government loans money; a lower rate pumps more cash into the economy.) In most industrialized countries, politicians know they cannot trust themselves with day-to-day decisions about printing money, which can solve political problems but fuel inflation. To enforce self-discipline and enhance public trust in the value of money, these decisions are turned over to a **central bank.**[12] The economists and technical experts who run the central bank seek to maintain the value of the state's currency by tightening money supply when growth is strong (to limit inflation) and loosening it when growth falters (to prime economic activity). Central banks have only private banks, not individuals and corporations, as their customers. The long-term, relatively nonpartisan perspective of central bankers makes it easier for states to achieve the collective good of a stable world monetary system.

Central bank decisions about interest rates have important international consequences. Higher rates tend to attract foreign capital. And if economic growth is high in a foreign country, more goods can be exported to it. So states care about other states' monetary policies. The resulting international conflicts can be resolved only politically (such as at G7 meetings), not technically, because each central bank, although removed from domestic politics, still looks out for its own state's interests.

---

[12] Blinder, Alan S. *The Quiet Revolution: Central Banking Goes Modern.* Yale, 2004. Sinclair, Peter, and Juliette Healey, eds. *Financial Stability and Central Banks.* Routledge, 2003.

Central banks operate under the control of national governments and work in the national interest (or the European interest in the case of the EU's central bank). But because of the importance of international cooperation for a stable world monetary system and because of the need to overcome collective goods problems, international regimes and institutions of global scope have developed in monetary affairs. As in security affairs, the main international economic institutions were created near the end of World War II. The **Bretton Woods system** adopted in 1944 established the International Bank for Reconstruction and Development (IBRD), more commonly called the **World Bank,** as a source of loans to reconstruct the Western European economies after the war and to help states through future financial difficulties. (Later, the main borrowers were countries in the global South and, in the 1990s, Eastern Europe.) Closely linked with the World Bank, the **International Monetary Fund (IMF)** coordinates international currency exchange, the balance of international payments, and national accounts (discussed shortly). The World Bank and the IMF continue to be the pillars of the international financial system.[13]

Bretton Woods set a regime of stable monetary exchange, based on the U.S. dollar and backed by gold, that lasted from 1944 to 1971.[14] The international currency markets operated within a narrow range around fixed exchange rates. The gold standard was abandoned in 1971—an event sometimes called the "collapse of Bretton Woods" but which was more an adjustment than a collapse. To replace gold as a world standard, the IMF created a new world currency, the **Special Drawing Right (SDR).** The SDR has been called "paper gold" because it is created in limited amounts by the IMF, is held as a hard-currency reserve by states' central banks, and can be exchanged for various international currencies. SDRs are linked in value to a basket of several key international currencies.

Unlike the UN General Assembly, the IMF and the World Bank use a *weighted voting* system—each state has a vote equal to a *quota* of reserves it deposits with the IMF based on the size of its economy. Thus the G7 states control the IMF, although nearly all the world's states are members. The United States has the largest vote, and Washington, D.C., is headquarters for both the IMF and the World Bank.

The IMF maintains a system of *national accounts* statistics to keep track of the overall monetary position of each state. A state's **balance of payments** is like the financial statement of a company: it summarizes all the flows of money in and out of the country. The system itself is technical and not political in nature. Essentially, three types of international transactions go into the balance of payments: the current account (trade balance), flows of capital (foreign investments), and changes in reserves (to make the accounts balance).

States often borrow or lend money beyond their borders. Borrowing money can help keep an economy going, but debt is the opposite of the pile of reserves that mercantilists would like to be sitting on. Why do states go into debt? One major reason is

---

[13] Fischer, Stanley. *IMF Essays from a Time of Crisis: The International Financial System, Stabilization, and Development.* MIT, 2004.

[14] Eichengreen, Barry. *Globalizing Capital: A History of the International Monetary System.* Princeton, 1996. Andrews, David M., C. Randall Henning, and Louis W. Pauly, eds. *Governing the World's Money.* Cornell, 2002.

to make up a trade deficit. A second reason is the income and consumption patterns of households and businesses. If people and firms spend more than they take in, they must borrow to pay their bills. The credit card they use may be from a local bank, but that bank may be getting the money it lends to them from foreign lenders. A third reason is government spending relative to taxation. Under the principles of **Keynesian economics** (named for the economist John Maynard Keynes), governments sometimes spend more on programs than they take in from tax revenue—*deficit spending*—to stimulate economic growth.[15] If this strategy works, increased economic growth eventually generates higher tax revenues to make up the deficit.

Government decisions about spending and taxation are called **fiscal policy;** decisions about printing and circulating money are called **monetary policy.**[16] These are the two main tools available for government to manage an economy. There is no free lunch: high taxation chokes off economic growth, printing excess money causes inflation, and borrowing to cover a deficit places a mortgage on the state's future. Thus, for all the complexities of governmental economic policies and international economic transactions, a state's wealth and power ultimately depend more than anything on the underlying health of its economy—the education and training of its labor force, the amount and modernity of its capital goods, the morale of its population, and the skill of its managers. In the long run, international debt reflects these underlying realities.

In recent years the United States has run very large and growing trade deficits as well as large budget deficits, going rapidly and deeply into debt. These trends have profound implications for the entire world political economy. They undermine the leading U.S. role in stabilizing international trade and monetary relations, in ensuring the provision of collective goods, and in providing capital for the economic development of other world regions. In a more decentralized, more privatized world economy with an uncertain U.S. role, collective goods problems could be harder to solve and free trade harder to achieve.

MULTINATIONAL BUSINESS

Although states are the main rule makers for currency exchange and other international economic transactions, those transactions are carried out mainly by private firms and individuals, not governments.[17] Most important among these private actors are MNCs.

Multinational corporations (MNCs) are companies based in one state with affiliated branches or subsidiaries operating in other states. There is no exact definition, but the clearest case of an MNC is a large corporation that operates on a worldwide basis in many countries simultaneously, with fixed facilities and employees in each. There is also no exact count of the total number of MNCs, but most estimates are in the tens of thousands worldwide.

---

[15] Markwell, Donald. *John Maynard Keynes and International Relations: Economic Paths to War and Peace.* Oxford, 2006.

[16] Kirshner, Jonathan, ed. *Monetary Orders: Ambiguous Economics, Ubiquitous Politics.* Cornell, 2003.

[17] Bernhard, William T., and David Leblang. *Democratic Processes and Financial Markets: Pricing Politics.* Cambridge, 2006. Braithwaite, John, and Peter Drahos. *Global Business Regulation.* Cambridge, 2000.

The role of MNCs in international political relations is complex and in some dispute.[18] Some scholars see MNCs as virtually being agents of their home national governments. This view resonates with mercantilism, in which economic activity ultimately serves political authorities; thus MNCs have clear national identities and act as members of their national society under state authority. An opposite version of this theme (popular among Marxists) considers national governments as being agents of their MNCs and state interventions (economic and military) as serving private, monied interests. Others, however, see MNCs as citizens of the world beholden to no government. Only in the case of state-owned MNCs—an important exception but a minority of companies worldwide—do MNC actions reflect state interests.

Giant MNCs contribute to global interdependence. MNCs prosper in a secure, stable international atmosphere that permits freedom of trade, of movement, and of capital flows (investments)—all governed by market forces with minimal government interference. Thus MNCs are, overall, a strong force for liberalism in the world economy, despite the fact that particular MNCs in particular industries push for certain mercantilist policies to protect their own interests.

MNCs do not just operate in foreign countries, they also own capital there—buildings, factories, cars, and so forth. Investments in foreign countries are among the most important, and politically sensitive, activities of MNCs. Figure 11.1 illustrates the growth of foreign direct investment worldwide. Unlike portfolio investment (on paper), **foreign direct investment** involves tangible goods such as factories and office

FIGURE 11.1   Foreign Direct Investment, World Total

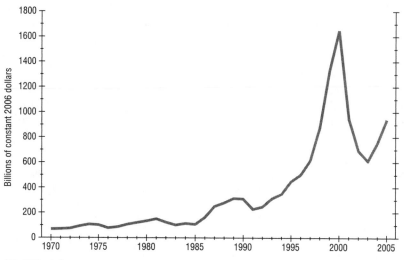

Source: World Bank data.

---

[18] Doremus, Paul N., William W. Keller, Louis W. Pauly, and Simon Reich. *The Myth of the Global Corporation*. Princeton, 1998.

buildings (including ownership of a sizable fraction of a company's total stock, as opposed to a portfolio with little bits of many companies).[19] Mercantilists tend to view foreign investments in their own country suspiciously. In poor countries, foreign direct investment often evokes concerns about a loss of sovereignty, especially for poor countries whose governments may be less powerful than the MNCs that invest there. These fears also reflect the historical fact that most foreign investment in the global South used to come from colonizers. Furthermore, although such investments create jobs, they also bring dislocations of traditional ways of life and cultures. But many poor and transitional states also court foreign investment because they desperately need capital to stimulate economic growth. In any case, most foreign investment is in industrialized countries.

A state in which a foreign MNC operates is called the **host country;** the state where the MNC has its headquarters is called its **home country.** MNC operations create a variety of problems and opportunities for both the host and home countries' governments. Conflicts between the host government and the MNC may spill over to become an interstate conflict between the host government and home government. For example, if a host government takes an MNC's property without compensation or arrests its executives, the home government may step in to help the MNC.[20]

THE INFORMATION REVOLUTION

Global telecommunications are profoundly changing how information and culture function in international relations.[21] These technological advances, at the center of globalization, are bringing the identity principle to the fore as communities can interact across distances and borders. Newly empowered individuals and groups are creating new transnational networks worldwide, bypassing states. International regimes have grown up around the regulation of international communications technologies.[22] For example, because radio waves do not respect national borders, the allocation of frequencies is a subject of interstate bargaining.

Unlike TV and radio, telephones and the Internet are two-way media through which users interact among themselves without any centralized information source—empowering individuals as international actors. Growth of phones and Internet use worldwide has been explosive in the past decade (see Figure 11.2), with cell phones

---

[19] Moosa, Imad A. *Foreign Direct Investment: Theory, Evidence and Practice.* Palgrave Macmillan, 2002. Phelps, Nicholas A., and Jeremy Alden, eds. *Foreign Direct Investment and the Global Economy: Corporate and Institutional Dynamics of Global-Localisation.* Routledge, 2002.

[20] Krasner, Stephen D. *Defending the National Interest: Raw Materials Investments and U.S. Foreign Policy.* Princeton, 1978. Gibbs, David N. *The Political Economy of Third World Intervention: Mines, Money, and U.S. Policy in the Congo Crisis.* U of Chicago, 1991. Lipson, Charles. *Standing Guard: Protecting Foreign Capital in the Nineteenth and Twentieth Centuries.* U of California, 1985.

[21] Allison, Juliann E., ed. *Technology, Development, and Democracy: International Conflict and Cooperation in the Information Age.* SUNY, 2002. Treverton, Gregory F. *Reshaping National Intelligence in an Age of Information.* Cambridge, 2001. Pool, Ithiel de Sola. *Technologies without Boundaries: On Telecommunications in a Global Age.* Edited by Eli M. Noam. Harvard, 1990.

[22] Franda, Marcus. *Governing the Internet: The Emergence of an International Regime.* Rienner, 2001. Braman, Sandra, ed. *The Emergent Global Information Policy Regime.* Palgrave, 2004.

FIGURE 11.2   World Phone and Internet Use, 1995–2006

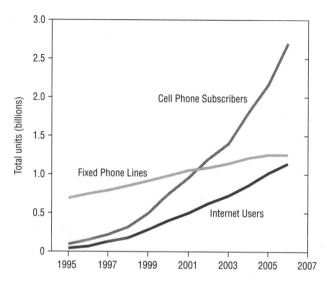

Source: International Telecommunications Union data.

leading this explosion of connectivity.[23] Nearly 3 billion people had cell phones in 2008, and more than a billion used the Internet—in each case representing a 25-fold increase in a decade. Taken on its own, the addition of phone and Internet capability in poor countries is impressive. But in comparison with rich regions, the gap is growing year by year (see Figure 11.3). A person living in the global North is four times as likely as a person in the global South to have a land line or cell phone, and eight times as likely to use the Internet. This gap, along with the gap in access to information technologies *within* countries, is known as the **digital divide.**[24] As the Internet wires parts of the world into a tight network centered on the United States, Europe, and East Asia—where more than 90 percent of Web users live—other regions are largely left out. Poor countries and poor people cannot afford computers, which cost the equivalent of years' worth of wages for a typical person in a poor country.

With more information traveling around the world than ever before, information has become an important instrument of governments' power (domestic and interstate).[25] Today's information technologies make it easier for governments to gather, organize, and store huge amounts of information. In this respect, the information revolution empowers governments more than ever. And as the cost of information technology decreases, it

[23] Data on information access are from the International Telecommunication Union (ITU) unless otherwise noted.

[24] Norris, Pippa. *Digital Divide: Civic Engagement, Information Poverty, and the Internet Worldwide.* Cambridge, 2001.

[25] Deutsch, Karl W. *The Nerves of Government: Models of Political Communication and Control.* Free Press, 1969.

FIGURE 11.3   The North-South Digital Divide, 1994–2006

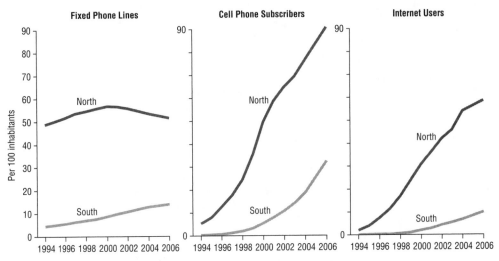

Source: International Telecommunications Union data.

comes into reach of more states. For example, high-resolution satellite photos are now available commercially and cheaply.

But information can also be used against governments—by foreign governments, NGOs, or domestic political opponents. New information technologies have become powerful tools of domestic opposition movements and their allies in foreign governments. This creates a dilemma for authoritarian regimes. Both Iran and China, for example, want the economic benefits of information on the Internet, but want to control its political effects. China, like several other developing countries, channels all access to the Internet through a few state-controlled service providers, and filters the hundreds of billions of instant text messages exchanged annually among 300 million Chinese cell phone subscribers.

Information technologies undermine realists' assumptions of state sovereignty and territorial integrity while, by empowering substate and transnational actors, they also undermine the centrality of states themselves in world affairs. The information revolution also helps states and interstate regimes, however. It greatly increases *transparency* in international relations. As a result, states do not need to arm against unknown potential threats because they know what the real threats are. Similarly, the ability to monitor performance of agreements makes collective goods problems easier to resolve because cheaters and free riders can be identified. Moreover, the ability of governments to bargain effectively with each other and to reach mutually beneficial outcomes is enhanced by the availability of instant communications channels. Increased transparency thus strengthens the reciprocity principle as a solution to IR conflicts. The complex monitoring and accounting required in international agreements based on reciprocity—from trade deals to arms control—comes much easier in a transparent world.

Telecommunications, with its ability to connect communities beyond geographic space, is also strengthening the identity principle in IR because people's identities have new sources and new avenues of expression that often transcend national borders. In the past, nationalism has tapped into the psychological dynamics of group identity in a powerful way that has legitimized the state as the ultimate embodiment of its people's aspirations and identity. Now the information revolution may aid the development of transnational or supranational identities.

Like international integration and globalization generally, global culture has its downside. The emerging global culture is primarily the culture of white Europeans and their descendants in rich areas of the world (mixed slightly with cultural elements of Japan and local elites in poor countries). This cultural dominance has been referred to as **cultural imperialism.**[26] For many people, especially in the global South, the information revolution carrying global culture into their midst is, despite its empowering potential, an invasive force in practice.

MANAGING THE ENVIRONMENT

Global threats to the natural environment are a growing source of interdependence. Actions taken by one state routinely affect other states' access to natural resources and to the benefits of a healthy environment.[27] Because environmental effects tend to be diffuse and long term and because such effects easily spread from one location to another, international environmental politics creates difficult collective goods problems. For example, the world's major fisheries in international waters are not owned by any state; they are a collective good. Because of a failure of international cooperation, fishing fleets have depleted a third of the world's seafood species with the rest projected to go by midcentury.[28] No world government exists to decide who can catch how many fish, so states must enter into multilateral negotiations, agreements, and regimes. Such efforts create new avenues for functionalism and international integration, but also new potentials for conflict and "prisoner's dilemmas."

This type of collective goods dilemma has been called the **tragedy of the commons,** a name taken from the shared grazing land in Britain centuries ago.[29] Each sheep benefited its owner, but too many sheep overgrazed the commons. Britain solved the problem by **enclosure**—splitting the land into privately owned pieces, on each of which a single owner would have an incentive to manage resources responsibly. (Similarly, the world's states have extended territorial waters to put more fish under the control of single states; see p. 172.) The *global commons* refers to the shared parts of the earth, such as the oceans and outer space.

---

[26] Maxwell, Richard. *Culture Works: The Political Economy of Culture*. Minnesota, 2001. Barber, Benjamin R. *Jihad vs. McWorld*. Times Books, 1995. Tomlinson, John. *Cultural Imperialism: A Critical Introduction*. Johns Hopkins, 1991.

[27] Sprout, Harold, and Margaret Sprout. *The Ecological Perspective on Human Affairs, with Special Reference to International Politics*. Princeton, 1965. Brown, Lester R., et al. *State of the World* (annual). Norton/Worldwatch Institute. Pirages, Dennis Clark, and Theresa Manley DeGeest. *Ecological Security: An Evolutionary Perspective on Globalization*. Rowman & Littlefield, 2003.

[28] Food and Agriculture Organization. *State of World Aquaculture 2006*. FAO, 2006.

[29] Hardin, Garrett. The Tragedy of the Commons. *Science* 162, Dec. 16, 1968: 1243–48.

As in other areas of IPE, solutions to environmental collective goods problems often rely on *regimes*.[30] Functional IOs specialize in technical and management aspects of the environment. Increasingly, these IOs overlap with broader communities of experts from various states that have been called **epistemic communities** (knowledge-based communities).[31]

In global environmental politics, it is hard to manage collective goods problems because of the large number of actors. The Commission on Sustainable Development monitors states' compliance with environmental agreements and hears evidence from environmental NGOs such as Greenpeace. But it lacks powers of enforcement over national governments—again reflecting the preeminence of state sovereignty over supranational authority.

The most important, and most intractable, international environmental problem is global climate change, or **global warming**—a slow, long-term rise in the average world temperature. Growing and compelling evidence shows that global warming is a real problem, that it is caused by the emission of carbon dioxide and other **greenhouse gases,** and that it will get much worse in the future. It is costly to reduce the emissions of these gases because they are a by-product of burning **fossil fuels**—oil, coal, and natural gas—to run cars, tractors, furnaces, factories, and so forth. Global warming presents states with a triple dilemma. First, there is the dilemma of short-term (and predictable) costs to gain long-term (and less predictable) benefits. Second, specific constituencies such as oil companies and industrial workers pay the costs, whereas the benefits are distributed more generally across domestic society and internationally. Third, there is the collective goods dilemma among states: benefits are shared globally but costs must be extracted from each state individually.[32]

This third dilemma is complicated by the North-South divide. Eighty percent of greenhouse gases now come from the industrialized countries—25 percent from the United States alone. Yet the most severe impacts of global warming are likely to be felt in the global South where hundreds of millions of poor people in densely populated countries such as Bangladesh stand to lose their homes and farmland under a rising sea.

All of these elements make for a difficult multilateral bargaining situation, one not yet resolved. The *Framework Convention on Climate Change* adopted at the 1992 Earth Summit set a nonbinding goal to limit greenhouse emissions to 1990 levels by the year 2000. That goal was not met. The 1997 **Kyoto Protocol** adopted a complex formula for reducing greenhouse emissions to 1990 levels in the global North over about a decade.[33] Countries in the global South received preferential treatment because their

---

[30] Speth, James Gustave, and Peter M. Haas. *Global Environmental Governance*. Island, 2006. Stevis, Dimitris, and Valerie J. Assetto, eds. *The International Political Economy of the Environment: Critical Perspectives*. Rienner, 2001. Schreurs, Miranda A., and Elizabeth Economy, eds. *The Internationalization of Environmental Protection*. Cambridge, 1997. Peterson, M. J. *International Regimes for the Final Frontier*. SUNY, 2005. Young, Oran R., ed. *The Effectiveness of International Environmental Regimes: Casual Connections and Behavioral Mechanisms*. MIT, 1999.

[31] Haas, Peter M. *Saving the Mediterranean: The Politics of International Environmental Cooperation*. Columbia, 1990.

[32] Fisher, Dana R. *National Governance and the Global Climate Change Regime*. Rowman & Littlefield, 2004.

[33] Victor, David G. *The Collapse of the Kyoto Protocol and the Struggle to Slow Global Warming*. Princeton, 2001.

FIGURE 11.4   Projected U.S. and Chinese Carbon Dioxide Emissions, 1990–2030

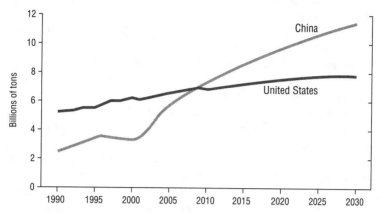

Source: International Energy Agency data.

levels (per capita) were much lower. Yet China and India, despite low emissions per person, have very large and growing total carbon dioxide emissions (see Figure 11.4). Despite a lack of U.S. participation, the Kyoto Protocol entered into effect in 2005. Mandatory carbon cuts under the Kyoto Protocol begin in 2008 and expire in 2012.[34] Since 1989 the UN-sponsored *Intergovernmental Panel on Climate Change* (IPCC) has served as a negotiating forum for this issue. It shared the 2007 Nobel Peace Prize. The dilemma of global warming remains fundamentally unsolved, though, and with weak enforcement mechanisms, even the states that signed the Kyoto Protocol may not meet their targets by 2012.

A second major atmospheric problem negotiated by the world's governments is the depletion of the world's **ozone layer,** which screens out harmful ultraviolet rays from the sun, by certain chemicals used until recently in refrigeration and in aerosol sprays.[35] This was another collective goods problem in that one state could benefit by allowing the use of Chlorofluorocarbons (CFCs) in its economy, provided that most other states prohibited their use. But the costs of replacing CFCs with other chemicals were much lower than the costs of addressing global warming, and the international community has had success. In the 1987 **Montreal Protocol,** 22 states agreed to reduce CFCs. Four times in the 1990s, as evidence of ozone depletion mounted, the timetable was accelerated, the agreement strengthened, and the signatories expanded. Rich countries stopped making CFCs in 1996 and have contributed $2 billion to help poorer countries make the switch. Scientists now expect the ozone layer to heal over the coming 50 years if current arrangements continue. The Montreal Protocol on CFCs is the most important success yet achieved in international environmental negotiations.

---

[34] Stowell, Deborah. *Climate Trading: Development of Greenhouse Gas Markets*. Palgrave, 2005.

[35] Litfin, Karen. *Ozone Discourses: Science and Politics in Global Environmental Cooperation*. Columbia, 1993.

Another major area of international environmental negotiation addresses **biodiversity**—the tremendous diversity of plant and animal species making up the earth's (global, regional, and local) ecosystems.[36] It has been difficult to reach international agreement on sharing the costs of preserving biodiversity. A 1992 treaty committed signatories to preserving habitats, and got rich states to pay poor ones for the rights to use commercially profitable biological products extracted from rare species in protected habitats (such as medicines from rain forest trees). However, the United States, afraid that the treaty could limit U.S. patent rights in biotechnology, never ratified it. International regimes to protect whales and dolphins have had limited success. The **International Whaling Commission** (an IGO) sets quotas for hunting certain whale species, but participation is voluntary and governments are not bound by decisions they object to. The *Inter-American Tropical Tuna Commission* (another IGO) regulates methods used to fish for tuna, aiming to minimize dolphin losses. The United States, the world's biggest tuna consumer, unilaterally requires that dolphin-safe methods be used for tuna sold in U.S. territory. But other countries have challenged this law through international trade organizations as an unfair trade restriction. Such conflicts portend future battles between environmentalists and free-trade advocates.[37]

Two types of habitat—tropical rain forests and oceans—are especially important to biodiversity *and* the atmosphere. Both are also reservoirs of commercially profitable resources such as fish and wood. International bargaining on the preservation of rain forests has made considerable progress. Most rain forests belong to a few states, and international bargaining amounts to agreements to shift costs from those few states onto the broader group of states benefiting from the rain forests.[38] Unlike rain forests, oceans belong to no state but are a global commons.[39] This makes the collective goods problem more difficult because no authority exists to enforce regulations against overfishing, dumping at sea, or oil spills on the **high seas** (nonterritorial waters). Preserving the oceans depends on the cooperation of more than a hundred states and thousands of nonstate actors. Free riders have great opportunities to profit. The **UN Convention on the Law of the Sea (UNCLOS)** established a 200-mile exclusive economic zone (EEZ) for economic activities, such as fishing and mining—placing a substantial share of the economically profitable ocean resources in the control of about a dozen states. Varying interpretations leave economic rights in dispute in a number of locations. Meanwhile *Antarctica* belongs to no state, but has caused few conflicts since its strategic and commercial value is limited.[40]

---

[36] Swanson, Timothy M., ed. *The Economics and Ecology of Biodiversity Decline: The Forces Driving Global Change*. Cambridge, 1998.

[37] Chambers, W. Bradnee, ed. *Inter-Linkages: The Kyoto Protocol and the International Trade and Investment Regimes*. Brookings, 2001. DeSombre, Elizabeth R. *Domestic Sources of International Environmental Policy*. MIT, 2000. Copeland, Brian R., and M. Scott Taylor. *Trade and the Environment: Theory and Evidence*. Princeton, 2003.

[38] Dauvergne, Peter. *Loggers and Degradation in the Asia-Pacific: Corporations and Environmental Management*. Cambridge, 2001.

[39] Borgese, Elisabeth Mann. *The Oceanic Circle: Governing the Seas as a Global Resource*. UN University Press, 1999.

[40] Stokke, Olav Schram, and Davor Vidas, eds. *Governing the Antarctic: The Effectiveness and Legitimacy of the Antarctic Treaty System*. Cambridge, 1997.

Air and water pollution generally creates collective goods problems that generally remain more local than global. In several regions—notably Western and Eastern Europe and the Middle East—states are closely packed in the same air, river, or sea basins and states must negotiate multilateral pollution controls.[41] Such regional agreements have worked fairly well, and in recent decades river water quality has improved in most industrialized regions.

Competition for natural resources, however, causes numerous conflicts both locally and globally.[42] For example, since the late 1990s, the Caspian Sea region has offered a new and largely untapped oil source, but one complicated by the division of the Soviet Union into independent states (see Figure 11.5). Oil and other energy resources are the most important commodity in world trade and vital to all countries' economies. The regions of

FIGURE 11.5   Dividing the Caspian Sea

The Caspian Sea is the world's largest inland body of water. It could be defined under international law as either a lake or a sea.[a] A *lake* has a joint area in the middle (on the left panel) that can be exploited only if the countries agree on terms. There are also coastal zones under each country's sole control. In a *sea* less than 400 miles across, the bordering countries' 200-mile Exclusive Economic Zones (EEZs) split up the whole sea (right panel). If the whole area is split as in the map on the right, the sectors can be defined by median lines (dashed line) or by a division into five sectors of equal area (dotted line), giving Iran a larger sector.

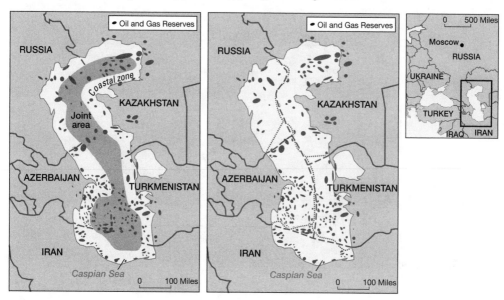

[a]Sciolino, Elaine. "It's a Sea! It's a Lake! No. It's a Pool of Oil!" *The New York Times*, June 21, 1998.

[41] Weinthal, Erika. *State Making and Environment Cooperation: Linking Domestic and International Politics in Central Asia.* MIT, 2002.
[42] Bannon, Ian, and Paul Collier, eds. *Natural Resources and Violent Conflict: Options and Actions.* World Bank, 2003.

the industrialized West are all large net importers of energy while the other six world regions are net exporters.[43] In the Middle East, colonial history and religious differences combine with oil to fuel ongoing international conflicts.

Increasingly scarce water supplies—rivers and water tables—often cross international boundaries; thus access to water is increasingly another source of international conflict. Sometimes—as when several states share access to a single water table—these conflicts are collective goods problems.[44] Conflicts over water, along with those over energy, pollution, and other environmental issues, have become a topic of growing interest in international security studies.[45]

POPULATION AND DISEASE

Projections of world population beyond a few decades have a range of uncertainty (see Figure 11.6). Population could level out around 9 to 10 billion in the next 200 years. Nearly all the increase in world population over the next two decades will be in the global South.[46] This makes population an important issue in global North-South relations.

Population growth results from a difference between birthrates and death rates. In agrarian (preindustrial) societies, both are high and population growth is thus slow. In the process of economic development, first death rates fall as food supplies increase and access to health care expands, and later birthrates fall as people become educated,

FIGURE 11.6   World Population Trends and Projections

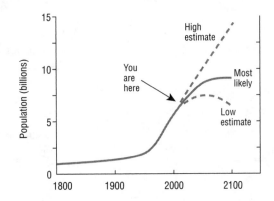

Source: Based on data from the UN Population Office.

---

[43] Yergin, Daniel. *The Prize: The Epic Quest for Oil, Money, and Power*. Simon & Schuster, 1991.

[44] Conca, Ken. *Governing Water: Contentious Transnational Politics and Global Institution Building*. MIT, 2005.

[45] Kahl, Colin H. *States, Scarcity, and Civil Strife in the Developing World*. Princeton, 2006. Dalby, Simon. *Environmental Security*. Minnesota, 2002. Lowi, Miriam R., and Brian R. Shaw. *Environment and Security: Discourses and Practices*. Palgrave, 2000. Homer-Dixon, Thomas F. *Environment, Scarcity, and Violence*. Princeton, 1999.

[46] UNFPA data. See United Nations. *State of World Population Report 2004*. UN, 2004.

FIGURE 11.7   The Demographic Transition

As income rises, first death rates and then birthrates fall. The gap between the two is the population growth rate. Early in the transition, the population contains a large proportion of children; later it contains a large proportion of elderly people.

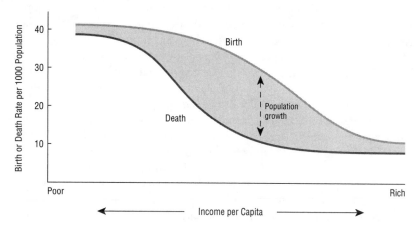

more secure, and more urbanized, and as the status of women in society rises. These changes are called the **demographic transition** (see Figure 11.7). At the end of the transition, as at the beginning, birthrates and death rates are fairly close to each other, and population growth is limited. But during the transition, population grows rapidly. Also, at the beginning and middle of the process, most of the population is young, but by the end, because adults live longer and families have fewer children, the average age is much older with a substantial elderly population.

The dilemma of the demographic transition is that rapid population growth and a child-heavy population drag down income per person, yet the best way to slow population growth is to raise income. Population growth thus contributes to a vicious cycle in many poor states, and tends to widen disparities of wealth. Countries that manage to raise incomes a bit enter an upward spiral—as population growth slows, income levels per capita rise more, which further slows population growth, and so forth. Meanwhile, states that do not raise incomes have unabated population growth; per capita incomes stay low, which fuels more population growth—a downward spiral. Globally, this disparity contributes to the gap in wealth between the North and South. Within the South, some countries manage to slow population growth and raise incomes while others fail to do so. Even within a single country, cities, richer classes, richer ethnic groups, and richer provinces tend to have low birthrates compared to the countryside and the poorer classes, ethnic groups, and provinces. These population trends contributed to differences within the global South that emerged in the 1990s, notably between Africa and Asia.

Population growth is also affected by epidemics of disease. Three mortality factors—AIDS, other infectious diseases, and smoking—exact high costs even if they do not much affect global population trends. In these cases, actions taken in the short term have long-term and often international consequences.

In the worldwide HIV/AIDS epidemic, one state's success or failure directly affects other states. During the delay of five to ten years after infection before symptoms appear, individuals can spread the virus internationally—through business, tourism, migration, and military operations. In Africa, already the world's poorest and most war-torn region, AIDS has greatly impeded economic development. In the global North, new drug therapies have dramatically lowered the death rate from AIDS since the late 1990s. But these treatments were too expensive to help much in Africa and other poor regions. India and Brazil began to export cheap generic versions of these drugs, violating patent rights of Western drug companies. After heated international bargaining among both states and NGOs, drug companies began offering lower prices to poor countries, but delivery of the drugs to millions of poor people remains painfully slow.

The global fight against AIDS also has not raised enough money from the world's countries. International efforts are coordinated primarily by the World Health Organization (WHO) and funded mainly by the industrialized countries, but the entire WHO budget is equivalent to that of a single midsize hospital in the global North. Overall, of worldwide spending on AIDS, less than 10 percent has been in the poor countries, where more than 80 percent of infected people live. Thus, AIDS has deepened the global North-South division. AIDS illustrates the transnational linkages that make international borders less meaningful than in the past. Effective international cooperation could save millions of lives and significantly enhance the prospects for economic development in the poorest countries in the coming decades. But once again, a collective goods problem exists regarding the allocation of costs and benefits from such efforts. A dollar spent by the WHO has the same effect regardless of which country contributed it.

Similar dilemmas arise for other international disease control efforts, which focus on tuberculosis (TB), malaria, hepatitis, dengue fever, and cholera—all of which have reemerged or spread in recent decades, often mutating into drug-resistant forms. Epidemics among animals also spread internationally. Britain lost billions of dollars during an outbreak of mad cow disease, and bird flu shut down poultry exports from several Asian countries. Scientists fear that bird flu could mutate and spread person-to-person, sparking a global pandemic that could potentially kill millions. On the positive side, vaccination programs have greatly reduced the incidence of both polio and measles in recent years, saving millions of lives.

The devastating effects of smoking mostly do not cross borders, but the tobacco trade makes smoking an international issue. Tobacco companies' recent marketing campaigns targeting women in the global South could produce a huge increase in smokers in that group, according to the WHO. In 2005, after overcoming initial U.S. opposition, the Framework Convention on Tobacco Control entered into force. Parties to the treaty are to ban tobacco advertising within five years and will be encouraged to raise taxes on tobacco 5 percent a year above the inflation rate.

Overall, demographic factors, population pressures, and environmental problems contribute in various ways to international conflicts and are receiving more attention from IR scholars. Such matters have moved squarely into the realm of international security affairs and not just humanitarian concerns. Clearly, their implications differ greatly in the global North and South, often deepening conflicts between the world's rich and poor countries.

CHAPTER 12

THEORIES OF DEVELOPMENT

BASIC HUMAN NEEDS

Countries in the global South, where most people live, are called by various names, used interchangeably: third world countries, less-developed countries (LDCs), underdeveloped countries (UDCs), or **developing countries.** The five regions of the global South differ on income level and growth. As Figure 12.1 shows, the regions experiencing the fastest growth—China and South Asia—are neither the highest- nor lowest-income regions. The Middle East is about as developed as China in terms of GDP per capita, but is growing at only half the rate. Thus the world's regions vary on both income and growth, with the two dimensions not correlated.

IR scholars do not agree on the causes or implications of poverty in the global South, nor on solutions (if any) to the problem. Thus, they also disagree about the nature of

FIGURE 12.1   Income Level and Growth Rate by World Region

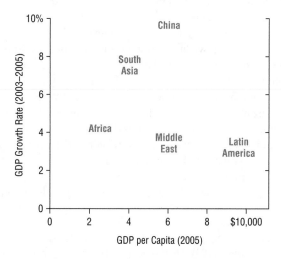

Note: For the global North overall, GDP per capita is $28,000.

Source: World Bank data.

FIGURE 12.2 **Rates of Access to Water and Food**

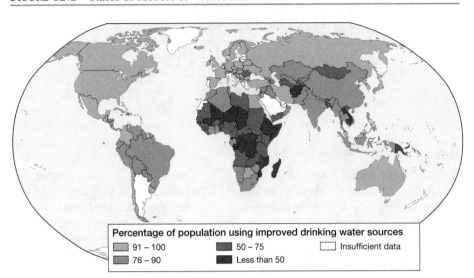

relations between rich and poor states (North-South relations).[1] Everyone agrees, however, that much of the global South is poor, and some of it extremely poor.[2] The widespread, grinding poverty of people who cannot afford necessities is more important than the dramatic examples of starvation triggered by war or drought, because chronic poverty affects many more people. The UN in 2000 adopted the **Millennium Development Goals,** which set targets for basic needs measures to be achieved by 2015 and measured against 1990 data. Progress has been uneven.[3]

For indicator after indicator, we find about a billion people, one-sixth of humanity, left behind with their basic needs unmet. Basically the bottom billion, most in rural areas, live in desperate poverty.[4] War in the global South—both international and civil war—is a leading obstacle to the provision of basic needs. War causes much greater damage to society than merely the direct deaths and injuries it inflicts. In war zones, economic infrastructure such as transportation is disrupted, as are government services such as health care and education. Wars drastically reduce the confidence in economic and political stability on which investment and trade depend.

Figure 12.2 maps the rates of access to safe water and food. The worldwide pattern somewhat resembles the map of wars in progress on p. 138. If indeed there is a relation-

[1] Seligson, Mitchell A., and John T. Passe-Smith, eds. *Development and Underdevelopment: The Political Economy of Inequality.* 3rd ed. Rienner, 2003. Thomas-Slayter, Barbara P. *Southern Exposure: International Development and the Global South in the Twenty-First Century.* Kumarian, 2003.

[2] UN Development Program. *Human Development Report.* Oxford, annual. World Bank. *World Development Report.* Oxford, annual.

[3] United Nations. *The Millennium Development Goals Report 2006.* UN, 2006.

[4] Collier, Paul. *The Bottom Billion: Why the Poorest Countries Are Failing and What Can Be Done about It.* Oxford, 2007.

FIGURE 12.2   (*continued*)

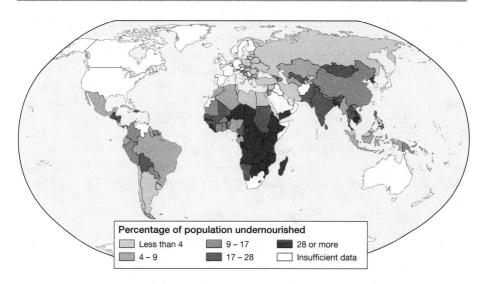

ship between recent or present warfare and a lack of basic needs (in turn correlated with income level), what really causes what? Does being at war keep a society poor and prevent it from meeting its population's basic needs? Or does being poor, with unmet basic needs, make a society more war-prone? Probably both are true. War is often part of a vicious circle for states unable to rise out of poverty.

Of all the basic needs of people in the global South, the most central is food.[5] Traditionally, rural communities have grown their own food—**subsistence farming.** Colonialism disrupted this pattern, and the disruption has continued in postcolonial times. States in the global South have shifted from subsistence to commercial agriculture. Small plots have been merged into big plantations, often under the control of wealthy landlords. By concentrating capital and orienting the economy toward a niche in world trade, this process is consistent with liberal economics. But it displaces subsistence farmers from the land. Wars displace farmers even more quickly, with similar results. Commercial agriculture relies on machinery, commercial fuels, and artificial fertilizers and pesticides, which must be bought with cash and often must be imported. To pay for these supplies, big farms grow **cash crops**—agricultural goods produced for export to world markets. Such crops typically provide little nutrition to local peasants; examples include coffee, tea, and sugar cane. When a plantation is built or expanded, subsistence farmers end up working on the plantation at very low wages or migrating to cities in search of jobs. International food aid itself can sometimes contribute to these problems. Agricultural assistance may favor mechanized commercial agriculture. And if an international agency floods an area

---

[5] Leathers, Howard D., and Phillips Foster. *The World Food Problem: Tackling the Causes of Undernutrition in the Third World.* 3rd ed. Rienner, 2004. Food and Agriculture Organization. *The State of Food Insecurity in the World 2006.* FAO, 2006.

with food, prices on local markets drop, which may force even more local farmers out of business and increase dependence on handouts from the government or international community. Also, people in a drought or famine often have to travel to feeding centers to receive the food, halting their work on their own land.

The displacement of peasants from subsistence farming contributes to a massive population shift that typically accompanies the demographic transition. More and more people move to the cities from the countryside—**urbanization.** They do so because of the higher income levels in the cities—economic opportunity—and the hope of more chances for an exciting life. They also move because population growth in the countryside stretches available food, water, arable land, and other resources. Many states have considered policies to break up large land holdings and redistribute land to poor peasants for use in subsistence farming—**land reform.**[6] Socialists almost always favor land reform, and many capitalists also favor it in moderation. The main opponents of land reform are large landowners, who often wield great political power because of their wealth and international connections to markets, MNCs, and other sources of hard currency.

Economic accumulation in poor countries is closely tied to the status of women in those societies.[7] This is a relatively recent revelation; most attention for decades had focused on men as supposedly the main generators of capital, because women's work often is not paid for in money and does not show up in financial statistics. But women in much of the world contribute substantially to economic growth and are central in providing basic human needs such as nutrition, education, health care, and shelter. States and international agencies have begun to pay attention to ending discrimination in schooling, ensuring women's access to health care and birth control, educating mothers about prenatal and child health, and generally raising women's status in society (allowing them a greater voice in decisions).[8]

The processes just outlined—basic needs deprivation, displacement from land, and urbanization—culminate in one of the biggest political issues affecting North-South relations: migration from poorer to richer states.[9] Millions of people from the global South have crossed international borders, often illegally, to reach the North. Someone who moves to a new country in search of better economic opportunities, a better professional environment, or better access to their family, culture, or religion is engaging in **migration** (emigration from the old state and immigration to the new state). Such migration is considered voluntary. The home state is not under any obligation to let such people leave, and, more important, no state is obligated to receive migrants. As with any trade issue, migration creates complex patterns of winners and losers. Immigrants often provide cheap labor, benefiting the host economy overall, but also compete for jobs with citizens of the host country.

---

[6] Deininger, Klaus W. *Land Policies for Growth and Poverty Reduction.* Oxford, 2003.

[7] Afshar, Haleh, and Deborah Eade. *Development, Women, and War: Feminist Perspectives.* Oxfam, 2004. Aguilar, Delia D., and Anne E. Lacsamana. *Women and Globalization.* Humanity, 2004. Rai, Shirin M. *Gender and the Political Economy of Development: From Nationalism to Globalization.* Blackwell, 2002.

[8] Basu, Amrita. *Two Faces of Protest: Contrasting Modes of Women's Activism in India.* California, 1992.

[9] Stalker, Peter. *Workers without Frontiers: The Impact of Globalization on International Migration.* Rienner, 2000. Meyers, Eytan. *International Immigration Policy: An Empirical and Theoretical Analysis.* Palgrave, 2004.

Most industrialized states try to limit immigration from the global South. Despite border guards and fences, many people migrate anyway, illegally. In the United States, such immigrants come from all over the world, but mostly from nearby Mexico, Central America, and the Caribbean. In Western Europe, they come largely from North Africa, Turkey, and (increasingly) Eastern Europe.[10] Many Western Europeans worry that the loosening of border controls under the process of integration (see p. 69) is letting in too many illegal immigrants.

International law and custom distinguish migrants from **refugees,** people fleeing to find refuge from war, natural disaster, or political persecution.[11] (Fleeing from chronic discrimination may or may not be grounds for refugee status.) International norms obligate countries to accept refugees who arrive at their borders. Refugees from wars or natural disasters are generally housed in refugee camps temporarily until they can return home (though their stay can drag on for years). Refugees from political persecution may be granted asylum to stay in the new state. Acceptance of refugees—and the question of which states must bear the costs—is a collective goods problem. It is not always easy to distinguish a refugee fleeing war or political persecution from a migrant seeking economic opportunity. In general, South-North migration of all types creates problems for the industrialized states that, it seems, can be solved only by addressing the problems of the South itself.

DEVELOPMENT EXPERIENCES

Economic development refers to the combined processes of capital accumulation, rising per capita incomes (with consequent falling birthrates), increasing skills in the population, adoption of new technological styles, and other related social and economic changes.[12] The concept of development has a subjective side that cannot be measured statistically—the judgment of whether a certain pattern of wealth creation and distribution is good for a state and its people. But one simple measure of economic development is the per capita GDP—the amount of economic activity per person. This measure is the horizontal axis in Figure 12.1 (p. 177), and change in this measure is on the vertical axis.

By this measure, in the new century growth has accelerated in the South and now outpaces the North (see Figure 12.3). This growth was uneven, however. South Asia joined China in rapid growth, 7–8 percent annually. Because China and South Asia together contain the majority of the population in the global South, this development is very important. This new growth shows that it is possible to rise out of poverty to relative prosperity. South Korea did so, followed by China, and India appears to be starting on the same curve (see Figure 12.4).

---

[10] Massey, Douglas S., and J. Edward Taylor. *International Migration: Prospects and Policies in a Global Market.* Oxford, 2004.

[11] UN High Commissioner for Refugees. *The State of the World's Refugees.* Oxford, annual. Loescher, Gil. *The UNHCR and World Politics: A Perilous Path.* Oxford, 2001.

[12] Stone, Diane. *Banking on Knowledge: The Genesis of the Global Development Network.* Routledge, 2001. Kothari, Uma, and Martin Minogue, eds. *Development Theory and Practice: Critical Perspectives.* Palgrave, 2002. Helpman, Elhanan. *The Mystery of Economic Growth.* Belknap, 2004.

FIGURE 12.3   Real GDP Growth of Selected Countries, 2006

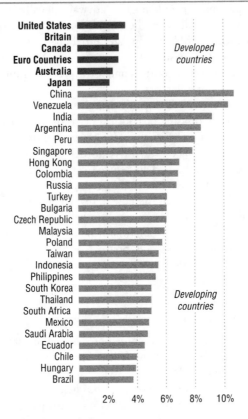

Source: World Bank. World Development Indicators.

Before China took off, a handful of poor states—called the **newly industrializing countries (NICs)**—achieved self-sustaining capital accumulation, with impressive economic growth.[13] These semiperiphery states (see pp. 108–109), which export light manufactured goods, posted strong economic growth in the 1980s and early 1990s. They suffered a setback in the 1997 Asian financial crisis because growth had been too fast, with overly idealistic loans, speculative investments, and corrupt deals (see p. 188). But the NICs quickly resumed growth and have developed much further and faster than most of the global South.

The most successful NICs are the **"four tigers"** or **"four dragons"** of East Asia: South Korea, Taiwan, Hong Kong, and Singapore. Each succeeded in developing particular sectors and industries that were competitive on world markets.[14] For different

[13] Amsden, Alice. *The Rise of the "Rest": Challenges to the West from Late-Industrializing Economies.* Oxford, 2001.
[14] Minami, Ryoshin, Kwan S. Kim, and Malcolm Falkus, eds. *Growth, Distribution, and Political Change: Asia and the Wider World.* St. Martin's, 1999.

FIGURE 12.4   Per Capita GDP of South Korea, China, India, and Ghana

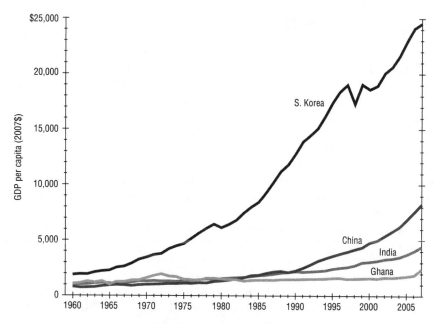

Source: Based on Penn World Tables; World Bank and IMF data.

reasons, each of these states holds a somewhat unusual political status in the international system. South Korea and Taiwan have been hot spots of international conflict, and came under the U.S. security umbrella during the Cold War. Both were militarized, authoritarian states intolerant of dissent then, although they later became democratic. U.S. spending in East Asia during the Cold War benefited South Korea and Taiwan. In these cases military conflict did not impede development. Hong Kong and Singapore, however, were both former British colonies, city-states, trading ports, and financial centers. They also were not democracies when their economies took off. It is unclear whether general lessons can be learned from the success of the "four tigers." Few equivalents exist elsewhere in the global South.

China, however, has proven that the successes of the NICs can be replicated on a larger scale. After decades of economic policy emphasizing national self-sufficiency and communist ideology, China since the 1980s has remade its economy on capitalist principles with foreign investment fueling export-oriented manufacturing. Economic growth has been rapid since these policies were instituted, and living standards have risen substantially.[15] However, China is also re-creating some of the features of capitalism that communist revolutionaries had overturned, including class disparities, unemployment, and corruption. Authorities have used harsh methods, including

---

[15] Lieberthal, Kenneth. *Governing China*. 2nd ed. Norton, 2004. Gore, Lance L. P. *Market Communism: The Institutional Foundation of China's Post-Mao Hyper-Growth*. Oxford, 1999.

military force in 1989, to suppress protests and maintain tight political control. Because its currency was not convertible, China weathered the 1997 Asian financial crisis despite its widespread problems with bad bank loans, money-losing state industries, and corruption. China's exports, which produced a large trade surplus, surpassed $1 trillion in 2007.

China's WTO membership is accelerating these trends but also raising new questions about how the ongoing Chinese opening of its economy to the world can coexist with continued political authoritarianism under communist rule. China's hundreds of millions of new Internet users and cell phone subscribers can communicate with overseas partners, monitor shipments, and follow economic trends globally. They can also potentially bypass government-controlled sources of political information. Some observers expect economic integration in an information era to inexorably open up China's political system and lead to democratization, whereas other experts think that as long as Chinese leaders deliver economic growth, the population will have little appetite for political change.

China's economic success has given it both more prestige in the international system and a more global perspective on international relations far from China's borders. Since 2004, Chinese leaders have made high-profile visits to resource-rich areas of the global South, reaching large-scale deals for minerals and energy to fuel China's growth, while boosting China's foreign aid to these areas. In 2007, China announced $3 billion in preferential loans to Africa, which, China emphasized, carry no political conditions (unlike Western loans, which often demand such policies as respect for human rights or fighting corruption). Several months earlier, China hosted a meeting for 48 African leaders. In recognition of China's new importance in the world economy, the G7 leading economies invited China to meet with them—a possible first step toward membership in the G7 (though China has been cool to full membership). China's rising international standing is also reflected in the selection of Beijing to host the 2008 Olympics.

For years it appeared that China's huge population would supply limitless cheap labor to foreign investors making goods in China. In recent years, however, China's growth has begun to squeeze the available labor force and push wages up somewhat. MNCs have begun to move some light manufacturing to other Asian countries with even cheaper labor, such as Vietnam.

It is unclear what lessons China's economic success over the past decade holds for the rest of the global South. The shift away from central planning and toward private ownership was clearly a key factor in its success, yet the state continued to play a central role in overseeing the economy (even more than in the NICs). These topics are being debated vigorously as China navigates its new era of rising prosperity and rising expectation, and as other poor states look to China's experience for lessons.

India, like China, deserves special attention because of its size and recent robust growth of 8 percent annually. India's decade of success still does not compare to China's nearly three decades, and India's GDP per person is still not much more than half of China's. But India's success has started it toward what could be, in the coming years, a repetition of China's rise out of poverty. India's economy was for decades based loosely on socialism and state control of large industries but on private capitalism in agriculture and consumer goods. The state subsidizes basic goods and gives special treatment to farmers. Unlike China, India has a democratic government, but a fractious one, with various autonomy movements and ethnic conflicts. India's government has suffered from corruption, although this has improved in recent years. Indian state-owned industries, like those elsewhere, were largely unprofitable. Furthermore, bureaucracy in India discouraged foreign investment. But after carrying out economic reforms, India saw robust economic growth in the late 1990s.

In the era of globalization, India's niche in the globalized world economy is in the service and information sectors. Although the service sector accounts for less than 30 percent of India's labor force (most of which is still in agriculture), it contributes 60 percent of GDP. Whereas South Korea specialized in exporting heavy manufactured goods and China in light manufactured goods, India specializes in exporting information products such as software and telephone call center services. Each country uses its labor force to add value to products that are exported worldwide, especially to the large American market. In India's case the labor force is well educated and speaks English. MNCs widely use India's labor force to answer phone calls from around the world, such as technical support calls.

India's future success or failure will bear strongly on several competing theories about economic development. In particular, China has had success under a harsh, centralized political system whereas India has a freewheeling democracy. Figure 12.5 compares China's and India's progress on two key indicators—infant mortality (a good overall measure of public health) and the fertility rate (see pp. 174–175). In both cases, China was able to make dramatic improvements very quickly because of its being an authoritarian government whose control (in theory) extended to every village and every bedroom. Thus, China relied on the dominance principle to force individuals to take actions that were in society's interest. Its successes in improving public

FIGURE 12.5   **Comparing Chinese and Indian Development**

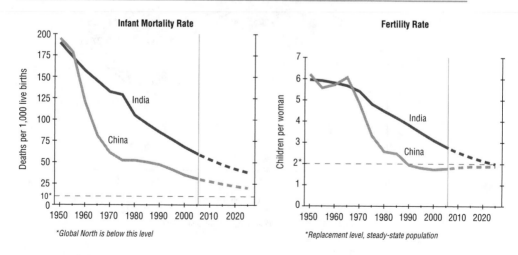

health and lowering fertility provided a foundation for China's subsequent economic success, although obviously at a cost to individual freedom. India, by contrast, relied more on the identity principle, getting people to change their preferences and *want* to have fewer children and help improve public health. Without a dictatorship to force compliance, India's progress has been slower. However, over time India is moving toward the same results as China, and doing so without giving up democracy.

Other sizable developing countries have had mixed results. Figure 12.6 shows the income levels and growth rates of the 16 largest countries by population in the global South. The graph parallels that for world regions in Figure 12.1 (p. 177). The five highest-income countries (Turkey, Iran, Thailand, Mexico, and Brazil) come from three of the four regions and are growing at 3–6 percent. The fastest-growing countries (India, Vietnam, Ethiopia, and Democratic Congo) at 7–9 percent were at the lower end of the income scale. Clearly China is developing faster than the other 15 large countries of the global South, although all posted solid growth, 5–9 percent for most. Clearly, too, regional location makes a difference. The fact that the five regions of the global South can be mapped onto single contiguous zones on this figure shows that whole regions are moving together in distinct patterns.

FIGURE 12.6 **Largest Countries' Income Levels and Growth Rates, 2006**

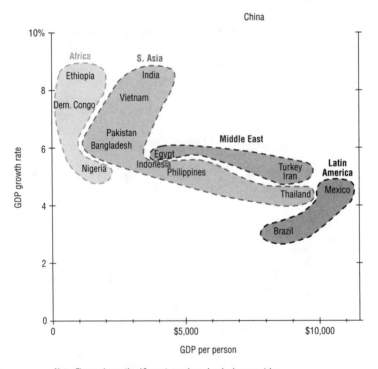

Note: Figure shows the 16 most populous developing countries.

CAPITAL ACCUMULATION

Throughout the global South, states are trying to use international trade as the basis of accumulation.[16] Through the creation of a trade surplus, a state can accumulate hard currency and build industry and infrastructure. One way to try to create a trade surplus, used frequently a few decades ago, is through **import substitution**—the development of local industries to produce items that a country had been importing. These industries may receive state subsidies or tariff protection. This might seem to be a good policy for reducing dependency—especially on the former colonial master—while shrinking a trade deficit or building a trade surplus. But it is against the principle of comparative advantage and has not proven effective in most cases. Some scholars think that import substitution is a useful policy only at a very early phase of economic development, after which it becomes counterproductive. Others think it is never useful.

More and more states have shifted to a strategy of **export-led growth,** which seeks to develop industries that can compete in specific niches in the world economy. These industries may receive special treatment such as subsidies and protected access to local markets. Exports from these industries generate hard currency and create a favorable trade balance. The state can then spend part of its money on imports of commodities produced more cheaply elsewhere. Such a strategy has risks, especially when a state specializes in the export of a few raw materials. The overall relationship between the prices of exported and imported goods—called the **terms of trade**—affects an export strategy based on raw materials. Because of both terms of trade and price fluctuations, states have looked to exporting manufactured goods, rather than raw materials, as the key to export-led growth. However, in seeking a niche for manufactured goods, a developing country must compete against industrialized countries with better technology, better educated workforces, and much more capital.

Manufacturing emerges as a key factor in both export-led growth and production for home markets. But one great difficulty in getting manufacturing started is that building factories requires capital. Authoritarian governments can sometimes squeeze the needed capital for manufacturing from the domestic economy by forcing reduced consumption, higher prices, and income disparities, but such policies can create political conflicts. The World Bank reviewed evidence on the effect of income inequality on economic growth and concluded that inequality holds back growth by wasting human potential. The Bank recommends extending access to health care, education, and jobs—as well as to political power—to the poorest people in societies of the global South in order to spur faster economic growth.[17]

A popular way to minimize the capital needs of manufacturing is to start out in low-capital industries such as *textiles*. The industry is fairly labor-intensive, giving an advantage to countries with cheap labor, and does not require huge investments of capital to get started. In 2005, textile tariffs were removed worldwide, and textile exporters in developing countries gained greater access to Western markets but also faced

---

[16] Easterly, William R. *The Elusive Quest for Growth: Economists' Adventures and Misadventures in the Tropics.* MIT, 2001.
[17] World Bank. *World Development Report 2006: Equity and Development.* World Bank, 2006.

intensified competition from China. An alternative, bottom-up approach to capitalization, **microcredit** (or *microlending*), uses small loans to poor people, especially women, to support economic self-sufficiency.

Capital can also come from foreign investment or foreign loans, but then profits must be shared with foreigners. Because of past colonial experiences, many governments in the global South have feared the loss of control that comes with foreign investments by MNCs. Sometimes the presence of MNCs was associated with the painful process of concentrating capital and the sharpening of class disparities in the host state. Although such fears remain, they are counterbalanced by the ability of foreign investors to infuse capital and generate growth. By the 1980s and 1990s, as models based on autarky or state ownership were discredited and the NICs gained success, many poor states rushed to embrace foreign investment. China has been the most successful of these.

Technology transfer refers to a poor country's acquisition of technology (knowledge, skills, methods, designs, and specialized equipment) from foreign sources, usually in conjunction with foreign direct investment or similar business operations. A developing country may allow an MNC to produce certain goods in the country under favorable conditions, provided the MNC shares knowledge of the technology and design behind the product. The state may try to get its own citizens into the management and professional workforce of factories or facilities created by foreign investment. Not only can physical capital accumulate in the country, so can the related technological base for further development. But MNCs may be reluctant to share proprietary technology.

Most poor states seek to build up an educated elite with knowledge and skills to run the national economy. One way to do so is to send students to industrialized states for higher education. This entails some risks, however. Students may enjoy life in the North and fail to return home. The problem of losing skilled workers to richer countries, called the **brain drain,** has impeded economic development in many countries.

Corruption is an important negative factor in economic development in many states. Corruption centers on the government as the central actor in economic development, especially in its international aspects. The government regulates the conditions under which MNCs operate, enforces worker discipline (calling out the army if necessary to break strikes or suppress revolutions), sets tax rates, and wields other macroeconomic levers of control over the economy. It may own sizable stakes in major industries—a monopoly in some cases. If state officials make these decisions based on private interests, such as taking a bribe from an MNC, their enrichment comes at the expense of the society.

Borrowing money is an alternative to foreign investment as a way of obtaining capital. Borrowing keeps control in local hands and does not impose painful sacrifices on local citizens, at least in the short term. But the borrower must service the debt—making regular payments of interest and repaying the principal over time. With foreign direct investment, a money-losing venture is the problem of the foreign MNC, but with debt it is the problem of the borrowing state. Failure to make scheduled payments, called a **default,** is considered a drastic action because it destroys lenders' confidence and results in cutoff of future loans.

Rather than defaulting, borrowers attempt **debt renegotiation**—reworking the terms on which a loan will be repaid. To do so, state creditors meet together periodically as the **Paris Club,** and private creditors as the **London Club,** to work out their terms. Through such renegotiations and the corresponding write-offs of debts by banks, poor states have largely avoided defaulting on their debts. However, the South still owes more than $2 trillion in foreign debt, and pays more than $300 billion a year to service that debt.

In recent years, activists and NGOs have called for extensive debt forgiveness for the poorest countries, most of which are in Africa. Critics say such cancellations just put more money in the hands of corrupt, inept governments. In 2005, G7 members agreed to eliminate all debts owed by 37 very poor countries to the World Bank and IMF—cutting almost in half the poorest countries' estimated $200 billion in debt. The IMF was considering a controversial plan to revalue its gold holdings (currently valued at $8 billion but worth 10 times that at market prices) as a source of finance for this debt relief.

ROLES OF INTERNATIONAL INSTITUTIONS

The International Monetary Fund (IMF) and the World Bank play an important role in funding the early stages of accumulation in developing countries. As a political entity rather than a bank, the IMF can make funds available on favorable terms. But the IMF first scrutinizes developing countries' economic plans and policies, withholding loans until it is satisfied that the right policies are in place. Its approval of a state's economic plans not only opens the door for IMF funding but is a "seal of approval" that bankers and MNCs use to assess the wisdom of investing in that state.

An agreement to loan IMF funds on the condition that the government adopt certain policies is called an **IMF conditionality** agreement. Implementation of these conditions is referred to as a *structural adjustment program*.[18] Dozens of developing countries have entered into such agreements with the IMF in recent decades. The IMF's terms are usually painful for the citizens (and hence for national politicians). It demands that inflation be brought under control, which requires reducing state spending and closing budget deficits. These measures often spur unemployment and require that subsidies of food and basic goods be reduced or eliminated. The IMF also demands steps to curtail corruption.

Because of the pain inflicted by a conditionality agreement—and to some extent by any debt renegotiation agreement—such agreements are often politically unpopular in the global South.[19] On quite a few occasions, a conditionality agreement has brought rioters into the streets demanding the restoration of subsidies for food, gasoline, and other essential goods. Sometimes governments have backed out of the agreement or have broken their promises under such pressure. Occasionally, governments have been toppled. The IMF formula for stability and success is remarkably

---

[18] Fischer, Stanley. *IMF Essays in a Time of Crisis: The International Financial System, Stabilization, and Development.* MIT, 2004. Vines, David, and Christopher L. Gilbert. *The IMF and Its Critics: Reform of Global Finance Architecture.* Cambridge, 2004.
[19] Haggard, Stephan, and Robert R. Kaufman, eds. *The Politics of Economic Adjustment: International Constraints, Distributive Conflicts, and the State.* Princeton, 1992. Vreeland, James R. *The IMF and Economic Development.* Cambridge, 2003.

universal from one country to the next. Critics of the IMF argue that it does not adapt its program adequately to account for differences in the local cultural and economic conditions in different states.

Most states of the global South see their economic future in a close interconnection with the world economy, and thus must play by the rules embedded in international economic regimes. But the WTO trading regime tends to work against poor states relative to industrialized ones. Over the course of the GATT/WTO regime, tariffs on manufactured goods came down sooner and faster than those on textiles and agricultural products, for which poor states had a comparative advantage. As a result, some developing countries had to open their home markets to foreign products, against which their home industries could not compete, yet see their own export products shut out of foreign markets. North-South conflicts over agricultural goods stalled the WTO's Doha Round for years.

Another criticism leveled at the WTO centers on the trade dispute system, in which states may bring complaints of unfair trading practices. Such legal disputes can cost millions of dollars to litigate, requiring expensive lawyers and a large staff at WTO headquarters in Geneva. Few states in the global South can afford this legal process, and therefore few use it to help their own industries knock down unfair barriers to trade. Recall that even if a state wins a WTO dispute, it gains only the right to place tariffs on the offending country's goods in an equal amount. For small states, this retaliation can inflict as much damage on their own economy as on the economy of the offending state. Attempts to compensate somewhat for these inequalities include the Generalized System of Preferences (see p. 152) and the EU's Lomé conventions, which relax tariffs on goods from the global South.[20]

The tenuous position of the global South in international economic regimes reflects the fact that the global North, with nearly two-thirds of the world's wealth, has more power than the South. To try to change the power balance, countries in the South have used the *UN Conference on Trade and Development (UNCTAD)*, which meets periodically but lacks power to implement major changes in North-South economic relations.

FOREIGN ASSISTANCE

Along with the commercial economic activities just discussed (investments and loans), **foreign assistance** (or *foreign aid* or *overseas development assistance*) is another major source of money for development. It covers a variety of programs—from individual volunteers lending a hand to massive government packages. Different kinds of development assistance have different purposes. Foreign assistance creates, or extends, a relationship between donor and recipient that is simultaneously political and cultural as well as economic. Foreign assistance can be a form of power in which the donor seeks to influence the recipient.

---

[20] Tussie, Diana, and David J. Glover, eds. *The Developing Countries in World Trade: Policies and Bargaining Strategies*. Rienner, 1993.

The majority of foreign assistance comes from governments in the North. Private donations provide a smaller amount, although sometimes a significant one. Of the more than $100 billion in governmental foreign assistance provided in 2005, more than 90 percent came from members of the **Development Assistance Committee (DAC),** consisting of states from Western Europe, North America, and Japan/Pacific. Three-quarters of the DAC countries' government assistance goes directly to governments in the global South as state-to-state **bilateral aid;** the rest goes through the UN or other agencies as **multilateral aid.** The DAC countries have set themselves a goal to contribute 0.7 percent of their GNPs in foreign aid. But overall they give less than half this amount. The United States gives the lowest percentage of GNP—about two-tenths of 1 percent. The world total in foreign assistance dropped substantially in the 1990s (see Figure 12.7), although it has risen modestly since the 2001 terrorist attacks.

In foreign aid, the donor must have the permission of the recipient government to operate in the country. This goes back to the principle of national sovereignty and the history of colonialism. National governments have the right to control the distribution of aid and the presence of foreign workers on their soil. Only occasionally is this principle violated, as when the United States and its allies provided assistance to Iraqi Kurds against the wishes of the Iraqi government following the Gulf War. International norms may be starting to change in this regard, with short-term humanitarian assistance starting to be seen as a human right that should not be subject to government veto.

Most of the multilateral development aid goes through *UN programs.* The overall flow of assistance through the UN is coordinated by the **UN Development Program (UNDP),** which manages 5,000 projects at once around the world (focusing especially

FIGURE 12.7   **Foreign Aid as a Percent of Donor Income, 2006 and 1960–2006**

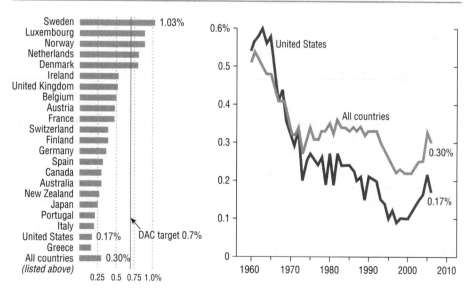

Note: Percent of Gross National Income, which is very close to GDP.
Source: The New York Times

on technical development assistance). Other UN programs focus on concentrating capital, transferring technology, and developing workforce skills for manufacturing. A major disadvantage faced by UN development programs is that they are funded largely through voluntary contributions by rich states. Each program has to solicit contributions to carry on its activities, so the contributions can be abruptly cut off if the program displeases a donor government. A second disadvantage of UN programs is their reputation for operating in an inefficient, bureaucratic manner.

Disaster relief is something of a collective good because the states of the North do not benefit individually by contributing, yet they benefit in the long run from greater stability in the South. Despite this problem and the large number of actors, disaster relief is generally a positive example of international cooperation to get a job done.[21] International norms regarding states' legal obligations to assist others in times of natural disaster and to accept such assistance if needed are changing.

Despite its humanitarian basis, foreign assistance can generate political conflicts among self-interested parties. For example, U.S. law requires that food aid for Africa be grown in the United States and shipped to Africa in U.S. vessels. In 2005, the Bush Administration proposed using U.S. funds to buy food locally in Africa, which would save a lot of money, deliver aid months faster, and help African farmers. But the proposal was opposed by the so-called Iron Triangle of food aid—U.S. agribusiness that profits from selling the food to the government, U.S. shipping companies that profit from shipping it, and U.S. charities (including CARE and Catholic Relief Services) that fund part of their budgets by selling in Africa some of the grain they ship from the United States. The charities, by becoming international grain merchants and flooding local markets with cheap food (both sold and given away), compete with local farmers and drive down local prices, harming long-term recovery. Yet because of the Iron Triangle's lobbying power, Congress killed off the proposal to allow purchase of food locally in Africa.

CONCLUSION

Ultimately the conflicts and dramas of international relations are the problems of human society—struggles for power and wealth, efforts to cooperate despite differences, social dilemmas and collective goods problems, the balance between freedom and order, and trade-offs of equity versus efficiency and of long-term versus short-term outcomes. These themes are inescapable in human society, from the smallest groups to the world community. The subject of international relations is in this sense an extension of everyday life and a reflection of the choices of individual human beings.

This book has shown that in IR, collective goods problems pose formidable challenges to successful cooperation among the large number of independent (state and nonstate) actors. With no central government to enforce order, actors in IR have developed three kinds of solutions to collective goods problems—our three core principles. Countries turn to the dominance principle most often in international security affairs, especially military force. The identity principle matters most in the remarkable

---

[21] Maynard, Kimberly A. *Healing Communities in Conflict: International Assistance in Complex Emergencies.* Columbia, 1999.

process of integration. Most important, however, is the reciprocity principle that underlies international treaties, law, and organizations from the UN to the WTO. Characteristic solutions based on the reciprocity principle are complicated, take a long time to agree upon, and require extensive monitoring of compliance thereafter. But woven together, these reciprocity-based agreements offer the basis for an international system that has moved over centuries from extreme war-proneness to ever-stronger peace and prosperity—notwithstanding the world's many serious remaining problems.

One major theme of this book is the nature of the international system as a well-developed set of rules based on state sovereignty, territoriality, and "anarchy"—a lack of central government. Yet state sovereignty is challenged by the principle of self-determination. International norms have begun to limit the right of government to rule a population by force against its will and to violate human rights. Territorial integrity is also problematic, because national borders do not stop information, environmental changes, or missiles. Information allows actors—state, substate, and supranational—to know what is going on everywhere in the world and to coordinate actions globally.

Technological development is just one aspect of the profound changes taking place in international relations. New actors are gaining power, long-standing principles are becoming less effective, and new challenges are arising for states, groups, and individuals alike. Nonmilitary forms of leverage, particularly economic rewards, have become much more important power capabilities. The post–Cold War era is a peaceful one, yet the peace is fragile. Will this era, like past postwar eras, lapse slowly into the next prewar era, or will it lead to a robust and lasting "permanent peace" such as Kant imagined?

In IPE, we see simultaneous trends toward integration and disintegration among states. People continue to speak their own language and to fly their own flag, and nationalism continues to be an important force. At the same time, however, although people identify with their state, they also now hold competing identities based on ethnic ties, gender, and (in the case of Europe) region. In international trade, liberal economics prevails because it works so well. States have learned that to survive they must help the creation of wealth by MNCs and other actors. Environmental damage may become the single greatest obstacle to sustained economic growth in both the North and South. Because of high costs, the large number of actors, and collective goods problems, international bargaining over the environment is difficult.

Meanwhile, North-South relations are moving to the center of world politics. Ultimately, the North will bear a high cost for failing to address the economic development of the South. Perhaps, by using computerization and biotechnology innovations, poor states can develop their economies more efficiently and sustainably than did Europe or North America.

Theories provide possible explanations for events in IR. Throughout this book, different theories have offered various possible explanations for outcomes. Theoretical knowledge accumulates by a repeated cycle of generalizing and then testing. A laboratory science, controlling all but one variable, can test theoretical predictions efficiently. IR does not have this luxury, because many variables operate simultaneously. Thus, it is especially important to think critically about IR events and consider several different theoretical explanations before deciding which (if any) provides the best explanation. The habit of thinking critically about world affairs is the most important "product" you can take from this book into your future studies and career.

INDEX

Boldface entries and page numbers indicate key terms. Entries for tables and figures are followed by "*table*" and "*fig.*" respectively.